Greenhill Books

A Soldier for Napoleon

*Dedicated to all those who still practise the ancient
and honourable art of writing letters*

We are especially grateful to Herr Dr Ernst Aichner and the staff of
the Bavarian Army Museum in Ingolstadt for the courtesy and
promptitude with which they supplied invaluable material on the 7th
Infantry Regiment and the Bavarian combat experience during the
Napoleonic epoch. We would also like to thank Herr Dr A. Fuchs of the
Bavarian Kriegsarchiv for his kind and swift assistance in providing a
copy of Franz's *Personalakt* (OP 78406)
and a wealth of other useful information.

Mr Peter Harrington also earned our gratitude for his always
friendly assistance in locating illustrations in the wonderful
Anne S.K. Brown Military Collection at Brown University in
Providence, Rhode Island, USA.

A SOLDIER FOR NAPOLEON

The Campaigns of
Lieutenant Franz Joseph Hausmann
7th Bavarian Infantry

TRANSLATED BY
CYNTHIA JOY HAUSMANN

EDITED BY
JOHN H. GILL

GREENHILL BOOKS, LONDON
STACKPOLE BOOKS, PENNSYLVANIA

A Soldier for Napoleon
first published 1998 by

Greenhill Books, Lionel Leventhal Limited,
Park House, 1 Russell Gardens, London NW11 9NN
and
Stackpole Books,
5067 Ritter Road, Mechanicsburg, PA 17055, USA

Introduction, and English translation of the letters and diaries of
Franz Hausmann © Cynthia Joy Hausmann, 1998
All additional text and maps © John H. Gill, 1998

British Library Cataloguing in Publication Data
A soldier for Napoleon : the campaigns of
Lieutenant Franz Joseph Hausmann, 7th Bavarian Infantry
1. Hausmann – Diaries 2. Hausmann – Correspondence
3. Napoleonic Wars, 1800–1815 – Personal narratives
I. Gill, John H.
940.2'7'092

ISBN 1-85367-336-6

Library of Congress Cataloging-in-Publication Data
Hausmann, Franz Joseph, 1789–1856.
A soldier for Napoleon : the campaigns of Lieutenant Franz Joseph
Hausmann, 7th Bavarian Infantry / translated by
Cynthia Joy Hausmann ; edited by John H. Gill
p.   cm.
Includes bibliographical references and index.
ISBN 1-85367-336-6
1. Hausmann, Franz Joseph, 1789–1856--Correspondence.
2. Napoleonic Wars, 1800–1815--Campaigns--Participation, German--Sources.
3. France, Armée--Officers--Biography. 4. Napoleonic Wars, 1800–1815--
Campaigns--Personal narratives, German
I. Hausmann, Cynthia Joy. II. Gill, John H. III. Title.
DC198.H37A4   1998
940.2'7--dc21   98-17740
                                                               CIP

Edited and designed by Donald Sommerville
Printed and bound in Great Britain by
Creative Print and Design (Wales), Ebbw Vale

CONTENTS

Maps

Illustrations
(between pages 128 and 129)

Preface

Franz Joseph Hausmann lived during one of the most important phases of Bavarian history and personally experienced many of the dramatic events that transformed that realm in the first fifteen years of the nineteenth century. Born in 1789, the year of the French Revolution, Franz first entered the army in 1799, the same year that Prince-Elector Maximilian IV Joseph assumed the Wittelsbach throne. Franz left active service in 1815 after the Battle of Waterloo, and finally departed the army in 1818 when the last Allied occupation troops came home from France. Through these years in uniform, he fought in every major Central European campaign of the French Empire: in 1805 against Austria and Russia, in 1806–07 against Prussia and Russia, in 1809 against Austria, in 1812 against Russia, and in 1813 against the combined Allied powers. Finally, in 1814, after Bavaria had changed sides and joined the Grand Alliance against Napoleon, he participated in the invasion of France with the Bavarian Corps of the Allied Main Army. Altogether this comprises a remarkable collection of military experiences for a young man of 25.

Through all the many trials and glories of these years, Franz maintained a detailed march journal and, from 1812, kept up a regular and lively correspondence with his parents, who were then living in Neuburg on the Danube. It is these often lengthy letters which form the foundation of this book. Though we know that some of the letters of 1812–14 have not survived because there are gaps in the sequence of numbers that Franz gave them, those that have remained provide unique insights into military life during the Napoleonic epoch, and we are pleased to offer them to the public for the first time.

The letters are supplemented by what Franz's family calls his 'military diaries'. Though some entries are nothing more than daily march destinations and distances, others provide rare first-hand glimpses into little-known corners of the period: the Bavarian combat experience in the Austerlitz campaign in 1805, for example, or the siege of Thorn (Torun) in 1813. To take advantage of these military diaries and to place the letters in context, we have structured this volume to include chapters on all of Franz's campaigns from 1805 to 1814. Each section begins with an historical overview and commentary on the Bavarian participation in the campaign; this is followed by the 'military diaries' for that year and, for 1812 through 1814, by the letters themselves.

The letters and diaries, written in a simple, practical style, come from a collection of Franz's papers held by his great-granddaughter, Cynthia Joy Hausmann. The diaries had been a part of Franz's life from his earliest years. After leaving Aachen with his parents when his regiment (the 4th Grenadiers) was being relocated to Bavaria, the boy-cadet Franz, not quite ten years old, began in January 1799 to record his daily marches, probably with his father's help, from just before Essen all the way to Munich and later to Neuburg on the Danube. While on campaign from 1805 through 1814, Franz evidently kept rough notes from which he transcribed the diaries at some subsequent date. As Cynthia has discovered, it is clear in some places that several pages were written at one sitting, and one passage, the entry of 16 May 1809, contains a comment that was obviously added later, 'The fate that befell the town of Schwaz and several villages can be seen today in the ruins that are still standing there.'

Wilhelm Hausmann was also an important influence in his son's letters. We cannot assert with certainty, but may assume with considerable confidence that Franz's comprehensive letters begin in 1812 because this was the first campaign in which Franz was separated from his father. A sergeant-major in the same regiment as Franz (now the 7th Line Infantry), Wilhelm had entered service in 1777 and participated in all of Bavaria's wars up to and including 1809. He and his young son thus campaigned together in 1805, 1806–07 and 1809. On 24 April 1809, however, at the Battle of Neumarkt in Bavaria, Wilhelm took an Austrian musket ball in his right foot. This painful wound and his performance during the fighting earned him the award of the French Legion of Honour, but his injury ended his active service with the field army. Wilhelm remained in uniform, but had to stay behind when Franz rode off to war against Russia in the spring of 1812, promising the old soldier that he would maintain an accurate account of his travels and engagements. For the information that follows, then, we may be grateful to a father's care and a loving son's unswerving dedication.

As a final introductory note for those who think of the Napoleonic era as a piece of ancient history only one step removed from the Roman Empire, it is worth recalling that Cynthia Hausmann is only Franz's great-grand-daughter. Considering that most of us have probably known one or more of our grandparents and some have even been blessed to know great-grandparents, this little observation helps bring home the fact that the age of Napoleon is not all that far removed in time from our own after all.

John H. Gill, 1998

Introduction

Franz Joseph Hausmann

My great-grandfather Franz Joseph Hausmann served as a young officer with the 7th Bavarian Infantry Regiment and was one of the fortunate few members of Napoleon's *Grande Armée* to survive the Russian campaign of 1812–13. Later, after the Bavarians changed sides and joined the Allies in the campaign against Napoleon, Franz fought his way across France up to the capitulation of Paris on 31 March 1814. It was Franz's good fortune on these military campaigns to be serving as adjutant to one or another of the Bavarian commanding officers, thereby greatly increasing his chance of survival.

From the Russian campaign, Franz wrote a series of 24 letters (21 of which survive), and from the French campaign a series of 11 (only 4 of which survive). These letters were written to his parents, who were then living at Neuburg on the Danube, the garrison town of the 7th Bavarian Infantry Regiment, where his father was assigned to the Reserve Battalion.

I first became aware of these letters after the death of my grandfather, Franz's youngest son, in 1951. Although the quality of the paper and ink was probably as good as one would encounter today, through the years the letters had clearly been lovingly pored over by Franz's children. In places they were torn or mended with small strips of brown or transparent paper, some pages were out of order, and here and there my grandfather had pencilled in comments, as was his wont. Although Franz's handwriting was quite good, he used the old-fashioned Gothic script, sometimes squeezed comments into the margins, and generally wrote in a very small hand – in later years he would admonish his children to write as small as possible, so as to save postage by not using much paper.

By 1951 Franz's only living descendants were in the United States, and only my father and I had sufficient linguistic interest to attempt a preliminary translation for the benefit of other family members. The older generation was thrilled to learn what an honourable young man Franz had been, and the younger generation by and large merely noted the fact that some ancestor had written letters during Napoleon's time. So matters remained, until I recently realised that my days were slowly running out and that I ought to make a serious effort to learn if there might be any outside interest in what had until then been considered strictly a family curiosity. I was fortunate enough to make contact with Lionel Leventhal of Greenhill Books and with Jack Gill, my co-author, who together have helped add another dimension to this material and place it in its broader military-historical setting. In the meantime family attics have also produced various other related treasures, notably Franz's military diaries, his voluminous later letters to his children, and the citations associated with his decorations.

In writing to his children, Franz often expressed his pride at being the third generation to serve in the Bavarian infantry. The first of the family to do so was Bartholomäus Hausmann (1724–1800), whose father was the assistant to the mayor of Heydeck, Bavaria and also had the unusual distinction of being able to read and write. In 1744 Bartholomäus joined the 4th Bavarian Grenadier Regiment at Neuburg and marched with them into garrison at Jülich, near Aachen in the Rhine Province, where he remained throughout his career. In the latter part of the 18th century Aachen was part of the Rhine Province that came under the protection of the combined Palatine-Bavarian Electorates. Bartholomäus' only son, Wilhelm Hausmann (1759–1841), was born in Jülich and joined the same regiment, now garrisoned at Aachen, where he married and had one son, Franz, in 1789.

A few months after Franz's birth in Aachen on 25 February 1789, the French Revolution erupted, and tensions between Revolutionary France and other European nations led to war in 1792. The ensuing fighting ebbed and flowed across the Rhineland region. Over the next few years Wilhelm Hausmann was engaged in campaigns against the French, particularly around Düsseldorf, which finally capitulated to the revolutionaries on 6 September 1795.

Franz did subsequently manage to attend primary school in Aachen for four years, but after that his father's regiment was ordered to march back to Bavaria, preparatory to helping fight the French in southern Germany. On 2 January 1799 Wilhelm, accompanied by his wife and son and whatever worldly goods they may have possessed, marched off from Aachen, arriving in Munich on 25 February 1799. After further moves within Bavaria, on 27 November 1799 the family finally arrived at Neuburg, which was to be the regiment's permanent garrison town. During the main period of relocation, from 1 January to 1 May 1799, ten-year-old Franz was carried on the payroll of the 3rd Company of the 4th Grenadier Regiment as a junior fourier or cadet (*Fourierschütze*).

Once settled in Bavaria, Franz lost his military status, and after arriving at Neuburg he spent four years attending the Latin School there. On 1 November 1804 he was then accepted as a fourier-trainee or cadet

(*Fourierpraktikant*) in the 7th Bavarian Infantry Regiment *Graf Morawitzky*, as his father's and grandfather's regiment was now called. In addition to learning his military duties, in this capacity Franz also participated in Bavaria's campaigns in alliance with France against Austria, Prussia and Russia during the period 1805–09. On 1 November 1806 he was promoted to full fourier in the 1st Grenadier Company of the 7th Royal Bavarian Infantry Regiment, and on 1 August 1809, during the campaign in Austria, he was advanced to second lieutenant with the Reserve Battalion of the 7th Infantry (now *Löwenstein*). On 1 September 1809 he was also appointed adjutant of this unit.

Wilhelm, meanwhile, continued to serve as a non-commissioned officer in the 7th Infantry. He was made a member of the French Legion of Honour, the notification of which was provisionally issued to him from Napoleon's headquarters at Ebersdorf on 13 May 1809, in recognition of his role in the Battle of Neumarkt on the Rott on 24 April of that year.

However, Wilhelm had received a severe wound in the foot at Neumarkt which would keep him out of active campaigning for the remainder of his long career in uniform. For most of the rest of this career, he was assigned to the Reserve Battalion of the 7th Infantry at Neuburg as a recruiting officer, although in June 1813 he was named lieutenant and adjutant of the 4th Battalion of the Rezat District Mobile Legion (later re-designated as the 17th National Field Battalion) and served in this capacity for a time. Promoted to captain on 26 October 1833, Wilhelm died in Neustadt on the Haardt (today Neustadt on the Weinstrasse) on 19 July 1841 as a retired officer in that rank.

When Franz marched out in March 1812 preparatory to the invasion of Russia, his father (owing to his injured foot) remained at Neuburg with the Reserve Battalion, and it was largely through military friends and couriers that the two corresponded with each other. As Franz's letters show, his father expected regular, well composed letters detailing the regiment's marching route, military engagements, personnel particulars and general living conditions in the field. Wilhelm's training and discipline are reflected in young Franz's pains to separate fact from rumour in his narrative, and in his apologies for not having the time (sometimes in the midst of battle!) to organise his material better. Throughout, Franz does his best to follow his father's advice to 'act with reason' and 'stand like a man'.

In the letters, young Franz's main concerns at first are about wearing the proper uniform and keeping correct account of his finances, but as his unit closes with the enemy he concentrates on describing the military engagements. The Bavarians, who formed part of the *Grande Armée*'s left flank, most notably succeeded in heading off the Russians under General Wittgenstein at the Battle of Polotsk, 18–19 August 1812, which Franz

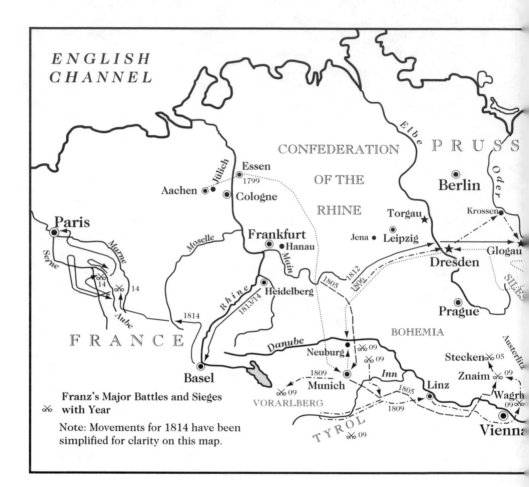

ENGLISH CHANNEL

CONFEDERATION OF THE RHINE

PRUSS

Elbe

Oder

Berlin

Essen
1799

Jülich

Aachen

Cologne

Torgau

Krossen

Paris

Moselle

Frankfurt

Hanau

Jena

Leipzig

Glogau

Dresden

SILE

Serne

Marne

Main

1812

1809

Rhine

Heidelberg

1805

Prague

Aube

1814

1813/14

BOHEMIA

14

14

Danube

Neuburg

09

09

Stecken

05

Austerlitz

FRANCE

Basel

Munich

1809

Inn

Znaim

09

1805

Linz

Wagram

VORARLBERG

TYROL

1809

09

Vienna

Franz's Major Battles and Sieges with Year

✂

Note: Movements for 1814 have been simplified for clarity on this map.

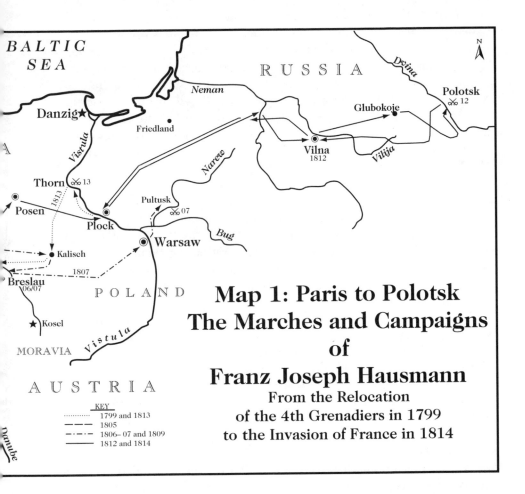

Map 1: Paris to Polotsk
The Marches and Campaigns
of
Franz Joseph Hausmann
From the Relocation
of the 4th Grenadiers in 1799
to the Invasion of France in 1814

treats at length. For his participation in this battle Franz was made a knight of the French Legion of Honour, the provisional notification of which was sent him on 25 September 1812 from Moscow, where Napoleon was at that time. During the following cruelly cold winter, Franz came down with typhoid fever on the disastrous retreat from Russia, a death march so horrible he says he cannot bring himself to write about it. Following the retreat, he suffered through the siege and capitulation of the fortress of Thorn (Torun) in Poland, and he was finally able to return to Neuburg on 13 July 1813. On his way home from Thorn Franz learned that he had been promoted to first lieutenant on 18 May 1813.

With the signing of the Ried Treaty on 8 October 1813, the Bavarians switched their allegiance away from Napoleon and joined the Allies. For the next few weeks, however, Franz himself enjoyed a respite from the wars, travelling around Bavaria from 8 October to 10 November 1813 and on 30 October coincidentally missing out on the battle of Hanau, where his battalion lost three officers dead and five more wounded. Franz met up with his unit at Heidelberg on 10 November 1813 to join in the invasion of France.

During the subsequent campaign, Franz writes about the battles where 'we met the enemy without flinching', including the battle of Chaumesnil, where 'the Emperor himself was in command against us'. Here Franz particularly reports on the fate of individual officers, since he believes that 'the newspapers will have already told you about our fortunate and unfortunate incidents'. After fighting his way across France to Paris, the provincial Bavarian was amazed to find the French capital 'fantastically large' and 'illuminated day and night by innumerable shops or boutiques'.

After Napoleon's abdication on 6 April 1814, Franz decided to leave the military, because he believed that the armed forces would be cut back in peacetime and that the chances of promotion would therefore be slim. As he would write on 27 June 1854 to his son Otto, who was by then fretting over his own slow promotion to first lieutenant in the artillery,

> Back then [when I was a lieutenant in the infantry] I allowed myself to be driven by dissatisfaction over the sudden insertion of four mobile legion battalions into my regiment and to be overcome with worry that I would not become a captain until I had grey hair and would even have to sacrifice for that with pay of 44 francs a month, and that is why I left the service.

Although Franz would go on to a distinguished career in the Bavarian civil service, he always showed a certain nostalgia for the military, and he encouraged several of his sons to consider military careers, with varying degrees of success.

On 1 December 1814 Franz went on leave status from the military and proceeded to Augsburg, where for the next four years he studied cameralistics (economics) at the university. Upon his graduation in 1818, he joined the Bavarian civil service and finally left the military on 30 April 1818.

All of Franz's civil service was spent in the Palatinate, which at that time formed part of the Kingdom of Bavaria (the elector of Bavaria having become King Maximilian I Joseph in 1806). Franz began his new career on 21 April 1818 with an assignment as actuary with the regional commission in Zweibrücken. There he married Catharina Chandon, the daughter of a local merchant, with whom he had three children who lived beyond infancy. On 16 September 1824 Franz was assigned to Kaiserslautern as inspector of the main prison, and on 17 March 1826 he was promoted to regional commissioner in Pirmasens. On 7 January 1834 he was assigned in the same capacity to Neustadt on the Haardt, where his wife died in childbirth later that same year.

On 10 October 1837 Franz took a second wife, Antonia Adolay, the daughter of a landowner and notary in nearby Frankenthal, with whom he had eight more children. Franz's career continued to prosper, and on 28 October 1843 he was appointed royal counsellor in Neustadt.

In 1848–49 revolutionary unrest sporadically swept across the Palatinate. On 20 July 1848, for example, Franz remarked to his son Otto that he had been busy pacifying a student mob that had marched over from Heidelberg. On 22 May 1849 Franz told Otto, who was assigned to nearby Fort Germersheim with the 2nd Artillery Regiment *Zoller* during this period, that the president of the Palatine government had fled to the fort, and that he (Franz) would soon seek refuge there.

By the autumn of 1849, Franz was back in Neustadt, and then, probably in late 1850, he was promoted to royal counsellor in Speyer, at that time the capital of the Palatinate, making him the second-highest government official in that jurisdiction (after the president). Franz held the counsellor's position until he died of a heart attack on 30 July 1856. Along the way he received several decorations from the Bavarian king, but the highlight of his career came on 25 October 1852, when King Maximilian II came to Speyer and personally dubbed Franz a knight of the Order of St. Michael, thereby entitling him (but not his descendants) to use the noble form 'von Hausmann'.

Throughout his life Franz strove to send his children to the best schools available, pointing out to them that, although he could not leave them any financial fortune, he was willing to give them the best education possible, so that they would become honourable and self-sufficient

15

members of society. For the boys this meant preferably a military education leading to a career in the army, while the girls were sent to finishing schools.

After initial disciplinary struggles as a cadet, the oldest boy, Otto (1830–1917), had a successful career in the Bavarian artillery (not the infantry, to his father's regret), dying as a retired colonel. The next two boys, Franz (1834–77) and Fritz (1838–62), had even greater difficulty adapting to military life and were in and out of various military schools and tutoring sessions. The other boys were too young when Franz died for him to have exerted any significant influence on their careers.

Upon his death in 1856, Franz senior's widow had to make do with a very small pension. Franz had estimated that it would amount to only some 300 francs annually, which was roughly as much as it had been costing him to send one child to boarding school for a year. It is therefore not surprising that most of the children emigrated to the United States, the land of opportunity, although some, either unmarried or without children, remained in Germany.

Of interest is the fact that Fritz and the next youngest boy, Eduard (1843–77), not only emigrated but on 22 April 1861 enlisted in Company D, 4th New York Volunteer Infantry, to fight in the American Civil War. Fritz was killed at the battle of Antietam on 17 September 1862; Eduard was wounded in the same battle and discharged, later to marry and settle in Chicago.

My grandfather, Julius (1849–1951), Franz's youngest child, emigrated in 1869, became an American citizen in 1874, and founded a successful importing business in New York. He spent long periods of time in Germany around the turn of the century, even maintaining a house there in Weissenburg (in Alsace, now Wissembourg in France) where his unmarried sisters lived. In approximately 1923, when travel between Germany and the United States again become possible after World War I, he came into possession of all his father's letters and diaries.

Presumably, these had previously been kept by his half-brother Otto, Franz's eldest son, who had remained in Germany. Otto, however, had no children, and after his death in 1917 my grandfather assumed responsibility for the family legacy. In the war-related interim before someone from my family could bring these papers and related mementos to the United States, they were probably kept by Franz's unmarried daughter, Mathilda who, by the time of her death in 1939, was the last of Franz's descendants living in Germany.

In his later letters to his children Franz makes it clear that he considers a military education the best preparation for a successful life, on one occasion pointing out to his son Otto that not only Napoleon, 'the greatest man of our times', but also Friedrich Schiller, 'the greatest poet', were products of military schools (letter of 16 May 1844). Elsewhere the concerned father exhorts his son serving in the artillery always to be 'pleasant and obedient to your superiors, friendly to everyone, as well as sociable and thoughtful toward your subordinates' (letter of 20 March 1851), to keep a clear conscience, and, above all, to trust fearlessly in God.

Although it did not hurt Franz's career that King Maximilian I Joseph took a special interest in his army and apparently also in Franz, and that Franz would continue to enjoy good relations with the king's son and grandson, Ludwig I and Maximilian II, it is evident that the military discipline and code of honour passed on to Franz by his father and grandfather must have contributed greatly to his later outstanding career, culminating in his becoming the king's top representative in the Palatinate.

The young Bavarian lieutenant who wrote the letters which appear later in this book was already demonstrating in them the moral principles and deep faith in God that humanised his life-long firm belief in orderly conduct and military obedience. I trust that those same admirable qualities are today still shared by many military officers around the world, and by many Hausmanns, young and old.

Cynthia Joy Hausmann, 1998

Conventions

In an effort to make this book a pleasant as well as an informative read, we have adopted the following conventions:

• Franz's erratic spelling of place names has been regularised and, in some cases, modernised. The Polish and Russian names used represent a compromise between modern accuracy and historical familiarity; readers will thus find Vilna instead of Vilnius and Polotsk instead of Polock or Polack. Where major Polish and Slovak towns have been renamed in the twentieth century, these new names are included in brackets after the old German names Franz knew – for example: Willenburg [Wielbark].

• German ranks have been rendered into English. Although this is a fairly straightforward process for ranks up to colonel (*Oberst*), it is important to keep in mind that a Bavarian *Generalmajor* (translated as major general) was a brigade commander and thus performed basically the same functions as a modern British brigadier or American brigadier general. Similarly, a *Generalleutnant* (translated as lieutenant general) would command a division as would a major general in the armies of the United Kingdom or the United States today.

• Original French and Austrian rank titles are preserved insofar as this is feasible and convenient. A table at the end of the volume relates these to current U.S. and British ranks.

• Ligne and Léger respectively are used for French line and light infantry units.

• Military units are often described in the text by both their number and their name (the Bavarian 4th Chevauxlegers are also the *Bubenhofen* Chevauxlegers).

• To minimise confusion between individuals and units, those units which were also known by the names of their proprietors or their commanders are shown in italics (for example, Oberstlieutenant von Butler commanded the Bavarian 5th Light Infantry Battalion *von Butler*).

• Battalions or squadrons are designated by Roman numerals (thus II/7th indicates the 2nd Battalion of the 7th Infantry Regiment).

• The term *Rheinbund* throughout refers to the Confederation of the Rhine.

• Occasional gaps or illegible sections in Franz's letters or diaries are shown thus [...].

• The authors are responsible for all translations: Ms Hausmann for Franz's material; Mr Gill for the translations in the commentary.

Chapter One

The Bavarian Army, 1805–14

Bavaria was a state in transition in the year 1805 when Franz Hausmann embarked upon his military career. A principality within the Holy Roman Empire under the rule of Prince-Elector Maximilian IV Joseph, it consisted of a diverse group of plots and holdings scattered across the face of western Germany from the Alps to the Meuse River. Many of the territories had no physical connection to the heartland of Old Bavaria (Altbayern) around Munich and the Danube – indeed, it was in a distant enclave between the Meuse and the Rhine that Franz had been born in 1789. Moreover, even the contiguous parts of the realm were speckled with countless principalities, duchies, ecclesiastical properties and other areas beyond the Prince-Elector's control. Within his own monarchy, he was opposed by entrenched estates and other interests whose rights and prerogatives were protected by the constitution of the decrepit old Empire. Maximilian thus found his authority constrained both externally and internally.

Like several other German states in the early nineteenth century, however, Bavaria was changing. Led by the chief minister, Maximilian Montgelas, the Prince-Elector and his government instituted a broad series of reforms that pushed Bavaria toward Montgelas' ideal of a modern, unitary, centralised state ruled by a powerful monarch and administered by an efficient bureaucracy. These sweeping reforms reached into every corner of the Bavarian state and society, including the military. Franz thus found himself entering an army that was rapidly modernising to meet the needs of this image of the state as well as the new demands of warfare on the cusp of the Napoleonic era.

The Nation's Army

Like the rest of Bavaria's institutions, the Bavarian Army changed dramatically between 1799 and 1814, transforming itself from a dynastic, essentially mercenary force into a truly national military. The first steps in this process began shortly after Max Joseph's accession as elector in 1799; that is, just around the time young Franz Joseph Hausmann was being entered on the rolls of the 4th Grenadier Regiment as a boy cadet.

Max Joseph found the army in dire need of reform. As a member of the Holy Roman Empire, Bavaria had contributed contingents to the Allied Coalition fighting against Revolutionary France from 1793 through 1797, but the Bavarian soldiers, though courageous, were poorly prepared for combat. Training, equipment, uniforms, supply and leadership were all grossly deficient. Training was perhaps the most glaring problem, and the Bavarian battalions in the Wars of the French Revolution demonstrated little fire discipline, complete ignorance of skirmishing tactics, and no ability to react to unexpected situations. Nor was the composition of the army encouraging. Bavaria drew its common soldiery from the very lowest elements of society by a mixture of voluntary recruitment (which took in numerous foreigners and mercenaries) and the draft; indeed criminals were often condemned to duty in the army. Discipline was correspondingly harsh and young men of any means at all purchased exclusion from military service. Small wonder, then, that the military occupied an unenviable position in the Bavarian social order.

Once in uniform, appalling inadequacies in the procurement of supplies and replacement equipment often left the men in pitiable condition, ragged, starving and unpaid. As a provincial commandant observed in 1795, 'naked and barefoot, the troops move about to the ridicule of the Austrian Army'.[1] Muskets were of poor quality and varying calibres, and the infantry's white uniform (designed by an American) was generally despised.[2] The army also suffered from serious manpower shortages brought on by the monarchy's chronic financial woes and compounded by desertion, poor pay and wretched conditions of service. In 1795, for example, the nine infantry 'regiments' mustered a total of only 776 soldiers fit for field duty.[3]

The officer corps did little to ameliorate the plight of the common soldier and generally proved helpless in the field. Many officers acquired their commissions through purchase, and promotions were often granted based on favouritism or aristocratic status rather than professional competence. As a result, the army's higher ranks were filled with men who had little prior military education or experience. When they attended to their duties at all, they frequently adhered strictly to the letter of the regulation books and seldom provided the imagination, drive and leadership necessary to overcome the army's deficiencies in training and administration.

There were, of course, exceptions to this broad picture. Not all of the aristocrats were incompetent; the minor nobility produced able offspring such as Generals Deroy and Wrede, for example, who performed well fighting against the French Revolutionary armies and would continue to demonstrate their leadership skills under Napoleon. Similarly, in terms of composition, the lower strata of the officer corps were somewhat variegated. For those of non-noble origin, however, the chances of promotion beyond the lowest officer ranks were slim. With neither the funds to buy higher positions nor the social connections to arrange advancement, they were consigned to spend their careers as lieutenants and captains, usually serving under men far junior to themselves in age and experience.

Indeed, Franz's family represents the new type of officer appearing in the Bavarian Army as Max's reforms took hold, men promoted on the basis of merit and experience. His grandfather, Bartholomäus (1724–1800), the son of a minor town official, had joined the army in 1744 and became a non-commissioned officer; his father, Wilhelm, enlisted in 1777, made sergeant in 1790, gained a promotion to second lieutenant in 1813, was pensioned as a first lieutenant in 1822 and was granted honorary captain's rank 11 years after his formal retirement; while Franz, though only a sergeant's son, was able to enter the officer ranks in 1805 at the age of sixteen.[4] It is also interesting to note that Wilhelm was not promoted until 1813, that is after the Russian debacle, when the Bavarian Army was searching for anyone with leadership experience to fill the depleted ranks of the regular officer corps and simultaneously to find leaders for its new militia battalions (the 'Mobile Legions').[5]

The years of war with France from 1793 to 1797 had only exacerbated the army's problems. When Max Joseph donned his Elector's cap in 1799, he therefore found that his army was hardly commensurate with his state, now once more at war with France (1799–1800). The artillery was in sad condition, there were only 700 horses for the eight cavalry regiments and the total available infantry numbered barely 8,000.[6] Trapped in a war he did not want – much of which would be fought on Bavarian soil – and fearing his ally Austria's predatory designs on his lands, the new Prince-Elector quickly realised that he would need to initiate a complete overhaul if he intended to play anything but a pawn's role on the German political scene. Moreover, modernisation of the military and improvements in the soldier's lot were completely in accord with his enlightened approach to governance.

Max Joseph recognised, however, that he himself was not suited by position or background to the task of drafting and implementing a comprehensive reform programme and therefore engaged the talents of a group of military and civilian experts to create a new army for Bavaria, one that fitted his new image of the state. This group included Montgelas (Prime Minister), General Johann Nepomuk von Triva (Minister of War), General Bernhard Erasmus Count von Deroy and General Karl Philipp

Baron von Wrede. Although Franz had no direct personal contact with such elevated personages as Montgelas and Triva, Deroy and Wrede were two of Bavaria's most senior and most talented generals. Their names accordingly appear frequently in Franz's letters and diaries as he served either with or under them in almost every one of his campaigns.

Max began initiating reforms almost as soon as the reins of state were in his hands. He started by forbidding the purchase of officers' commissions, a crucial step that paved the way for later improvements in the standards of the officer corps. He also replaced the unpopular and uncomfortable white uniform with a new pattern in Bavaria's traditional cornflower blue and introduced the high-crested helmet (*Raupenhelm*) which would be the distinctive headgear of the Bavarian army for many years to come.

The new war with France (1799–1800) and the disastrous defeat at Hohenlinden (3 December 1800) delayed further military reforms, but in 1804–05, Max and his advisers introduced a broad series of measures which transformed the Bavarian Army into a modern, national force. Key to these reforms was the announcement of general conscription in 1804. Under this law, all physically fit men between 16 and 40 years of age, and at least 5 feet 2 inches tall, were liable for military service (in practice most were between 18 and 36 years old). Once conscripted, the soldier was committed to eight years in uniform with one year of war counting as two years of peace. There were no provisions for evading duty by hiring a substitute or paying a fee, although Mennonites and Jews could purchase an exemption for 185 gulden. Numerous other exemptions meant that the lower classes continued to supply most of Bavaria's ordinary soldiers; government officials, teachers, students, artisans and many others, for example, were not subject to conscription. These exemptions notwithstanding, the recruiting base was considerably enlarged, resulting in an army that was more representative of its nation. Furthermore, the recruitment of foreigners was discouraged and criminals were no longer sentenced to join the army. Service to King and Country thus became the honourable duty of each Bavarian citizen.

To make the army more attractive, increase its effectiveness and enhance its public image, conditions for officers and soldiers were significantly improved. Under Max's paternal eye (his men referred to him as 'Father Max' or 'Our Max'), steps were also taken to modernise the army's administration, organisation and medical services. Corporal punishment was retained, but its impact was palliated and channels were established through which soldiers could raise complaints of maltreatment. Under a new, more liberal relationship between officers and their men, the soldiers were to be motivated by the honour of national service and regimental pride rather than fear of physical abuse. These noble impulses were to be further stimulated by the creation of service medals for officers and men and, in 1806, by the founding of the Military Order of Max Joseph. Soldiers were thus no longer simply mercenaries or criminals (or both), but citizens in the service of their country; officers were no longer merely young nobles who received responsibility by virtue of wealth or social connections, but men of proven military ability who attained their ranks by merit. For example, one sergeant who distinguished himself in 1805, was promoted to lieutenant in 1809 and concluded his career as a colonel – a nearly impossible level of advancement under previous conditions.[7]

Another set of innovations brought better treatment of soldiers and their families. Terms of service were reduced, pay was increased (albeit marginally), a veterans' home was founded and pensions were decreed for both officers and men. Moreover, the state began to demonstrate greater concern for army families by establishing funds to support the widows and orphans of soldiers killed on active duty. Though hardly perfect or foolproof, these steps did much to alleviate the nagging financial insecurity felt by the common soldier and his family.

While reforms such as these addressed the composition of the army and the everyday well-being of the soldier, others were aimed at improving its combat performance. Structurally, the infantry and cavalry regiments were completely reorganised and the entire army was expanded to a size more appropriate to Bavaria's international position. For Franz Hausmann, the immediate impact of these structural changes was the disappearance of his former regiment, the 4th Grenadiers, from the Bavarian order of battle and the creation of the unit that would be his home for the next ten years, the 7th Line Infantry Regiment.[8]

Tactically, the Bavarians modernised by consciously following the French model, adopting the use of small, flexible columns to enhance battlefield manoeuvrability, and introducing skirmishing as a standard element of the tactical commander's repertoire. Twenty especially clever and agile men in each company were designated as 'Schützen' to perform light infantry duties; granted short green plumes and other distinctions (*see* illustrations), they held elite status similar to the company of grenadiers in each battalion. In 1809 the number of Schützen per company was increased to 36, and 1811 saw the creation of a separate Schützen company for each light and line battalion. Deroy was the principal architect of the new infantry regulations, but the section on skirmishing was almost entirely Wrede's work. Together, they effected the transition in the Bavarian infantry from the stiff, linear forms of eighteenth-century combat to the fast, adaptable tactics of the Napoleonic age.[9]

The organisation, training and equipment of the artillery were also significantly improved by borrowing from the French. Here the credit belongs to General Jakob Count von Manson, an expatriate Frenchman and student of his countryman, the renowned Jean Baptiste Vacquette, Comte de Gribeauval. Count Manson formed his guns into permanent batteries, increased the overall number of artillerists, reintroduced light artillery (albeit not true horse artillery as only some of the crew were mounted, the remainder riding on the equipment) and promoted the tactical employment of guns en masse. In addition, a train battalion was raised in 1806 to provide greater mobility in the field. These innovations greatly improved the effectiveness of the formerly deplorable Bavarian artillery, making it a valuable adjunct to the infantry and cavalry arms.[10]

Franz thus embarked upon his military career at a time of great activity and change, and the army he came to know was dramatically different in structure, composition, spirit and even appearance from that which his father and grandfather had joined many years before. By the autumn of 1805, when Franz fought his first campaign, this reorganised and reformed army numbered some 26,000 men divided among 13 line infantry regiments (each of two battalions), six light infantry battalions, two dragoon regiments, four chevauxlegers regiments and three artillery battalions. With some transitory exceptions (a 7th Light Infantry Battalion existed from 1807–11 for example), this general structure remained constant for the next eight years (*see* Appendix 6, pages 252–3).

Absorbing the lessons of its campaigns and profiting from the example of its French allies, the army steadily improved. Under the pressure of Napoleon's demanding standards and the heat of combat in the campaigns of 1805, 1806 and 1807, a new Bavarian army was forged. Fighting the first and last battles of the 1809 war against Austria, it experienced its most successful campaign, winning the recognition of friend and foe alike for its battlefield performance. Three years later, it impressed all observers, Napoleon included, as it marched into Russia, but the horrors and hopelessness of that campaign drained its strength and spirit. Small shadow remnants fought on with honour in 1813 under French eagles, but the tide was turning against France and by October that year, Bavaria had switched sides, joining the Allied effort to evict Napoleon from Germany and ultimately participating in the invasion of France in 1814.

The Bavarian defection in 1813 was mostly the result of simple political calculation – Napoleon had been badly defeated and Max Joseph hoped to preserve his crown and lands by siding with the Allies in a timely fashion – but it was also an expression of mounting Bavarian dissatisfaction with their distinctly subservient position in the Napoleonic galaxy.[11] In the early years of the alliance, most Bavarians had welcomed the close ties to France as a safeguard against Austrian designs and felt honoured to serve under the banners of the greatest soldier of the age.

Curiously, Max Joseph's son and heir apparent, Crown Prince Ludwig, was an embarrassingly vocal exception. He had always detested Napoleon and all things French and became increasingly vociferous, outspoken and incautious over time. 'It is well known that I would rather fight against the French than for them!' he once declared.[12]

Sentiments such as these, initially rare, gradually became more common as disappointment and frustration began to outweigh enthusiasm. The causes were many. Napoleon's insistence on appointing Frenchmen as the senior commanders of the Bavarian contingents was one major irritant, as were the seemingly endless French demands for money, logistic support and ever more soldiers. But the French tendency to treat the Bavarians, indeed all non-French troops, as second class fighting men was perhaps the most annoying feature of the relationship – many Bavarians complained that they were given the dull or onerous campaign chores (such as secondary sieges or line of communication protection) rather than the more dangerous, but also more prestigious, battlefield tasks.

French dominance even manifested itself in all manner of everyday matters. Correspondence between the Bavarian division commanders and their King was conducted in French, for example, as were the communications exchanged among the Bavarian generals. On outpost duty, pickets and guards were instructed to use the French challenge '*Qui vive?*' rather than the German '*Wer da?*' ('Who goes there?'). In 1809 even the official seals of the three Bavarian divisions showed the arms of Bavaria surmounted by the words '*première* [or *deuxième* or *troisième*] *division bavaroise*'.[13] Some of these measures were simply practical expedients in a composite, multilingual army (the use of a common challenge, for example), but they still rankled, injuring Bavarian pride.

Overlooked in the victorious early campaigns, annoyances such as these festered over time and began to creep into the open in the latter part of 1809. Although the main, conventional campaign of 1809 against the Austrian regular forces was Bavaria's most glorious experience as a French ally, disagreements over operations against the pertinacious Tyrolean insurgents that year left a corrosive legacy of mutual suspicion. What had been minor irritations became ugly affronts to national sovereignty and the well of Bavarian tolerance began to dry up. Most military men still retained their commitment to the alliance and their faith in Napoleon as they marched for the River Neman [Niemen] in 1812, but the Russian catastrophe effectively expunged pro-French sentiment for most of Max Joseph's soldiers. The dreadful retreat from Russia and the gruelling 1813 campaign in Germany brought more disputes and Max Joseph's decision to side with the Allies in October seemed to many a decision long overdue.[14]

Disaffection and defection notwithstanding, the Bavarians proved valuable allies to France right up to the close of their association. If perhaps not as vigorous and durable as some of the other German contingents or as impetuous as the French themselves, they were solid, courageous, reliable soldiers.

Much of the credit for their contributions belongs to the re-invigorated Bavarian officer corps. Deroy was a thorough, conscientious, proficient veteran, and Wrede, if ambitious and sometimes obstreperously independent, was an excellent leader on the battlefield. Even the difficult Crown Prince performed satisfactorily, especially when assisted by able staff officers such as General Clemens von Raglovich. The cavalry brigadiers were particularly noteworthy, consistently exhibiting keen tactical judgment and a sure ability to motivate their troopers in the most trying circumstances.

The infantry was steady, the cavalry determined in the attack (if not always wise in defence) and the artillery both brave and capable. Moreover, all three arms displayed a fine grasp of flexible tactical manoeuvre. Their weaknesses included outpost duty, marching, and commanders' initiative, and they acquired an unpleasant reputation for being hard on the local populations wherever they were quartered (including in Bavaria).[15]

Even in enumerating their failings, however, it is important to note the brilliant exceptions. Indeed, inspired by leaders such as Wrede at his best, Bavarian troops performed marvels. His own division's astonishing march to Wagram in 1809 or the steadfast performance of isolated Bavarian detachments in the sieges of Thorn and Danzig [Gdansk] in 1813–14 are but two examples. Max Joseph's army may not have been the best of *Rheinbund* contingents, but during nine years of almost uninterrupted warfare, Napoleon and the French owed no little debt to the fidelity, competence and valour of the Bavarian Army.

Vignettes of Military Life

In closing out this brief introduction to Franz Hausmann's letters, it seems useful to provide some insights into how the Bavarian Army's officers and men lived during the Napoleonic period. While some of the practices and incidents described below were common to many armies of the era, others were uniquely Bavarian; in both cases they serve to fill in the background detail of the military panorama portrayed in Franz's correspondence.[16]

Lodgings A variety of different types of lodgings was available to Franz and his compatriots depending upon rank and circumstances. In peacetime, officers would normally live in their own homes or rent suites of rooms within their means. Men on long-term furlough (to reduce the burden on the state's exchequer, a significant percentage of a unit's strength could be on extended leave at any one time) would usually return to their home towns or wherever they could find temporary employment.[17]

Those men who remained in the regimental garrison, however, lived in conditions that seem very primitive indeed to the modern observer. Often old, cramped and dilapidated, barracks offered the individual soldier almost no privacy. Men slept two to a bed and did not even have a wardrobe to store their belongings, rather their equipment and personal effects were kept on bare shelves above their beds or hung from nails on the walls.

Soldiers' wives shared the barracks room with their husbands' comrades. Married non-commissioned officers (NCOs) might enjoy the luxury of a partition to afford some sense of personal space, but common soldiers and their spouses were fortunate to have a curtain round their beds. Children were brought into the world in this near-public barracks environment and most women evidently received medical attention there as well.

In some cases at least, sergeants' wives seem to have played a major, and sometimes deleterious, role in the lives of their husbands' companies. Major General Franz Joseph von Gaza, for instance, Inspector General of the Infantry and one of the early reformers of the Bavarian Army, was staunchly opposed to NCO marriages, evidently owing to some extraordinarily negative experiences with termagants. In his opinion, permitting an NCO to marry was detrimental to unit morale and performance because 'then not only is he punished, but the company as well'.[18] Given Gaza's testimony, poor pay, and limited quarters, it is perhaps not surprising that NCOs and soldiers were discouraged from marrying, and that soldiers of all ranks were required to pay a significant marriage fee to the state if they did decide to wed. This official scepticism notwithstanding, the number of authorised wives per company was raised from four to six in 1804.

Women frequently accompanied their husbands' companies on campaign, sharing the hardships of marches and the dangers of the battlefield. A veteran remembered seeing a soldier's wife hurrying by his battery during a battle in 1809 with her small brandy cask and an apron full of bread. When he and his comrades asked her for some schnapps, she replied 'no, I have only been able to round up a little and my company needs it, my people are under fire and I must be with them.'[19]

When on campaign, officers and men alike would either receive quarters in towns along the route of march or would bivouac under the open skies. Billeting in towns and villages was a fairly regularised affair in theory. The soldier received a 'lodging billet' which authorised him room and board in some local citizen's home; the citizen then exchanged the billet for his allotted remuneration. That, at least, was the system in theory. In practice, the system was open to all manner of abuses, and the incessant quartering of French troops on the local populace was a key source of German complaints about the alliance with Napoleon. In difficult circumstances, such as the retreat from Russia, all such orderliness could collapse completely, but even in better times, a company would sometimes have to employ its bayonets to enforce its right to its assigned barn.

When lodgings under a proper roof (however crowded) were unavailable, units would establish camp in a convenient field or wood. Except on peacetime manoeuvres, tents were not carried, but if they arrived early enough, the men might erect rude shelters constructed from local materials, vegetation, for example, or a nearby farmer's fences, sheds and home.[20]

If a unit were to be in one place for an extended period of time, these temporary structures would acquire more permanent features; Franz describes just such an encampment in his letter of 9 July 1812. The French were justly renowned for constructing tidy regimental villages given time and resources, and an envious Saxon officer admired the lodgings of some fellow Germans assigned to garrison Passau during the 1809 campaign,

> Behind the newly-constructed fortifications, we recognised our close countrymen of Gotha, who had built themselves huts of straw and branches under the shade of some fruit trees and were savouring the contents of a great tun [of beer] which the nimble serving girl could hardly tap fast enough.[21]

Food Officers and men who were billeted on the populace also received their meals from their temporary hosts. Alternatively, the home owner might be required to provide the soldiers some space around the fire to prepare whatever rations the men had been issued with. The host's responsibilities in this regard were explicitly outlined. For a soldier quartered in a town on a long-term basis in peacetime, a typical day's provisions in 1807 were to include a nourishing soup, vegetables and half a pound of meat or an equally satisfying replacement; bread and drink were not included. For this fare, the soldier was to pay the householder three kreuzer. If the soldier was on field duty, the host was responsible for providing a loaf of bread (one and a half pounds in weight) and a pint of beer daily in return for six kreuzer (three from the soldier, three from the government).[22]

Hosts were frequently required to supply a small amount of brandy or similar libation as well, this as a 'vitaliser' to be consumed first thing in the morning. Bavarians passing through Passau in 1809 must have been annoyed to notice fellow Germans from the small Thuringian principalities, such as the troops from Gotha with their admirable beer keg, whose daily ration was two pounds of bread and one pound of meat, plus vegetables and a quart of beer![23]

The Bavarians cherished their bread and beer. Bread was the army's key staple, but commanders also used it as an incentive, issuing double rations of bread (often accompanied by brandy) to units as a reward for good performance. To keep the men properly provisioned, a September 1808 edict authorised three bread wagons for each battalion. With 632 loaves per wagon, these three vehicles were considered sufficient to supply the battalion with bread for four days. Logistical arrangements quickly deteriorated in the Russian campaign, however, and the scarcity of bread in 1812 was the cause of innumerable complaints, leaving memoirists to blame the contingent's lethargy and high sickness rate on the insufficiency of this crucial item.[24]

Beer was another important part of the army's diet and beer of poor quality was certain to excite bitter grumbling. In Poland in 1807, for example, the troops were distressed to find that 'under the name of beer a dreary beverage was set before them in which plums and brandy formed the principal local ingredients'.[25] Two years later, weak beer was determined to be the cause of a regiment's poor physical condition,

> The French marshal [François Lefebvre, appointed by Napoleon to command the Bavarian VII Corps in 1809] gave his whole attention to the condition of the troops. During the reviews of the 1st and 3rd Divisions, he observed that soldiers were collapsing from exhaustion during manoeuvres; he concluded, correctly, that the inadequate provisions were the cause. During the resulting investigation it became clear that the food provided in the quarters among the villages and hamlets occupied by our regiment was very bad, and that the beer in particular was unpalatable and thinned with water. This explained the high sickness rate of 39 men in our regiment as compared to other units.[26]

Troops garrisoning Salzburg later in 1809 experienced similar problems. As one common soldier of the 5th Infantry remembered,

> We are here in the barracks, the officers in quarters; even in the barracks all would have been pleasant and tolerable if things had remained as they had been promised to us – one pound of meat, two litres of beer, as well as brandy, peas, lentils, etc. – but all this was often provided to us in a most parsimonious fashion. The beer was discoloured water, the peas as hard as wood, the meat and all was not

worthy of the name; we were, after all, enemies in the rich city of Salzburg.[27]

Curiously, there were even problems in Moravia in 1805, the soldiers being distressed to find that, other than water, the only liquid refreshment available was poor brandy.

As might be expected food supply was often highly problematic when the army was bivouacking. Despite the bread wagons, regular rations were frequently unavailable or were not delivered on time or in edible condition. Indeed, the military commissary department (*Kriegskommissariat*) proved inadequate in almost every campaign from 1805 through 1814.[28]

Even when the army supplied reasonable rations, the men would raid the local countryside for supplementary comestibles – sometimes despoiling their own country. At the opening of the 1805 campaign, for example, Wrede remonstrated sternly with his subordinates,

> … the commanding generals will have convinced themselves today of the unauthorised excesses, nearly resembling absolute plundering, that have been committed here. The 3rd Infantry Regiment stood out especially, and the 7th Infantry Regiment committed similar excesses during its entry into Pietenhausen.[29]

Poor logistical support had driven the men to this unacceptable behaviour. They had apparently received no bread for the previous three days and could not prepare a meal that morning (8 October 1805) because the wagons with the cooking equipment had not caught up with the marching columns.

These problems with food and utensils persisted, and an artillery drummer recalled rustling a chicken during the early stages of the 1809 campaign while his battery was still in Bavaria. To make matters worse, he stole a kettle so he and his comrades could cook his catch. As NCOs and soldiers normally ate some type of soup or stew and commonly took their meals seated or lying around a large kettle over their campfire, this drummer offered the eminently practical advice that a soldier should always have three or four spoons at hand; otherwise, he would have to wait to use one of his comrades' spoons, by which time his share of the soup might not be a substantial one.[30]

The kettles and pans used by the men for cooking were originally transported in company wagons. In the spring of 1806, however, as part of a general effort to cut down the size of the army's baggage train and thereby increase mobility, these vehicles were eliminated and the weighty pots were distributed among the soldiers to carry. The beneficial effect of this measure was enhanced by a simultaneous reduction in the number of officers' baggage wagons from six two-team rigs per regiment to two four-team vehicles. On the debit side, however, was the tendency of some troops (such as the drummer above) to discard these encumbrances at the first opportunity in the hopes of always acquiring a substitute from the local population.

Pay As with most armies of the day, pay in Bavarian service was low and often in arrears. Although increased early in Max Joseph's reign, the common soldier's garrison pay remained a mere 5 kreuzer a day or 2 gulden and 30 kreuzer per month (60 kreuzer made one gulden) as late as 1811. According to at least one source, this daily sum was utterly inadequate as the soldier needed at least 3 kreuzer to buy a decent pea soup with bread and the remaining 2 kreuzer were not enough to pay for a glass of beer.[31] Soldiers were thus left with little option but to supplement their income by taking on additional jobs in their garrison towns.

The situation was somewhat better for officers. An infantry lieutenant like Franz would have earned 30 gulden per month, more than ten times a private's pay. An artillery colonel, on the other hand, drew 188 gulden a month (cavalry officers drew the highest pay, followed by artillery and engineers, and lastly infantry). An officer, however, had to cope with a variety of additional expenses. Not only was he required to provide his own uniform, he would have to purchase and maintain one or more horses with all their tack and would need to hire a servant or two at his own expense (without a servant to take care of small administrative matters such as food, forage, equipment maintenance and equine care, an officer would have no time to attend to his duties). If a soldier was assigned as an officer's orderly, he was meant to receive extra pay from his employer. Small wonder, then, that the middle class men who were filling the officer ranks in increasing numbers often had difficulty meeting their expenses.[32] A typical officer's numerous expenses and limited financial resources also help explain why Franz later took such care to advise his son Otto in the minutest facets of fiscal management.

The army also received occasional supplements in the form of cash 'gratifications' or material goods. Although these usually came at the conclusion of a campaign or particularly noteworthy battle, one such occasion was the betrothal of Napoleon's step-son, Eugène de Beauharnais, to Max Joseph's daughter Auguste Amalie in January 1806. This union brought a tangible reward to the army in the form of a cash 'wedding gift' to the 50 private soldiers who wished to wed and who had most distinguished themselves in the recent campaign. According to a royal decree of 5 February, each of these deserving men received 500 gulden cash (nearly four year's pay for an ordinary soldier!) from the monarchy's coffers, assuming their brides met certain qualifications and that they agreed to give the names 'Eugen' or 'Auguste' to any children resulting from their marriage. Two privates of the 7th Infantry were selected for this honour and sent off to Munich in July to collect their gift.

In terms of material rewards, shoes and shoe soles were probably the most common recompense on less exceptional occasions, but other clothing items could also be offered as incentives. In December 1805, for instance, each NCO received several ells of requisitioned cloth from Austrian magazines to repair or enhance his uniform. Similarly, in February 1807, an Imperial announcement promised the Bavarian contingent 450 ells of cloth for officers, 6,277 ells for the soldiers and 1,674 pairs of shoes.[33]

Equipment The army specified in considerable detail what each man was to carry with him when he was on campaign. The following table from 1809 shows what an officer such as Franz would have been expected to have at his disposal in the field.[34] It is interesting to note the items Franz mentioned in his letters that do *not* appear in this table, in particular some of the articles he valued highly, such as his prized coffee pot and cook set.

In Portmanteau or Valise	Worn on the March	Carried by Orderly
1 uniform	1 shirt	1 overcoat rolled
4 waistcoats	1 white neck stock	or in backpack
3 pairs of breeches	1 black neck stock	1 shirt
7 shirts	1 pair of underwear	2 pairs of socks
3 pairs of underwear	1 pair of blue trousers	2 white neck stocks
7 handkerchiefs	1 pair of socks	1 set of field utensils
6 white neck stocks	1 pair of boots	1 small salt cellar
1 black neck stock	1 waistcoat	1 drinking glass with
3 hand towels	1 coat	case
8 pairs of socks	1 sash	1 pair of slippers
1 pair of boots	1 black sword belt	1 comb
1 pair of shoes	1 sword	2 brushes
1 pair of black gaiters	1 handkerchief	1 hand towel
1 small writing kit	1 briefcase	old linen
1 razor	1 pair of gloves	for use as bandages
1 clothing brush		
2 shoe brushes		
2-3 books		
5-6 maps		
1 helmet		

Uniforms Though it was similar to that of other contemporary armies in most respects, the Bavarian uniform featured several distinctive characteristics. The most striking item was the tall *Raupenhelm*

(literally 'caterpillar helmet'), a high black leather helmet with a black caterpillar crest made of lamb's wool (soldiers) or bearskin (officers).[35] Although this headgear pleased Bavarian sartorial tastes and warded off sabre blows, it was heavy and ungainly and the fur crest soaked up water like a sponge in the rain. It did, however, provide NCOs a convenient storage place for their notebooks.

The cornflower blue base colour of the line infantry's uniform coat was also unusual. Traditionally Bavarian, it set the army apart from its allies and enemies at a time when most continental soldiers (including Bavaria's light infantry, cavalry and artillery) were clad in green, white or some shade of dark blue.

Another curious feature was the system for designating officer rank. Where most countries adorned their officers with epaulettes to show their grades, Bavaria relied upon a system of horizontal gold or silver bars reaching back from the front edge of the high collar on the uniform coat. As a second lieutenant, Franz would thus have worn a single gold bar on his collar, with a second added when he was promoted to first lieutenant in 1813. Additionally, all officers wore a distinctive waist sash woven of light blue and silver thread. This was officially replaced by a gorget in 1812.

Common to many European armies, a gorget was a crescent-shaped metal plate a few inches wide usually decorated with a national emblem or regimental device. Suspended from a chain attached to each end, it hung outside the clothing on the breast indicating the bearer's status as an officer. Franz and his comrades, however, were clearly in no great hurry to effect this change, preferring their traditional sashes to the new gorget.

Hair styles also changed as Franz was learning his responsibilities as a soldier. From 24 December 1805, queues were abolished and hair was to be cut 'round'. One of the Bavarian detachments returning from Austria after the Austerlitz campaign decided to implement this new regulation on the march; the soldiers thus cut one another's queues during a halt, leaving the road and ditches littered with these curious reminders of the transition from one era to the next. The rather vague definition of 'round', however, left officers enormous latitude in hair style, the most popular fashion being to let one's locks fall across the brow in a wild and unruly manner.

Moustaches were permitted for the cavalry, but this right was also granted to NCOs, soldiers and musicians of the infantry and artillery in 1811. Officers, however, had to wait until 1826 before they could grow legal moustaches.[36] Beards, on the other hand, were a special perquisite of the chevauxlegers' officers, and senior commanders occasionally had to remonstrate with members of the other arms,

Numerous officers of the infantry, artillery and dragoons have permitted themselves to grow beards, which is entirely against the wishes of His Majesty the King, whose desire it is that only chevauxlegers officers should wear beards. For all other officers these are forbidden, and those who have allowed themselves to grow one will have it removed.[37]

Curiously, throughout this period, officers were also forbidden to wear eyeglasses. In 1817 this injunction was relaxed to the extent that spectacles could be worn if specific permission were granted by the army high command after review of medical evidence. The army noted, however, that the use of glasses constituted a physical infirmity and could result in denial of promotions.[38]

This, then, was the army young Franz joined as a boy cadet in 1799, this the army he accompanied on his first campaign in 1805 and which would be his home for ten more years of war.

❖ ⚜ ❖

Notes to Chapter One

[1] Quoted in Ernst Aichner, 'Das bayerische Heer in den Napoleonischen Kriegen', in Hubert Glaser, ed., *Krone und Verfassung*, Munich: Hirmer, 1980, vol. III/1, p. 241. The discussion throughout this chapter draws heavily on Dr Aichner's excellent survey monograph.

[2] Benjamin Thompson Count von Rumsford was an American who had fought for the British during the American War of Independence. Entering Bavarian service in 1784, he enjoyed great favour from Prince-Elector Karl Theodor and eventually reached the post of Chief of Staff. He attempted to introduce a comprehensive series of army reforms, including a white uniform of his own design.

[3] Aichner, p. 241.

[4] Notes on Wilhelm Hausmann from his *Personalakt* (OP 78408) in the Bavarian War Archives, courteously provided by Herr Dr A. Fuchs. Later in these pages, we will encounter another officer who rose from the ranks, Lieutenant Franz Xaver Loe, Franz's companion on the final stage of the retreat from Russia, promoted from sergeant in 1809.

[5] Wilhelm Hausmann's talents brought him promotion despite the wound to his foot and being nearly blind in his left eye. He was, however, hardly fit for unrestricted campaign service and was thus posted to the Mobile Legion

of the Rezat District as a battalion adjutant on 1 March 1813 (communication from Dr Fuchs).

[6] Camille Sauzey *Nos Alliés les Bavarois*, vol. V of *Les Allemands sous les Aigles Françaises*, Paris: Terana, 1988, p. 5.

[7] Josef Deifl, *Infanterist Deifl*, Munich: Beck, 1939, p. 21.

[8] The regiment was also known as *Zedtwitz-Stengel* after its initial proprietor (*Inhaber*). In 1804, Lieutenant General Max Count von Morawitzky-Topor briefly served as the 7th Infantry's proprietor; in 1806, it was assigned the former proprietor of the 12th Infantry, Lieutenant General Dominik Konstantin Prince von Löwenstein-Wertheim, when the 12th was disbanded for mutiny.

[9] Oskar Bezzel, *Geschichte des Königlich Bayerischen Heeres unter König Max I. Joseph von 1806 (1804) bis 1825*, vol. VI/1 of *Geschichte des Bayerischen Heeres*, Munich: Schick, 1933, pp. 197–9.

[10] Ibid., pp. 65–73; Aichner, p. 243.

[11] Kurt Uebe presents a detailed study of the shift in Bavarian attitudes in *Die Stimmungsumschwung in der bayerischen Armee gegenüber den Franzosen 1806–1812*, Munich: Beck, 1939.

[12] Egon Corti, *Ludwig I of Bavaria*, Evelyn B. Graham Stamper, trans., London: Thornton Butterworth, 1938, p. 75.
For Austrian attempts to recruit Ludwig in 1808–09, see Eduard Wertheimer, 'Berichte des Grafen Friedrich Lothar Stadion ueber die Beziehungen zwischen Oesterreich und Baiern (1807–1809)', *Archiv für Oesterreichische Geschichte*, vol. 63, Vienna: 1882.

[13] F. von Fabrice, *Das Königlich Bayerische 6. Infanterie-Regiment*, vol. II, Munich: Oldenbourg, 1896, p. 164.

[14] Bavaria's position as a 'front-line state' on the frontiers of Austria (and perhaps its military potential) allowed it to escape the onerous requirement to send troops to the cauldron of the Peninsular War. The only Bavarian troops to participate in that dreadful conflict were about 65 train personnel who were incorporated into the French 3rd Train Battalion in 1808; a mere 27 returned home in 1814. Recounted in Rudolf von Xylander, *Geschichte des 1. Feldartillerie-Regiments*, Berlin: Mittler, 1909, pp. 118–20.

[15] Wrede repeatedly complained about the inadequacy of local security measures during 1805 (Auvera, *Geschichte des Kgl. Bayer. 7. Infanterie-Regiments*, vol. I, Bayreuth: Ellwanger, 1898, p. 356), a deficiency that continually appears in reports written by the contingent's French commanders. Excesses against civilians and unsatisfactory discipline were most serious in 1806–07 (Bezzel, p. 187; Uebe, pp. 25–41).

[16] For a wonderful account of the French Army's practices (many of which are applicable to other militaries of the era), see John R. Elting, *Swords Around A Throne*, New York: The Free Press, 1988.

[17] For example, when the 1st Grenadier Company of the 13th Infantry Regiment returned home after the 1806–07 campaign, it began to adjust to

peacetime conditions and, by early January 1808, it had only 5 NCOs and 56 men available for duty out of the 10 NCOs and 167 men on its muster rolls. Of the remainder, 4 NCOs and 85 soldiers were on furlough; 1 NCO and 26 men were in hospital. Figures from Hauptmann Zoellner, *Geschichte des K. B. 11. Infanterie-Regiments 'von der Tann'*, Munich: Lindau, 1905, p. 52.

[18] Aichner, pp. 241–2, 247.

[19] Nikolaus Reichold, *Soldaten-Sohn und das Kriegsleben von 1805 bis 1815*, Munich, 1851, pp. 93.

[20] Sheltered in tents during the large exercises in the autumn of 1808 (see Chapter Four), the troops were pestered by swarms of mice and swamped by heavy rains. See the various regimental histories, particularly Max von Prielmeyer, *Geschichte des k. b. I. Infanterie-Regiments König*, Munich: Huttler, 1881, p. 139.

[21] Diary of Otto Rühle von Lilienstern, 12 May 1809, in Friedrich M. Kircheisen, ed., *Feldzugserinnerungen aus dem Kriegsjahre 1809*, Hamburg: Gutenberg, 1909, p. 97. The French constructed some remarkable camps in Poland and Prussia during 1807–08; see for example, the descriptions in Jean-Roche Coignet, *The Note-Books of Captain Coignet*, London: Greenhill, 1989, pp. 149–52; and François-René Pouget, *Souvenirs de Guerre*, Paris: Plon, 1895, pp. 124–7.

[22] Franz Berg, *Geschichte des Königl. Bayer. 4. Jäger-Bataillons*, vol. I, Landshut: Rietsch, 1887, p. 201.

[23] Hans von Döring, *Geschichte des 7. Thüringischen Infanterie-Regiments Nr. 96*, Berlin: Mittler & Sohn, 1890, p. 120.

[24] See, for example Paul Holzhausen, ed., 'Tagebuch des Hauptmanns Joseph Maillinger im Feldzuge nach Russland 1812', *Darstellungen aus der Bayerischen Kriegs- und Heeresgeschichte*, Heft 21, Munich: 1912, pp. 68, 75, 83, 154. Also Holzhausen, *Die Deutschen in Russland 1812*, Berlin: Morawe & Scheffelt, 1912, p. 62; Uebe, p. 103.

[25] M. Ruith, *Das K. Bayer. 12. Infanterie-Regiment 'Prinz Arnulf'*, Ulm: Ebner, 1902, p. 20.

[26] Fabrice, p. 165.

[27] Deifl, p. 27.

[28] Bezzel, p. 38.

[29] Wrede, march disposition for 8 October 1805, in Auvera, p. 353.

[30] Reichold, pp. 85–9. In other words the soldier who had to wait would often get little more than broth, his comrades having consumed whatever meat, vegetables and bread there might have been in the pot.

[31] Aichner, p. 247.

[32] With thanks to John Elting for making this cogent observation.

[33] Auvera, pp. 367, 373, 388.

[34] Printed in Auvera, p. 407.

[35] Officers wore common bicorne hats until September 1805, when the casque was introduced for officers up to the rank of colonel.

[36] M. Ruith, *Das k. bayerische 10. Infanterie-Regiment 'Prinz Ludwig'*, Ingolstadt: Ganghofer, 1882, p. 144. Bezzel, pp. 156–7.

[37] Order of the Bavarian 3rd Division, 5 April 1809, quoted in Berg, p. 212.

[38] Bezzel, p. 157.

Chapter Two

War with Austria and Russia in 1805

Franz Hausmann's first campaign was also Bavaria's first experience as an ally of Napoleonic France. The War of the Third Coalition, that culminated in the Ulm/Austerlitz Campaign, was nearly two years in the making, a convoluted series of diplomatic and military manoeuvrings that led to the creation of a new alliance against France in the summer of 1805.[1] The chief members of this coalition, Russia, Austria, Great Britain, Naples and Sweden, concocted a complex and grandiose operational plan to move against Napoleon while his principal army was supposedly settled on the Channel coast preparing for an invasion of England. A key component of this plan, particularly from the Austrian point of view, was the early invasion and occupation of Bavaria. A large Habsburg force would then station itself along the River Danube in central Bavaria to await the arrival of Russian reinforcements, while other Coalition armies advanced in Italy and northern Germany. Casting a covetous eye on Max Joseph's territories, Vienna intended either to force Bavaria into the Coalition or to 'devour' it.[2]

Simultaneously, Napoleon was pressuring Max to enter into an alliance with France. Desiring only neutrality, but caught between the two antagonists, Max vacillated. In the end, however, Napoleon's blandishments, and Max's own deep-seated apprehensions about Austria, led him to chose the lesser of two evils by agreeing to a secret treaty of alliance with France in late August 1805. Having promised to provide Napoleon with 20,000 men as well as various types of logistical support, Max spent two anxious weeks desperately resisting clumsy Habsburg threats. Still temporising and dissembling when Austrian troops invaded his realm on 8 September, he and his court were forced to flee to Würzburg that night to escape the potential comforts of Habsburg hospitality. Twenty days later, Marshal Jean Baptiste Bernadotte and the French I Corps marched into the same city, the left flank of an army of 165,000 men that was sweeping across central Germany towards the Danube.

The war had begun.

Early Encounters

As the Austrian battalions made their way from the River Inn to the Danube, the Bavarian Army hastened to assemble. Hoping to avoid antagonising Vienna, Max had delayed issuing mobilisation instructions. Furloughed officers and men were not recalled until 5 September and the actual order to concentrate the army was only released on the 7th, one day before the Austrians crossed the border. As a result, regiments had to leave their garrisons before they could come close to completing their preparations for war. This unseemly haste caused problems for the duration of the campaign, as clothing and equipment were often either lacking entirely or in poor repair. Footwear was the most pressing deficiency, and as early as 13 October, the commanders of the 3rd and 7th Infantry Regiments were reporting that 'each regiment most urgently requires 400 pairs [of boots] as many NCOs are already nearly bare- . foot'.[3] The historian of the 7th Infantry gives a sense of the atmosphere in early September 1805, 'The feverish activity which surrounded our regiment escalated to panicked confusion when marching orders arrived on 14 September.'[4]

Furthermore, many men could not reach their garrisons before their regiments had to depart. In a remarkable testimony to the loyalty and dedication of the Bavarian soldiery, however, hundreds of men made their way through the Austrian army (and in defiance of Austrian penalties) to join their regiments in their appointed assembly areas. The 5th Infantry, for example, numbered only 440 men when it marched hurriedly out of Landshut on 9 September just ahead of the advancing enemy; by the middle of the month with some 1,800 men in its ranks, it was almost at full strength.[5]

Initially concentrating in two groups at Amberg and Ulm, the army soon moved farther north to place itself as far as possible from the Austrians and await the arrival of the French. By 1 October, therefore, the entire army, a total of some 26,000 men in six brigades, was gathered along the River Main between Bamberg and Würzburg under Deroy's command.[6]

Franz's 7th Infantry Regiment[7], along with the 3rd Infantry, the 2nd Light Battalion and the 1st Chevauxlegers, made up the 3rd Brigade under Major General Paul Count von Mezzanelli. Commanded by Colonel von Pierron, the 7th Infantry had 1,421 officers and men in its two field battalions, with an additional 234 in the two companies that made up the depot. It also had a large wagon train: 12 regimental vehicles (for baggage, ammunition, medical supplies and staff personnel), 10 company wagons (for baggage, cooking gear, etc.), 10 bread wagons, and one wagon for officers who could not march, all requiring 53 civilian drivers and 117 horses.[8] At first quartered in towns along the Main east and south of Würzburg for several days (the depot companies were sent to Würzburg itself), the regiment marched for the Danube on 2 October to embark on its first campaign.

As agreed in the treaty of alliance signed in August, Napoleon placed the the Bavarian Army under the command of a Frenchman, in this case, the proud and quarrelsome Marshal Bernadotte. The Bavarians were quickly added to Bernadotte's I Corps as he headed for the Danube to form the extreme left wing of Napoleon's great envelopment (though the 4th Brigade remained in Würzburg to guard Max Joseph and his court).

To avoid a time-consuming detour, Bernadotte crossed the neutral Prussian territory of Ansbach in accordance with Napoleon's instructions. He employed the Bavarian troops under Wrede as his vanguard as he committed this intentional breach of international norms, probably because having Bavarians in the lead meant that they were the first to violate Prussian neutrality, thereby generating Bavarian–Prussian tension and increasing Max Joseph's reliance on Napoleon. The Bavarian commanders, painfully aware of their country's predicament, tried in vain to avoid this onerous task, but obediently executed their orders with as much dignity and conscientiousness as possible.

As the rapid advance continued, however, Bernadotte kept the Bavarians in the van, according them the honour of being the first to enter Max Joseph's capital, which they did to much popular jubilation on 12 October, Max's saint's day.[9] Wrede performed well as an advance-guard commander during this fast-paced drive on Munich, taking more than 1,400 prisoners and 19 guns from the retreating Austrians between the 11th and 13th.[10] A brief operational pause then ensued as Napoleon prepared for the next phase of the war but, by the 26th, I Corps was on the move again, pushing for the line of the Inn and Salzach Rivers and seizing Salzburg on the 29th.

From this point, the activities of the Bavarian units diverged in two different directions. While Bernadotte and part of the Bavarian contingent left Salzburg on 3 November to participate in the march on Vienna and the subsequent manoeuvres in Bohemia-Moravia, three Bavarian brigades were assigned to assist in the conquest and occupation of the Tyrol. Under Deroy's command, therefore, the 1st, 2nd and 6th Brigades engaged in a number of small actions against Austrian regulars and Tyrolean militia through November and December to protect the main army's strategic right flank and its line of communications on the way to Vienna. As the French and their allies established control over the Tyrol, however, the 2nd Brigade was recalled to join Wrede in Moravia. Similarly, the 4th Brigade was released from its duties in Würzburg in late October and directed to join Wrede as well.

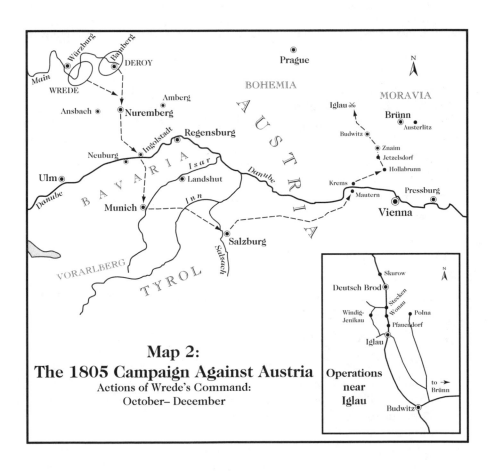

Map 2:
The 1805 Campaign Against Austria
Actions of Wrede's Command:
October– December

On the Edge of Austerlitz

Meanwhile, I Corps, including Wrede's command (*see* Appendix 7, page 255), headed north and east into the Danube valley. Along the way, Wrede replaced Franz's brigade commander, bringing in Major General Hippolyth von Marsigli and sending Mezzanelli back to take over the 2nd Brigade.

The weather was cold and snow frequently covered the ground, but operations began to move at a brisk pace as the climactic battle approached. Keeping up with the hurrying French, Wrede's division reached Mautern on 14 November, crossed the great river on the 16th and 17th, arrived in Hollabrunn that evening (27 miles) and pushed on to Jetzelsdorf with its main body the following day (11 miles), while Wrede himself with his three cavalry regiments pressed as far as Znaim and Budwitz (10 and 17 miles respectively). Wrede was astonished at the exertions expected of his soldiers, writing to Max Joseph on the morning of the 19th,

> If I did not actually see myself here this morning, I would consider it an impossibility that a force which only crossed the Danube the day before yesterday could already be here today and could already have a patrol of 100 troopers posted in Iglau.[11]

Passing through Znaim, Wrede had an opportunity to see Napoleon. After reviewing the Bavarian cavalry regiments, the French Emperor granted the Bavarian general an audience.

> One could not be more graciously treated than I was yesterday by His Majesty the Emperor,

he reported to Max Joseph,

> As I approached Znaim, I sent Major Rechberg ahead to report my arrival and request permission to pass through His Majesty's head-quarters with my cavalry. His Majesty saw fit to send his adjutant Bertrand to me and to say that he would review my cavalry with pleasure, but that he also wished to see me. After the review, I had a very long audience in which His Majesty spoke of the various manoeuvres still to be conducted against the enemy, of the present and future geographic situation of Your Highness' realm and of Your Highness' army.[12]

After this satisfying discussion, Wrede continued north towards Iglau. Expecting a major battle with the combined Austro–Russian army and knowing that Austrian Archduke Ferdinand was in command of a force near Prague, Napoleon wanted to ensure the security of his strategic left flank. He therefore ordered Bernadotte to draw closer to the *Grande Armée* at Brünn with his two French infantry divisions and to post the Bavarians on the road north of Iglau as a shield against anything Ferdinand's corps of some 10,000–12,000 men and 30 guns might undertake.[13] When Bernadotte's French troops marched for Austerlitz on the 29th therefore, Wrede's two brigades, with only 5,950 infantry, 800 cavalry and six guns, came to form the extreme left of the army, far from succour and outnumbered.[14]

Fearing that his small force would be outflanked, Wrede withdrew from his advanced position around Skurow and established himself at Pfauendorf just north of Iglau on 1 December, with outposts at Wonau. The forward position at Wonau, manned by the 2nd Light Battalion, came under attack on 2 December as Ferdinand advanced in three columns via Windig-Jenikau, Wonau and Polna. Its outposts surprised and captured, the 2nd Light regained its position under Wrede's leadership. The cost, however, had been high – 253 Bavarian casualties – and the skirmish could have proved disastrous had the Austrians exploited their initial advantage more vigorously.[15]

The dawn brought news of the Austrian column moving though Windig-Jenikau, thus confirming Wrede's concern about his flanks. Wrede also learned that his hoped-for reinforcements were being diverted to the *Grande Armée*. A message from General Mezzanelli reported that the 2nd Brigade, en route to Iglau, had received orders to march to the main army at Brünn. The Bavarians were thus in an unenviable position, outnumbered, outflanked and with no hope of imminent reinforcement.

Wrede, who may have already known of Napoleon's overwhelming victory at Austerlitz on the 2nd, boldly decided to resolve this operational dilemma by attacking.[16] The attack, launched by the 3rd and 5th Brigades at 1 p.m. on 3 December, was a complete success. In drawn-out fighting that continued into the night, the Bavarians pushed Ferdinand's troops beyond Stecken and caused the Austrian archduke to call back his flanking columns and retire to Deutsch Brod. The 7th played a key part in the fight, especially the 1st Battalion, which seized a wood near Stecken 'with rare determination' according to Wrede's report, while the I/8th pushed into the town itself and the 2nd Light struck the Austrian left. Bavarian losses for the day were less than 100 dead or wounded (2 wounded and 36 missing for the 7th Line), astonishingly light given the length of the engagement and the nature of the outcome.[17]

Combat was renewed on the 5th with a sudden Austrian attack against the Bavarian position at Stecken. That morning, the 7th Infantry was posted with its 1st Battalion in Stecken and the 2nd in a support position some distance behind the town. Moving through the thick woods, the Austrians again succeeded in surprising and capturing the Bavarian outposts (this time including those of the 7th Infantry). Indeed, the Austrian advance was so unexpected that the 1st Battalion in Stecken barely had time to conduct a somewhat disordered retreat on the 2nd Battalion. Fortunately, a timely charge delivered by the *Kurprinz* Chevauxlegers and the accurate fire of the 7th's own Schützen gave the struggling battalion some breathing space. The Bavarians soon recovered their composure and even made some local counterattacks, but the Habsburg troops gained ground steadily and threatened to outflank the entire position.[18] Wrede, who arrived after the engagement had opened, therefore had no choice but to order a withdrawal to Iglau.

To cover his infantry and guns as they pulled back, Wrede now collected his five cavalry regiments and delivered a short but fiery speech, concluding with,

> I would rather be trampled under the hooves of your horses than let the enemy celebrate a single trophy! Swear that you will stand and fight to the last man![19]

Inspired by Wrede's determination, the Bavarian troopers repeatedly charged the advancing Austrians over the snow-clad fields through the gathering evening and on into the night.[20] From 4 p.m. on the 5th to 2.30 a.m. on the 6th, the cavalry clashes rolled back and forth across the Moravian hills under the moonlight with varying results, but they sufficed to hold off the Austrians long enough for the rest of the Bavarian division to retreat to Budwitz in safety.[21]

Against Austrian losses of approximately 750 men, the 20-hour struggle had cost the Bavarians heavily: 200 dead or wounded and some 600 captured or missing. The 7th Line alone lost 199 captured or missing (as compared to only 18 dead or wounded). These men were probably taken prisoner when the 1st Battalion made its hasty withdrawal under pressure from Stecken. Both sides now learned of the armistice between Austria and France and its allies and these prisoners accordingly became an item of contention. Wrede had to threaten to reopen hostilities before Ferdinand would agree to return them. The armistice also required the two armies to redeploy, and, by 10 December, Wrede was back in Iglau, finally joined by the 2nd and 4th Brigades.[22] The Bavarians remained in the area for two more weeks, before setting off for home on Christmas Day 1805, and mostly returning to their garrisons by mid-January.[23]

Observations

Having crushed his opponents on the battlefield, Napoleon proceeded to exploit his victory at the peace table. The Treaty of Pressburg, signed on 26 December, thus imposed harsh terms on the defeated Habsburg

Empire, essentially evicting Austrian influence from Italy and Germany while levying a heavy war indemnity. His army broken, his allies in retreat and his exchequer in ruins, Austrian Emperor Franz had little choice but to accept the humiliating French terms.

While Austria reeled under Napoleon's demands, however, his German allies enjoyed the fruits of the victory. Bavaria received the lion's share of the rewards, acquiring the Tyrol, the Vorarlberg, the Prussian territory of Ansbach (whose neutrality Bavarian troops had violated in October) and numerous small enclaves in and around its traditional lands.[24] These acquisitions not only rounded out the monarchy's borders and removed innumerable impediments to Max's rule, they also dramatically increased its population, stature and income, permitting Napoleon to establish this newly enhanced Bavaria as an independent kingdom with Max Joseph elevated from prince-elector to king. Utterly defeated, Bavaria's hereditary foe, Austria, had no real choice but to recognise its neighbour's new royal status.

Furthermore, Napoleon bound the royal house of Bavaria, the Wittelsbachs, to his own by arranging for his step-son, Eugène de Beauharnais, the Viceroy of Italy, to marry Max Joseph's daughter Auguste Amalie in January 1806. Enlarged, consolidated, provided with more defensible borders and basking in Napoleon's grace, Bavaria, therefore, could only be satisfied with the outcome of the war.

The army, too, gained from the experience of 1805. Marching side-by-side with their veteran French allies under one of the greatest commanders of all time, the Bavarians learned first-hand how warfare was changing. It was a dramatic introduction to the speed and violence of Napoleonic combat. The key lessons for the Bavarian Army, however, were in security and mobility rather than tactics.

As in earlier wars, Bavaria's soldiers proved themselves courageous on the battlefield and, in most cases, tactically competent as well. Some of the small scale operations in the Tyrol were particularly well executed, and Wrede's command performed superbly on 3 and 5 December, these engagements being highlighted by excellent co-operation among infantry, cavalry and artillery. Outpost operations and field security, however, proved to be serious weaknesses. Wrede's men, for example, were inexcusably surprised on at least two occasions, and his command was fortunate that its Austrian opponents were not more enterprising.

The endurance Napoleon expected of his men also came as a shock. French Général de Division Marie François Caffarelli du Falga, an officer on the Imperial General Staff, thus remarked to Napoleon that,

> the Bavarian troops are well motivated and have fought very well in a number of skirmishes, but they do not march like those of Your Majesty and must always be pushed.[25]

Poor march discipline and an excess of baggage and vehicles were major problems, leading Bernadotte in an especially egregious case to remove Colonel Karl Baron von Buseck from the head of the 4th Infantry Regiment during a march and send him off under arrest. Though he tried in vain to have Buseck reinstated, General Deroy acknowledged that Bernadotte's assessment of Buseck had been accurate and that the regiment's officers contributed to its poor appearance,

> promoted from the ranks, old, fat from too much beer-drinking, clumsy, with long uniform coats down to their ankles and even longer overcoats which they can only drag through the mud with difficulty... moreover, they have long displayed an overly relaxed attitude toward the other ranks, which has caused discipline to deteriorate.[26]

The 7th Infantry earned some especially harsh criticism from Wrede on 4 October,

> With displeasure I noted today the utterly unacceptable disorder in which the 7th Regiment marched. Not only had the regiment numerous stragglers, but I also noticed many companies with no officers, and I saw nearly half of the officers riding in wagons...

Four days later, the situation was no better,

> I give a final warning to the 7th Regiment, which never marches closed up and in sections as prescribed.[27]

Indeed, problems like this remained a factor all the way through the campaign, so that Wrede felt it necessary to chastise his officers once more in mid-December,

> I must express my displeasure to the brigade commanders that many regimental commanders, contrary to standing orders, rode in the midst of the columns in carriages with horses, and tolerated almost all of their subordinate officers riding behind their regiments in wagons rather than marching with their companies.[28]

These deficiencies notwithstanding (and it is worth recalling that the army was still in the process of reforming itself), Napoleon expressed his sincere thanks to Max Joseph for the contributions Bavaria's soldiers had made to the triumph over Austria.

> My brother!
>
> At the moment when Your Majesty's troops re-enter your king-dom and cease to come under my orders, I would like to express my satisfaction with their services and the courage they displayed in the

various affairs against Kienmayer's corps before the passage of the Inn and later at the engagements at Lofer and Iglau.

Desiring to give them a proof of that satisfaction, I ask you, my brother, to permit me to award General Deroy a pension and to make General Wrede a Grand Officer in my Legion of Honour, and to permit me to give to those who most distinguished themselves 40 places in my Legion of Honour, 20 to officers and 20 to soldiers, with the enjoyment of appropriate pensions according to the constitution of the Legion.

These recompenses are not proportionate to the services they have rendered, but they are a proof of my esteem and of the respect with which I regard your army. They were animated by the justice of our cause and by the knowledge that they were defending their sovereign and their fatherland. They are worthy to be a part of the *Grande Armée*.[29]

In this hard school of war, the Bavarian Army thus came to understand that Napoleon expected every exertion of officers and men all the time, that nothing was to be considered impossible, and that distinct rewards and punishments would be the consequences of every soldier's action or inaction.

The army that returned to its home garrisons in January 1806 was still growing, just beginning to adjust to the shifting nature of war, but its own accomplishments and its association with the stunning success of the campaign allowed its soldiers to march with a new sense of self-respect and self-confidence.[30] Casting aside many outdated notions along with their queues, they came home as victors for the first time in many years, feeling part of something greater than themselves and ready for the next challenge.

Military Diary of
FRANZ JOSEPH HAUSMANN
for the
FIRST AUSTRIAN CAMPAIGN
From 14 September 1805,
when the 7th (Fürst Löwenstein) Line Infantry Regiment
marched out, until its return to the garrison
on 17 January 1806.

September 1805

14 September To Donauwörth in Bavaria.

15 September To Gundelfingen in Bavaria.

16 September To Unterstotzingen in Bavaria.

17 September To Schneidheim in Bavaria.

18 September To Ellwangen in Württemberg, where the 19th was a day of rest.

20 September To Rappersdorf.

21 September To Orlach.

22 September To Kreitshausen.

23 September To Untereichenroth.

25 September To Onsfeld.

26 September To Rindensheim.

27 September To Kitzingen.

28 September Our army joined up with that of the French, and because of the hard marches the Bavarian Corps had to remain in place on this day.

29 September To Wiesenbronn.

30 September To Kleinlangheim. On these two days the army assembled en masse near Kitzingen.

October 1805

1 October Marched all afternoon and night, after which we

2 October arrived at Kitzingen at 5 o'clock in the morning, but in the afternoon we set out again and spent the night at Briksenstadt.

3 October To Lonnerstadt. Crossed the Aisch.

4 October Bivouac near Niederndorf in Prussia.

5 October Near Schwabach.

6 October	Near Spalt.
7 October	Near Weissenburg.
8 October	At the fork near Ingolstadt. Crossed the Altmühl.
9 October	Bivouac at Unser Herr. Today to Ingolstadt and crossed the Danube there.
10 October	Bivouacked near Holzenkam.
11 October	Bivouac near Schleissheim.
12 October	Arrived in the city of Munich, crossed the Isar, and bivouacked near Neuwirtshaus.
13 October	Bivouacked in the woods near Anzing. The Army Corps had to remain here; during this time, on the 23rd the victory of the seizure of Ulm was celebrated.
26 October	Near Ebersberg.
27 October	To Wasserburg.
28 October	Crossed the Inn and bivouacked near Altenmark.
29 October	Near Teisendorf.
30 October	Salzburg taken, and bivouacked 1½ hours from Salzburg near Einödhöfen.

November 1805

3 November	The Corps reconnoitred toward Hof and immediately came back.
4 November	Camp near Frankenmarkt.
5 November	Camp near Lambach.
6 November	Camp near St Peter.
7 November	Camp near Steyer.
8 November	Camp near Seitenstetten.
9 November	Camp near Hausmening.
10 November	Camp near Steinakirchen.
11 November	Camp near the Mölk monastery.
12 November	Camp near St Pölten.
14 November	Camp near Ambach.
15 November	Camp near Mautern.
18 November	Here crossed the Danube. Through Stein and Krems, across the battlefield near Schöngrabern.
19 November	Marched until almost morning, then bivouacked near Hollabrunn. Set out again at noon and bivouacked near Budwitz in Moravia.[31]
20 November	Grossbietetzka.

23 November	To Wangen.
26 November	To Holzmühlen near Iglau.
27 November	To Dirn in Bohemia.
28 November	To Linden. Here the division took up a position on the road to Prague, in order to cover it and to halt any enemy that might try to break through.
29 November	It was learned that the Austrian Archduke Ferdinand was threatening to throw a large corps of his from Prague against our corps, and therefore

December 1805

1 December	we took up a defensive position near Pfauendorf and went into bivouac there.
2 December	The (von Metzen) Light Infantry Battalion,[32] which had passed ahead of us in the woods, was attacked by the enemy, and since it suffered considerable losses it was replaced by our regiment. On the evening of this day we were commanded to withdraw until behind Pfauendorf, where several hundred cords of wood had been piled up. The corps stood at arms throughout the night, while from time to time enemy patrols shot at us.
3 December	Lieutenant General von Wrede had us take the offensive, and when we came to within half an hour's distance from Stecken, we met up with the enemy. After a short but heavy skirmish the enemy withdrew past Stecken toward Linden, and we took up a position on the heights in front of Stecken.
4 December	We remained quietly where we were.
5 December	At about 2 o'clock in the afternoon the Austrians attacked our right flank with such a superior force that the troops that had been in the outposts had to abandon Stecken
	and sought to take the heights on this side. Owing to its weakness, the corps had to fear new flanking movements from the enemy's superior strength at any moment in this wooded and uneven terrain, so we hung around on the above-mentioned heights until 5 o'clock in the evening and took advantage of the night for our gradual withdrawal. The rear-guard skirmish lasted until 2 o'clock in the morning, while the corps retreated through Iglau to Budwitz, where we arrived at 8 o'clock on the morning of the 6th.

6 December	The news arrived that on the 4th a cease fire had been agreed upon between His Majesty the Emperor of the French and His Majesty the Emperor of Austria at Austerlitz, and that according to it the advantages obtained by Archduke Ferdinand were therefore not valid, and that the prisoners as well as the captured territory had to be returned. Therefore
7 December	after Archduke Ferdinand would not agree either to releasing the prisoners he had taken or to turning over the terrain he had seized, we again moved forward to Neu-Cerowitz.
8 December	The Bavarian brigade under General Baron Karg [4th Brigade] that had been sent to us arrived, and we also received reinforcement from several units from French Marshal Berthier's [actually Bernadotte's] Corps.
9 December	Again advanced as far as Stannern, and there
10 December	His Highness Archduke Ferdinand not only turned over the 500 prisoners he had taken but also withdrew the Imperial Austrian Corps to Deutsch Brod. Our corps thereupon marched into cantonment, specifically our regiment to Ruschenau. As peace was concluded between the supreme monarchs during this cease fire, all corps had to remove themselves from the Austrian provinces, and we therefore marched
27 December	to Königseck in Bohemia.
28 December	To Tomani in Bohemia.
29 December	To Wienau near Gratzen in Bohemia.
30 December	To Bömdorf.
31 December	To Harmannschlag. The division remained here until 1 January 1806. Peace was officially announced, and the Prince-Elector of Bavaria was rendered homage as King, whereupon we marched

January 1806

2 January	to Leopoltschlag in Bohemia.
3 January	To Engewitzdorf in Upper Austria.
4 January	To Linz in Austria. Crossed the Danube.
5 January	To Wels in Austria.
6 January	To Unterfils in Austria.
7 January	To Oberleithen in Austria.
8 January	To Altheim in Austria.

9 January	To Oberrottenbuch in Bavaria.
10 January	To Taufkirchen.
11 January	To Pilsting.
12 January	To Straubing.
13 January	To Pfatter.
14 January	To Pröll near Regensburg.
15 January	To Pullach near Vohburg.
16 January	To Ingolstadt.
17 January	Crossed the Danube and into the garrison at Neuburg.

Notes to Chapter Two

[1] For a detailed overview of the diplomatic background see Paul W. Schroeder, *The Transformation of European Politics*, Oxford: Clarendon Press, 1994, chapter 5.

[2] Quoted in Marcus Junkelmann, *Napoleon und Bayern*, Regensburg: Pustet, 1985, p. 89.

[3] Joint report by Colonel Pierron (7th) and Colonel Neumann (3rd), 13 October 1805, in Auvera, p. 355.

[4] Ibid., p. 346.

[5] Some units did, however, experience problems with desertion (the 2nd Light had 58 deserters), and strict orders were issued to tighten security around the field encampments (Ibid., p. 350).

[6] Max Leyh, *Die Feldzüge des Bayerischen Heeres unter Max I. (IV.) Joseph von 1805 bis 1815,* vol. VI/2 of *Geschichte des Bayerischen Heeres,* Munich: Schick, 1935, pp. 7–9.

[7] General Count von Morawitzky had relinquished his post as regimental proprietor on 25 January 1805 and Max had not yet appointed a replacement, so the regiment fought through 1805 with no title other than its number (Auvera, p. 343).

[8] Ibid., pp. 349–50.

[9] The army celebrated Max's saint's (christening) day every year with all manner of festivities, including special religious services, banquets and balls (just as the French marked Napoleon's birthday).

[10] A small controversy surrounds Wrede's actions before entering Munich. French General Auguste Ameil, then an officer in the 5th Chasseurs, claims in his recollections that Wrede intentionally paused outside of Munich to allow the Austrians to escape (extracts printed in Sauzey, pp. 373–8). Bavarian authors, on the other hand, maintain that Bernadotte ordered Wrede to halt (for example, Leyh, p. 16).

[11] Leyh, p. 38.

[12] Ibid.

[13] One of Bernadotte's two French infantry divisions was commanded by Général de Division Jean-Baptiste Drouet, Count d'Erlon, who would serve first as chief of staff and then as commander of the Bavarian VII Corps in 1809.

[14] These figures taken from Leyh (pp. 37, 43), Völderndorff disagrees, stating that there were only some 4,500 infantry and 400 cavalry (Völderndorff und Waradein, Eduard Freiherr von, *Kriegsgeschichte von Bayern unter König Maximilian Joseph I*, Munich, 1826, Book 3, p. 287).

[15] Völderndorff, Book 3, pp. 289–91.

[16] Leyh concludes that Wrede already knew of Napoleon's victory, but Völderndorff maintains the Bavarian commander did not receive word of Austerlitz until the 5th. Auvera (p. 365) states that two couriers arrived on the morning of 6 December with news of Austerlitz and the armistice. Franz recorded that news of the armistice arrived on the 6th, but he makes no mention of the Battle of Austerlitz.

[17] Auvera, pp. 360–1, describes the 7th's participation.

[18] For the 7th Infantry's part in the battle, see ibid., pp. 362–5.

[19] Ludwig von Madroux, 'August von Floret', *Archiv für Offiziere aller Waffen*, Band II, Munich: 1846.

[20] The 2nd Dragoons and a battery had arrived by forced marches on the 4th (Leyh, p. 45).

[21] Two companies of the 4th Infantry sent by Mezzanelli played a key role, holding the town of Iglau while their comrades filed through during the night (Völderndorff, Book 3, p. 302).

[22] Note that Franz's diary entry of 8 December only mentions the 4th Brigade, which was commanded by Major General Theodor Baron von Karg-Bebenburg.

[23] The 7th Infantry, for example, returned to Neuburg on 17 January. Note that a number of units were ordered to occupy the newly-acquired Tyrol and thus did not return to their previous peacetime garrisons.

[24] Bavaria gained more than one million inhabitants in its new territories, but also lost some 500,000 in giving up Würzburg (to Grand Duke Ferdinand, a Habsburg) and Berg (to French Marshal Joachim Murat).

[25] Leyh, p. 53.

[26] Reports from Deroy, late October 1805, in Auvera, pp. 370–1.

[27] Wrede, march dispositions for 4 and 8 October 1805, in ibid., p. 353.

[28] Ibid., pp. 48, 54; also Bezzel, p. 147.

[29] Letter to Max Joseph, 6 January 1806 in Napoleon I, *Correspondance*, Paris: Plon, 1858–70, no. 9,652.

[30] Leyh, p. 56.

[31] Small discrepancies between Franz's dates here and those in Leyh's account probably result from the Bavarians marching in long, strung-out columns so that trailing units might not reach a given point until a day or two after the lead unit had passed through. However, Franz seems to have got the sequence backwards as regards Hollabrunn and Schöngrabern; the regimental history has the 7th Infantry passing through Hollabrunn first, which is almost certainly correct.

[32] Franz mistakenly calls this unit Light Battalion *von Metzen* (that is, the 1st Light), it was actually the 2nd Light Battalion, commanded by Lieutenant Colonel von Dietfurth.

Chapter Three

War with Prussia and Russia, 1806–07

Unfortunately, we have neither letters nor diaries from Franz for the 1806–07 war against Prussia and Russia. However, a review of Bavarian participation in this conflict will serve to round out our understanding of Franz's military career and to place his other experiences in context.

Between the conclusion of the Austrian war of 1805 and the opening of the struggle with Prussia nine months later, Bavaria's relationship with France had altered significantly. Where Max Joseph's troops had marched against Austria under the terms of a strictly bilateral treaty arrangement with Napoleon, by the autumn of 1806 the kingdom had entered into a multilateral security organisation under French leadership, the Confederation of the Rhine or *Rheinbund*. The *Rheinbund* provided Napoleon with a means to expand his influence in central Germany at the expense of the Habsburg and Hohenzollern monarchies.

In essence, the *Rheinbund* was a military organisation. Although Napoleon's original plans called for the confederation to embrace political, social, economic and judicial institutions, as well as military, from the very outset, the security aspect was paramount and the other proposed features quickly fell into dormancy, never progressing beyond the concept stage. According to the 'constitutional act' signed by France and the other fifteen original members on 12 July 1806, each member state committed itself to providing a contingent for the common defence in case of crisis or war. These ranged in size from the 200,000 Frenchmen promised by Napoleon as the 'Protector' of the confederation to the 29 owed by the Prince von der Leyen's miniature monarchy. Bavaria, as the largest of the German states, was assessed the largest military contingent and was thus required to supply 30,000 men when called upon to meet supposedly common dangers. These troops were Napoleon's chief concern; as he told Montgelas in December 1807, 'The only thing that matters is having the 30,000 Bavarian soldiers.'[1]

In ratifying the *Rheinbund* agreement, Max Joseph gained a myriad of territories that brought some 500,000 new citizens into his kingdom. He also bolstered thereby his centralising monarchy's internal sovereignty and integrity by sweeping away the last trammels of the Holy Roman

Empire. These benefits had their price, however, and by entering the confederation, Max had to accept two painful, if unstated, conditions: tight constraints on his external sovereignty and almost inescapable involvement in any war Napoleon should decide to undertake.[2] October 1806 thus found Bavarian battalions en route to war with Prussia, a state which, unlike Austria, did not pose an immediate and vital threat to Bavaria's interests, a state, indeed, toward which the Bavarians had looked for help (albeit in vain) as recently as 1805.

The creation of the *Rheinbund* was also one of the causes of the war that now arose between Prussia and France. In Berlin, this step toward consolidation of French power east of the Rhine was considered a dangerous affront and, combined with the continued presence of the *Grande Armée* in southern Germany, was taken as a direct threat to Prussian interests. Moreover, many in Prussia were convinced that Napoleon intended a war of conquest against their state as soon as such a campaign was practicable. For this body of opinion the only recourse was an immediate pre-emptive offensive against the French forces in Germany.

The final straw came in the form of reports from the Prussian ambassador in Paris indicating that Napoleon was considering depriving Prussia of Hanover, the coveted province which the French Emperor had handed to the Prussian king only several months earlier.[3] Desperately bellicose, the Prussian government issued an ultimatum demanding, among other things, the immediate withdrawal of all French troops west of the Rhine. Napoleon answered by directing 200,000 men toward Berlin.

Opening Marches

In the late summer of 1806, the Bavarian Army was organised in three divisions, each with a separate and distinct mission (*see* Appendix 7, pages 255–6). The 1st Division, under Deroy, was initially detailed to watch the border with Austria. The 2nd Division, on the other hand, was immediately called to join the *Grande Armée* on the march into Prussian territory. Wrede had been designated for this command, but a sudden illness kept him at home, and it was March 1807 before he was fit enough to join the army. Napoleon, who showed Wrede much favour, was disappointed, writing to the Bavarian general on 3 November,

> I am most annoyed with your illness, I had counted on you in this campaign as I know your zeal and your talent, proofs enough of which you gave me last year.[4]

In Wrede's stead, Major General Mezzanelli (Franz's brigade commander at the beginning of the 1805 campaign) led the division in the initial weeks of the war. Finally, a Reserve Division was established under Lieutenant General Georg Count von Ysenburg-Büdingen to garrison the Tyrol and key fortresses.[5] This organisation changed significantly several times during the war, and, by the time hostilities ceased, almost the entire Bavarian Army had been committed to one or another of the theatres of war.

The several reorganisations notwithstanding, Franz's 7th Infantry Regiment remained in Major General Franz Xaver von Minucci's 2nd Brigade of the 2nd Division throughout the conflict. When it marched to war, however, the 7th Infantry had both a new proprietor and a new commander. On 31 May Lieutenant General Dominik Prince von Löwenstein-Wertheim had become the regimental proprietor, and Colonel Karl Baron von Stengel was named to command the regiment just before it left Neuburg for the campaign. Although the previous commander, Colonel von Pierron, soon moved on to assume command of the 4th Infantry, more than five months would pass before von Stengel was able to join his new regiment deep in Poland.

Like many other *Rheinbund* troops, the Bavarian contingent played a decidedly secondary role in the first phase of the war. While the 1st Division observed the Austrians, the 2nd Division followed the right hand column of the *Grande Armée*. Arriving in Bayreuth on 9 October, it was placed under the command of Napoleon's youngest brother, Jérôme, charged with the task of reducing Plassenburg, a Prussian-occupied fortress on one of the principal roads leading into Thuringia. The blockade, however, did not require an entire division, so the 13th Infantry was detached to observe the tiny fortress (which finally surrendered on 25 November), while the rest of the division hurried ahead to reach Schleiz on 13 October. The division spent several days in this town, guarding the road to Leipzig in Napoleon's rear during the Battle of Jena–Auerstädt on the 14th and giving Jérôme an opportunity to inspect his first land command, reporting to his brother,

> I have reviewed 4,367 infantry and 1,235 cavalry and have found them in good condition, excellently trained and full of the desire for combat.[6]

On 18 October the Bavarians marched for Dresden to occupy the Saxon capital and protect the army's right. Enjoying a few day's rest in Dresden, they learned that Napoleon had placed Jérôme in command of the 'Allied Army' to consist of the 1st and 2nd Bavarian Divisions and the Württemberg contingent. The 1st Division was already en route for Dresden, having left Ingolstadt on 19 October, but the fast pace of the war was dragging the *Grande Armée* east into Poland, so the 2nd Division could not await the arrival of its compatriots. Instead, it left Dresden on

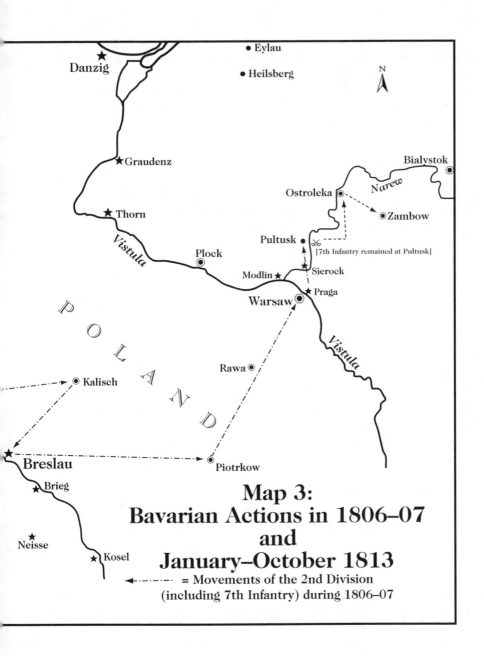

Eylau

Heilsberg

Danzig

N

Graduedz

Bialystok

Narew

Thorn

Ostroleka

Zambow

Vistula

Pultusk

[7th Infantry remained at Pultusk]

Plock

Modlin

Sierock

Warsaw

Praga

Vistula

Rawa

Kalisch

Breslau

Piotrkow

Brieg

Map 3:
Bavarian Actions in 1806–07
and
January–October 1813

Neisse

Kosel

= Movements of the 2nd Division
(including 7th Infantry) during 1806–07

the last day of October and pushed on to reach the Oder River at Krossen [Krosno] on 4 November. Here Jérôme was finally able to unite his new command, because the Bavarian 1st Division and a Württemberg Division under Lieutenant General von Seckendorff arrived on the 7th and 8th.[7] Rapidly reorganising by pulling the Bavarian and Württemberg light cavalry regiments out of their various mixed formations and forming them into three independent brigades (Mezzanelli was designated to lead one of these new cavalry brigades, so command of the 2nd Division devolved to Minucci), the 'Allied Army' left Krossen between 5 and 9 November for Silesia.

Silesian Sieges, 1806–07

Jérôme and most of his command spent the remainder of the war in Silesia, reducing Prussian fortresses and conducting a 'lieutenant's war' of small but vicious meeting engagements and ambushes.[8] The first target was Glogau [Glogow] which was invested on 10 November and fell on 2 December. From Glogau, the Bavarians shifted to Breslau [Wroclaw], with the 2nd Division arriving before the city on 8 December followed by the 1st Division ten days later. The Schützen of the 7th Infantry participated in an attempt to storm the walls in the predawn hours of the 23rd along with Schützen from the 3rd Light Battalion, the 2nd and 3rd Infantry Regiments, and a Württemberg detachment. Unfortunately, the materials available to cross the fortress' wet ditch proved inadequate, and by the time more had been brought forward, the morning light had revealed the struggling Schützen to the city's defenders. Deluged with artillery fire, the Bavarians and Württembergers were forced back to their trenches. The failed assault cost the Bavarians 76 casualties and Jérôme settled into a desultory siege, fending off several Prussian relief efforts before the fortress surrendered on 7 January.

Most of the 2nd Division remained in Breslau as its garrison while the other elements of Jérôme's command, now honoured by Napoleon with the title 'IX Corps of the *Grande Armée*', proceeded to invest Brieg, Schweidnitz and Kosel [Brzeg, Swidnica, Kozle]. Brieg fell on 17 January and Schweidnitz a month later, but the commandant of Kosel did not sign a capitulation until June and the fortress was still in Prussian hands when the war ended in July.

Skirmishes and small sieges continued in southern Silesia from March through June 1807 as the 1st Bavarian Division and the Württembergers endeavoured to overcome or neutralise Prussian forces around the fortresses of Glatz, Neisse and Silberberg [Klodzko, Nysa, Swieciechow]. Despite the energetic leadership of the Prussian Governor General, Major Friedrich Wilhelm Count von Goetzen, Jérôme's men were generally successful, winning most of the engagements in the open field and forcing the surrender of both Glatz and Neisse. Though constantly reduced by drafts sent to the 2nd Division in Poland, they therefore accomplished their mission of securing Napoleon's right flank, and, when the peace treaties with Russia and Prussia were signed at Tilsit in July, only the insignificant citadel of Silberberg remained unconquered.[9]

While the Bavarian 1st Division and the Württembergers were establishing control over the southern half of Silesia, the 2nd Division was participating in operations in Poland.[10] The division departed Breslau approximately 7,000 strong on 22 February 1807 to join Général de Division Anne-Jean-Marie-René Savary's thinly stretched French V Corps shielding Napoleon's far right flank along the Vistula [Wisla] and Narew Rivers. Arriving in Warsaw on 8 March, the 2nd Division was granted two days of rest before moving to its assigned sector running from Praga through Sierock [Serock] to Pultusk.

Several important changes in the division's command and structure took effect during this period. In the first place, Crown Prince Ludwig, Napoleon's inveterate and intemperate foe, had arrived in Warsaw in late January, and now assumed titular command of all Bavarian forces in Poland. Wrede, however, having recovered from his illness, was the true guiding hand once he appeared on the scene on 4 April. Secondly, after long delay, the 7th Infantry was able to welcome its new commander, Colonel von Stengel. Former commander of the 4th Light, von Stengel had been appointed to take over the 7th Line back in October, but was diverted to temporary assignment with the headquarters in Silesia and only joined the regiment on 13 April.

Finally, the entire division underwent yet another reorganisation in order to accommodate the numerous reinforcements it had received. Its 15 battalions and 8 squadrons were now divided among three infantry brigades and a cavalry brigade, with a total strength of some 13,300 men supported by 24 guns. As for the 7th Infantry, it numbered 38 officers, 74 NCOs, 17 musicians and 1,571 soldiers in the two field battalions in Poland and an additional 7 officers, 7 NCOS, 3 musicians and 342 men with the two depot companies in Bavaria.[11]

March and April passed quietly for V Corps, now under Marshal André Massena, but Russian movements prompted Napoleon to seek a firmer grip on the Narew. He therefore ordered Massena to cross the river, secure the far bank and attack any Russian force that sought to impede his advance. Under the overall command of French Général de Division Jean Le Marois, Colonel Pierron's Brigade therefore crossed the Narew at Sierock on 10 May, established a bridgehead, constructed a bridge over the river and pushed three battalions forward in an advanced position. The Russians did not react immediately, but waited until the night of 13/14 May to launch a powerful attack against the Bavarian brigade. In heavy fighting that cost over 100 casualties (including Pierron, former commander of the 7th Infantry, mortally wounded), the Bavarians were driven back on the works of the bridge-head before they could bring the Russian attack to a standstill. The 14th Infantry, only formed the preceding autumn, manned the defences and was instrumental in repelling the Russian attack.

At 4 a.m. on the 14th, Colonel Lessel's 2nd Brigade (including the 7th Infantry) crossed the river near Pultusk under the eyes of the Crown Prince.[12] Surprising the Russians, the Bavarian infantry quickly over-came light resistance to clear the eastern bank. As at Sierock, the Russians again gave the 3,000 Bavarians time to construct a bridge and to begin securing their position with field works; moreover, competent reconnaissance carried out by the Bavarians during the 15th had pro-vided advance warning that their enemies might undertake something the next day. As a result, the Bavarians were not entirely unprepared when strong Russian columns (totalling some 10,000 men in five infantry regiments, a hussar regiment, a Cossack regiment, and two or three artillery pieces) debouched from a large wood to advance against the bridgehead around noon on the 16th.

Outnumbered, the foremost Bavarian troops (3rd Light, I/3rd and I/7th from left to right) formed squares on Wrede's orders and coolly fell back to their half-completed breastworks. Once behind this partial pro-tection, the infantry halted and redeployed to turn a steady musketry on the advancing Russians. Combined with excellent support from their superior artillery in the bridgehead, on an island and across the river, the Bavarian foot soldiers proceeded to break up three attempts to storm their field fortifications. Unable to throw the Bavarians back across the river, the Russians withdrew in the late afternoon, cautiously followed by the Bavarians who were content to re-occupy their original positions. The repulse of this attack at Pultusk cost the Bavarian brigade 322 men (of these 3 dead, 72 wounded, and 22 captured were from the 7th Infantry), but represented a tidy little victory which ensured the security of Napoleon's flank, substantially enhanced the confidence of the troops and provided the Crown Prince with his first combat experience.[13]

The second half of May passed with only a few skirmishes as Bavarian reconnaissance probes attempted to gather information about Russian strength and intentions. In June, however, when Massena learned of Napoleon's decisive victory at Friedland on the 14th, V Corps began to advance. Leaving the 7th Infantry behind at Pultusk, the corps slowly followed the retreating Russians toward the borders of the Tsar's realm.[14] Although the Bavarian division led the advance, there were no encounters of any significance and the campaign came to a close when news of the Franco-Russian armistice (signed on 21 June) reached Massena on the 27th.

For both Bavarian divisions, there now followed a long period of occupation duty. Placed under Marshal Adolphe-Édouard Mortier's VIII Corps in Silesia, Wrede's Division filled its days with intensive training and numerous inspections, highlighted by a 22 September divisional exercise at Leuthen where Wrede had his men re-enact Frederick the Great's famous oblique assault on the Austrian left flank during the Battle of Leuthen in December 1757; a battle in which the linear ancestor of the 7th Infantry, the *Churprinz* Regiment, had partici-pated. Deroy's men, on the other hand, left Silesia in late August 1807 for the area between Berlin and Stettin [Szczecin], but not before the 2nd Chevauxlegers had been accorded the special honour of escorting Napoleon on his return trip from Glogau to Saxony (mid-July).

The two divisions remained in these locales until November and finally returned to their garrisons in late December after an absence of some 16 months. The return of the 7th Infantry provided Neuburg with an occasion for a day of festivities. Cannon thundered, people cheered, the militia paraded, the city and the Danube bridge were caparisoned with flags, and the regiment passed in review before two royal princesses and other dignitaries. Immediately thereafter, however, the the regiment returned to its peacetime strength with numerous men being sent off on furlough.

Distant Diversions

Although not directly related to Lieutenant Franz Hausmann and the 7th Infantry Regiment, the little-known actions of two other Bavarian units deserve mention.

While the bulk of the Bavarian contingent was occupied in Silesia and Poland, a single regiment represented the kingdom in the larger battles and manoeuvres of the *Grande Armée*. When the Bavarian contin-gent was reorganised in Krossen in early November 1806, the 1st Chevauxlegers had been detached to form a light cavalry brigade with the French 11th Chasseurs à Cheval. Initially commanded by Général de Brigade Pierre Watier, the brigade participated in the main army's December offensive to the Narew, in the winter campaign of 1807 that culminated in the ugly struggle at Eylau, and in Napoleon's concluding summer offensive. Assigned to the cavalry reserve under Marshal Joachim Murat, the 1st Chevauxlegers thus fought at Eylau and Heilsberg, but missed the final triumph at Friedland. Bavarian veterans fondly recalled Napoleon saying 'I value the Bavarian cavalry as highly as the infantry of my Guard, it is the best in the world.'[15]

The other unit was the brigade of Major General Karl von Vincenti which served briefly on the Baltic coast. Composed of the 9th Infantry Regiment, the 1st Light Battalion, the 4th Chevauxlegers and an artillery battery, the brigade was called north to reinforce Marshal Guillaume Brune's 'Observation Corps of the *Grande Armée*', a multinational command containing French, Dutch, Spanish and German (from Bavaria, Berg, Hesse, Nassau, and Würzburg) troops posted in northern Germany to counter enterprises by Prussia's allies, Britain and Sweden.[16]

On leaving Bamberg on 5 June, Vincenti reported that his 3,200 soldiers were motivated by 'the best will and true patriotic feeling'.[17] The brigade, however, found almost no opportunity to express its patriotism on the field of battle. Other than some brief and minor skirmishing on 13 July, during Brune's invasion of Swedish Pomerania (the Swedish king persisted in maintaining the war even after learning of the peace treaties and despite the departure of his British and Prussian allies), Vincenti's men spent their weeks in guard, patrol, occupation, and other support duties along the Baltic and on the island of Rügen. Finally departing in the second half of November, Vincenti's Brigade returned home in late December 1807 like the other elements of the Bavarian contingent.

Observations

As in 1805, the Bavarian campaign experience in 1806–07 was almost exclusively associated with protecting the flanks and rear of the *Grande Armée*. Deroy's and Wrede's men were afforded no opportunities to test their mettle in a major combat, and none of the army's leaders had a chance truly to display his skills. At the same time, the experience was different from that of the preceding campaign. Where the war against Austria and Russia in 1805 had been primarily one of arduous marches and swift manoeuvres, for the Bavarian contingent the conflict with Prussia and Russia was characterised above all by siege warfare. Small-scale forays which placed a premium on junior-level leadership were also an important feature of this war and the Bavarians consistently showed themselves in good light during the many little engagements that punctuated their Silesian sojourn. They also did well in Poland, where even the newly-formed 14th Infantry demonstrated admirable firmness. As Bavarian historian Max Leyh points out, the consistently good performance of the Bavarian troops was founded on confidence in themselves and in their leaders, based on their previous experiences in 1805 as well as the glowing reputation of Napoleon and his army.[18]

Outpost duty remained, however, a significant exception to this generally favourable picture. The Prussians seem to have surprised and seized Bavarian pickets and guards with relative ease, and French commanders continued to lament the Bavarian Army's lax approach to field security and reconnaissance.[19]

Although not without the frictions attendant upon almost any military alliance or coalition (particularly with Jérôme's Chief of Staff, Général de Division Gabriel Comte d'Hedouville), Bavarian relations with their French allies remained generally good.[20] The Bavarians rightly felt that the French frequently treated them like second-class soldiers, and this sentiment brought occasional expressions of disgruntlement but, with minor exceptions (such as the Crown Prince), these complaints were not manifestations of some pervasive, deep-seated anti-French ire. Indeed, beyond the annoyance with inadequate logistical arrangements and preferential treatment for French troops, much of the Bavarian displeasure arose from the perception that they were sometimes denied their fair share of honour and glory for their achievements. That is to say that, even in this war where the issue had no relation to Bavarian national interests, the army in general did not object so much to fighting for Napoleon, as to not having an opportunity to demonstrate its martial prowess in the principal theatre of operations (Vincenti's Brigade, for example), or to not receiving its due rewards and recognition for its role in the victory.[21]

If the Bavarian Army's combat performance was satisfactory, its comportment off the battlefield was often less than admirable. Every army of the era had units or individuals whose treatment of civilian populations was questionable if not disgraceful, but the Bavarians acquired an especially poor reputation during this war, most notably during their march through Saxony.[22] There were important exceptions, however, and Vincenti's men earned sincere gratitude from their French commanders, as well as from civilian authorities, for their discipline and honourable behaviour.[23]

Gaining steadily in experience and tactical skill, if still weak in outpost duties, the Bavarian Army could take pride in its contributions to the successful conclusion of the 1806–07 conflict with Prussia and Russia. Most of its laurels, however, had been gathered in dull siege work on secondary fields, far from the eye of the Emperor, far from the great battles. Officers and men thus felt frustrated and looked forward to an opportunity to prove themselves in a major contest in close association with the *Grande Armée*. Their moment would not be long in coming.

Notes to Chapter Three

[1] Quoted in Junkelmann, p. 155.

[2] However, it is important to note that Bavaria was not entirely a vassal of France. It was, for example, one of the few *Rheinbund* states that did not end up sending a significant part of its army to Spain.

[3] As part of the territorial settlement following the victory over Austria, Prussia gave up Ansbach to Bavaria and gained Hanover, while Bavaria passed over its remaining Rhenish lands to Napoleon who turned them into Marshal Murat's Grand Duchy of Berg.

[4] Quoted in Leyh, p. 116.

[5] Note that one Bavarian military historian claims that he could find no reference to Ysenburg's Division in the Bavarian archives (G. Paulus, 'Bayerische Kriegsvorbereitung, Mobilmachung und Einleitung zum Feldzuge 1809', *Darstellungen aus der Bayerischen Kriegs- und Heeresgeschichte*, Heft 2, Munich: 1893, pp. 99–100). Max Leyh, on the other hand, writing some 30 years later with equal access to archival materials, includes Ysenburg's Reserve Division in his account of Bavaria's preparations for the war with Prussia. As the units intended to comprise this division were quickly distributed elsewhere and as Ysenburg retained his regional command, the answer may be that the 'Reserve Division' was merely a concept that was never actually implemented.

[6] Leyh, p. 71.

[7] Left behind in Bavaria, the officers of the 4th Chevauxlegers appealed (in vain) to their king to be allowed to join one of the divisions destined for combat (Georg Leisner, 'Die Bayerische Brigade Vincenti in Schwedisch-Pommern und auf Rügen im Jahre 1807', *Darstellungen aus der Bayerischen Kriegs- und Heeresgeschichte*, Heft 16, Munich: 1907, p. 121).

[8] The following drawn primarily from Leyh, pp. 71–101.

[9] Note that in June the commandants of Glatz and Kosel had both signed agreements to surrender their fortresses in July if there was no sign of relief. The expiry dates of both agreements fell after the 9th when Prussia signed the peace treaty, so both were still occupied by Prussian troops when hostilities ended. In Jérôme's area of operations, therefore, only tiny Silberberg had the honour of finishing the war without a capitulation (ibid.).

[10] Ibid., pp. 101–8.

[11] Auvera, p. 391.

[12] The force that actually crossed the river and participated in the battle the following day consisted of the I/3rd Infantry, 7th Infantry, 13th Infantry, 3rd Light, two squadrons of the 3rd Chevauxlegers and three guns (Völderndorff, Book 4, pp. 169–73).

[13] Description drawn from Auvera, pp. 390–4; Völderndorff, Book 4, pp. 170–4; and the Crown Prince's battle report to Massena, 17 May 1807

(in Jean Baptiste Koch, ed., *Mémoires d'André Masséna*, Paris: Bonnot, 1966, vol. V, pp. 434–6). Völderndorff details the Russians as one grenadier regiment, one Jäger regiment, three infantry regiments, a cossack pulk, the 'brown hussars' (presumably the *Akhtyrsk* Hussars), one gun and one howitzer under General Count Schuvalov; the Crown Prince's report estimates the Russian strength at 7,000 to 8,000 and lists the artillery as two guns and a howitzer; Auvera says there were 10,000 Russians.

[14] For this operation, the 2nd Division was reinforced by the French 34th Ligne and 15th Dragoons (Leyh, p. 107).

[15] Ibid., p. 109. If accurate, this recollection demonstrates Napoleon's extraordinary sense of leadership; even if it is apocryphal, it serves to highlight the honour and pride German troops gleaned from their association with Napoleon and the *Grande Armée*.

[16] The brigade had been Major General Marsigli's up to the spring of 1807. The 8th Infantry joined the brigade in mid-August in northern Germany.

[17] Leisner, p. 134.

[18] These observations are based primarily on Leyh's analysis (pp. 115–7).

[19] Sauzey, pp. 92–3.

[20] The Bavarians were especially irritated at Hedouville for allowing French officers to receive the capitulations of several fortresses even though the besieging troops were exclusively or mostly Bavarian (Uebe, pp. 30–2).

[21] I agree here with Leyh's assessment that 'These small frictions, which necessarily appear in all coalitions, particularly in a long war and especially in siege warfare, should not be accorded too much importance. They were overcome without damaging the general political situation...' (p. 117). Uebe (pp. 25–41), on the other hand, highlights every Bavarian complaint (sometimes to the point of exaggeration – he overlooks, for instance, the fact that many French regiments were suffering the same privations) in an effort to conclude that 1806–07 represents the first indication of broad Bavarian dissatisfaction with the Napoleonic alliance.

[22] Bezzel, p. 187; Sauzey, pp. 55–7, 92–3; Uebe, pp. 25–41.

[23] See Leisner.

Chapter Four

Renewed War with Austria in 1809

The year 1808 afforded the Bavarian Army twelve months of much-needed recuperation. The only interruption was a brief mobilisation in the late summer and autumn when Napoleon called out the larger *Rheinbund* contingents to discourage Austria from any aggressive action.[1] Royal orders of 10 and 12 August directed the mobilisation of the army and its concentration in three divisions at Plattling (Deroy), Augsburg (Wrede's Division, including the 7th Infantry) and Nuremberg (Ysenburg) under the guise of autumn manoeuvres.[2] By the end of August, the three divisions were assembled and opened their exercise period with formal parades, reviews and artillery salutes.

Though Napoleon had commanded the Bavarian mobilisation as part of a larger effort to overawe Austria, the army took good advantage of this opportunity to increase its combat readiness. Closely monitored by officers of the general staff, the training was divided into three phases, starting with fundamentals to accommodate the numerous recruits recently called up (as many as 25 per cent in some regiments). The first phase progressed from individual instruction to company, battalion and regimental drill and exercises. This was followed by brigade and division level manoeuvres in the second phase. Unfortunately, the third phase, field duties, was curtailed by dreadful weather, so the army was not able to practice the outpost and security tasks which had been its weakest points in previous campaigns.

The poor weather – incessant, torrential rain – also forced a change in living conditions. To spare the populace, the infantry was initially established in large tent camps across the countryside but, by 29 September, Deroy was reporting that some tents were under water and that even in those which had escaped the flood the men's straw bedding was completely soaked through and was giving off an intolerable odour. In addition, one of Deroy's regiments, the 1st Infantry, complained of being overrun by an invasion of mice. Conditions in the other camps were no better. Under these circumstances, Max ordered the infantry into billets on 1 October, and on the 12th cancelled the exercises entirely. Even so the 1808 mobilisation served the monarchy well as it allowed the army and the state bureaucracy to practice at some leisure the measures they would need to implement in haste four months later. Likewise, the ensuing exercise period, though not completed, not only improved the army's level of training, but also provided an opportunity to integrate new recruits and to familiarise units and commanders with the order of battle they would use in the coming war.[3]

Like Berlin in 1806, Vienna was all abuzz with talk of war in 1808–09.[4] For many in the Habsburg capital, Napoleon's invasion of Spain in the spring of 1808 seemed to offer an irresistible opportunity to launch a sudden offensive into Germany and Italy, soundly defeat the reduced French forces in both areas, and thereby re-establish Austrian influence along the Rhine and the Adige. Through a bold strike, the Habsburg monarchy would thus revenge itself upon France's parvenu emperor and recoup the humiliating loss of status and resources inflicted on it since the beginning of the Wars of the Revolution.

Moreover, many in Austria were convinced that their state would be Napoleon's next target as soon as he was finished with his affairs on the Iberian Peninsula. A pre-emptive attack seemed to them the only conceivable remedy to their intolerable situation. Like Prussia in 1806, therefore, Austria's approach to the coming conflict took on a desperate character, and Austria's leaders entered into offensive planning with little clear idea of what they wanted from the war or how their still unprepared army would achieve its undefined objectives.[5] Nonetheless, the men of the Austrian Main Army (*Hauptarmee*) under the Archduke Charles were in hopeful good spirits when they crossed the River Inn into Bavaria on the morning of 10 April 1809 to open what would be Franz Hausmann's third war in four years.

Repelling the Invasion

Aware of Austria's armaments, but uncertain of its intentions, Napoleon had written to the *Rheinbund* princes from Spain in January 1809 to 'invite' them to mobilise their contingents. Thanks to its recent experiences, the Bavarian Army's transition from a peacetime to a war footing proceeded fairly smoothly and, by 20 March, its three divisions were posted along the River Isar from Munich to the Bohemian border as the strategic advance-guard of Napoleon's army. Indeed, unlike in the two previous conflicts, the French Emperor found himself relying heavily on his German allies when the war of 1809 began. With most of the former *Grande Armée* committed for the moment to the Iberian imbroglio, the number of immediately available French troops, particularly veterans, was limited.[6] The German contingents, above all the Bavarians, thus found themselves in the forefront of the fighting in April 1809.

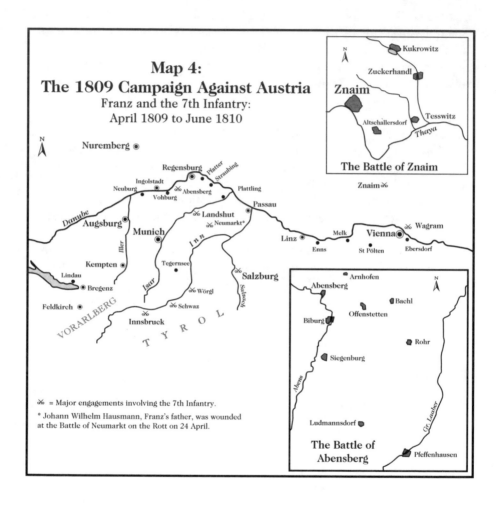

Map 4:
The 1809 Campaign Against Austria
Franz and the 7th Infantry:
April 1809 to June 1810

The Battle of Znaim

Kukrowitz
Zuckerhandl
Znaim
Altschallersdorf
Tesswitz
Thaya

N

Nuremberg

Regensburg *Pfatter* Straubing
Ingolstadt
Neuburg
Vohburg Abensberg
Plattling
Passau
Danube
Augsburg
Landshut
Neumarkt*
Munich
Iller
Inn
Linz
Melk
Vienna Wagram
Enns St Pölten Ebersdorf
Kempten
Tegernsee
Lindau
Bregenz
Wörgl
Salzburg
Isar
Salzach
Feldkirch
Schwaz
Innsbruck
VORARLBERG
T Y R O L

Znaim

The Battle of Abensberg

Arnhofen
Abensberg
Bachl
Offenstetten
Biburg
Rohr
Siegenburg
Abens
Gr. Laaber
Ludmannsdorf
Pfeffenhausen

✂ = Major engagements involving the 7th Infantry.

* Johann Wilhelm Hausmann, Franz's father, was wounded
at the Battle of Neumarkt on the Rott on 24 April.

As in the 1808 manoeuvres, in the spring of 1809 the Bavarians were organised into three mixed divisions, this time under the Crown Prince (1st), Wrede (2nd) and Deroy (3rd). Each composed of two infantry brigades and a cavalry brigade, the divisions were placed under the overall command of French Marshal François Lefebvre, the Duke of Danzig, as VII Corps of the 'Army of Germany'. Lefebvre, an Alsatian who spoke German (albeit with an unfamiliar accent as far as the Bavarians were concerned), was a good choice for this post and Napoleon bolstered the corps command team by assigning the experienced and thorough Général de Division Jean-Baptiste Drouet, Comte d'Erlon, as Lefebvre's Chief of Staff. The selection of a Frenchman for the command disappointed King Max, who had hoped to see his son at the head of the monarchy's corps, but Napoleon was adamant,

> I must speak to you frankly. The Crown Prince, whatever advantages he may have by nature, has never learned or made war; he cannot know it. You give me the privilege of utilizing your 40,000 men, but not of putting at their head a man who is sure and firm. I have named as commander the Duke of Danzig, who is an old soldier. The Bavarian troops are too numerous and the situation is too grave for me to conceal my thoughts from Your Majesty. If the Crown Prince had been through six or seven campaigns, then he could command them.[7]

As in 1807 and 1808, Franz's regiment was included in Wrede's 2nd Division, this time as part of the 2nd Brigade commanded by Major General Karl Count von Beckers (who had served in the 4th Grenadiers as a junior officer before Franz was born). Colonel von Stengel and the 45 officers and 1,929 men of the 7th Infantry departed Neuburg on 17 March to occupy their allotted position at Pfatter near Straubing. Stengel, however, did not long remain with the regiment he had commanded since 1806. Promoted to Major General on 1 April, he was posted to lead the 2nd Brigade of Crown Prince Ludwig's 1st Division, and Colonel Friedrich Count von Thurn und Taxis, elevated from command of the 6th Light Battalion, took his place at the head of the 7th Infantry on the 19th.

By the time Colonel von Thurn und Taxis took command of the 7th, however, the war was already into its second week, and the Bavarian Army had fought its first significant engagement. Defending the line of the River Isar against the slowly advancing Austrians at Landshut on 16 April, the men of Deroy's 3rd Division proved themselves both tough and tactically competent, delaying the crossing of the river by the main body of Archduke Charles' army and then conducting a model withdrawal under pressure against vastly superior numbers.

71

The Bavarians, along with the other *Rheinbund* contingents and their French allies, kept frantically busy from 10 to 18 April as Marshal Alexandre Berthier, in de facto command in Bavaria until Napoleon could arrive from Paris, marched and counter-marched the Army of Germany's constituent elements in a vain effort to obey his Emperor's instructions. Wrede's men thus dashed all about the area south of Regensburg for several days and were trudging drearily across the Danube at Vohburg late on the night of the 17th when there was a sudden stumbling, shouting and cursing as the long lines halted in the midst of their passage. New orders had arrived directing the 2nd Division to occupy positions above the Abens River and prepare for battle. It was 2 a.m., and considerable confusion ensued as the weary men were turned round and marched back to the line they had left only four hours earlier. But the cold, damp night air was also full of decision and expectancy; Napoleon had arrived and there would be no more retreats.

The next five days were a whirlwind of rapid marches and brutal combats across hilly, wooded terrain where the enemy situation was usually vague or unknown. The success that crowned these engagements despite formidable obstacles and frequent misperceptions is a testimony to Napoleon's genius, the tactical skill of his army, and the spirit he instilled in his men, French and German alike.

As the sun rose on 19 April, Lefebvre's mission was to tie down as many Austrians as possible along the Abens so that Napoleon could assemble the dangerously separated pieces of his army. For the 7th Infantry and the most of Wrede's Division, this meant long hours spent helplessly enduring Austrian artillery fire, while the 1st Division sparred with Austrian probes off to their left at Arnhofen.

Napoleon renewed the struggle the following day in a series of actions known collectively as the Battle of Abensberg. This time, however, his intent was entirely offensive. While the Bavarians struck the Austrian line from the front, Marshal Jean Lannes would drive in the enemy's right flank with a powerful ad hoc force of veteran French infantry and heavy cavalry. Before launching them against the Austrian positions the Emperor gathered the Bavarian commanders together on a low hilltop and delivered an energetic speech,

> Bavarian soldiers! I stand before you not as the Emperor of France but as the protector of your country and of the *Rheinbund.* Bavarians! Today you fight alone against the Austrians. Not a single Frenchman is in the first line, they are in reserve and the enemy is unaware of their presence. I have complete faith in your bravery. I have already expanded the borders of your land; I see now that I have not yet gone far enough. I will make you so great that you will not need my protection in any future war with Austria. For 200 years, the

Bavarian flag, supported by France, has fought heroically against Austria. We will march to Vienna, where we will punish Austria for all the evil it has caused your fatherland. They want to divide your land and enroll you in Austrian regiments!

Bavarians! This war will be the last one you fight against your enemies. Attack them with the bayonet and destroy them![8]

The effect on the Bavarian troops was immediate. A Bavarian artillery lieutenant recalled the scene,

Around this time [approximately 9 a.m.] the most remarkable event of my life occurred. A general jubilation announced the arrival of His Majesty the Emperor of the French and, as if struck by a bolt of lightning, the entire army was suddenly filled with joy and hope. From every eye shone forth the purest, most unmistakable joy, the certainty of an imminent victory. Never before had my eye beheld this rare mortal, and yet I recognised him – not so much from the similarity to the busts of him which I had seen – rather from the simplicity of his uniform.[9]

Inspired by the speech (translated by Crown Prince Ludwig and relayed to the troops by their officers), the Bavarian corps advanced with vigour and, in a fine display of tactical ability, steadily pushed the Austrian left wing under Feldmarschall-Leutnant Johann von Hiller out of its strong defensive positions. The 7th Infantry was in the centre of the action and, having thrown the Austrians back some six miles, the men were settling in for a well-deserved rest when new orders arrived at around 10 p.m. for Wrede to seize the town of Pfeffenhausen on the Laaber River that very night.

With the 6th Light in the lead, supported by a squadron of the *König* Chevauxlegers and the II/7th Infantry, Wrede set off into the dark, wet woods, chased away some nervous Austrian pickets, and surprised the town, which quickly fell into his hands with a large haul of prisoners and baggage. Thoroughly exhausted but satisfied with their success, the men snatched a few precious moments of sleep in the predawn hours. Wrede praised the regiment in his battle report,

This regiment stood under fire without a break from noon until 7 in the evening, resisted the attacks and renewed attacks of the enemy, and chased the enemy from wood to wood with a courage I cannot adequately describe.[10]

The 2nd Division drove south to Landshut on the 21st in the wake of Hiller's hurriedly retreating troops, and participated in the seizure of the town, the Bavarians competing with the French and Württembergers to be the first to enter. The next day, Wrede was detached with Général de

Division Gabriel Molitor's French division under Marshal Jean-Baptiste Bessières to pursue the broken Austrian left wing to the south, while Napoleon and the bulk of the available troops turned north to engage Archduke Charles and the remainder of the Habsburg host. To the surprise of the French and Bavarians, however, Hiller was able to restore order to his wounded command and return to the attack on the 24th. The result was a tough battle at Neumarkt on the Rott River. Bessières having sent the Bavarians forward across the river where Molitor could not support them effectively, Wrede's men were outnumbered when Hiller's columns appeared from the south at approximately 9 a.m. With desperate bravery and considerable skill, Wrede and his division held off the Austrians for several hours but, by noon, retreat had become the only viable course of action. The 7th Infantry, assigned as the rear-guard to protect the rest of the division as it struggled over the one narrow bridge across the Rott, lost 120 men killed and wounded, including its new commander, Colonel von Thurn und Taxis, as Wrede led it forward repeatedly to gain time for the withdrawal.

Among the wounded was Franz's father, Sergeant-Major Wilhelm Hausmann, who took a ball in his right foot. In the congestion and confusion of the retreat, the regiment might have lost its colours as well, had a Sergeant Schmidt not had the presence of mind to leap into the water with the standard and swim to the opposite bank. He received Bavaria's Military Service Medal in Silver for his quick thinking and courage. Wilhelm Hausmann also distinguished himself in the battle and was rewarded with the Cross of the Legion of Honour for his bravery. Casualties for the division totalled 795 for the day, and the now chastened Bessières allowed the Austrians to slip away on the 25th.

The pursuit resumed in earnest several days later and Wrede, operating virtually as an independent commander at this point, drove his men hard to seize Salzburg at the end of the month. The other two Bavarian divisions of VII Corps reached the city shortly thereafter, having marched from Regensburg via Munich. Both had participated in the Battle of Eggmühl on the 22nd while Bessières and Wrede were chasing Hiller, and the 1st Division had marched through Munich with prisoners and captured guns to the acclaim of patriotic crowds.

Using Salzburg as a base, the entire VII Corps now launched an offensive to reconquer the Tyrol. In a long-planned move, Tyrolean militia had risen up against Bavarian rule as soon as the first Austrian regulars crossed the border on 10 April. In a matter of days, the Bavarian garrisons had been killed or captured almost to a man, and the jubilant Tyroleans even succeeded in surrounding and forcing the surrender of a column of raw French conscripts en route to join the Army of Germany. With the assistance of a small detachment of Habsburg troops, the

Tyroleans began to organise a defence and even launched a few raids into southern Bavaria.

The arrival of VII Corps at Salzburg, however, presaged the end of this first Tyrolean 'liberation'. Instructed to clear out the Austrians, quell the rebellion, and open the lines of communications between Italy and Germany, Lefebvre sent his divisions up the Inn valley on 10 May. What followed was a war of the utmost bitterness. Although they easily scattered the poorly handled Austrians and were generally successful in driving off the Tyrolean insurgents, the Bavarian soldiers encountered fanatic opposition from the entire populace. Men, women and children took up arms against the 'invaders', annihilated isolated detachments and murdered anyone who strayed from his battalion,

> I saw boys of 12 to 14 years who fired at us with pistols; I noticed men and women on rooftops who hurled tiles and stones at us.[11]

The Bavarians, appalled at this 'unfair' and 'dishonourable' way of making war, treated the rebels as criminals who were resisting the lawful rule of their due sovereign. The result was 'theft, murder, plunder, etc.' as a private in the 5th Infantry recalled.

The advancing Bavarian divisions left a swath of destruction and death in their wakes and, through malice or accident, Tyrolean towns such as Schwaz and Wörgl were almost completely razed by uncontrolled fires. As Franz noted, 'wherever the slightest resistance was encountered, everything was devastated and burned down'. Nine days after launching their offensive, Lefebvre and the Bavarians made their formal entry into Innsbruck, the Tyrolean capital. Resistance seemed to have dissipated and in late May the 1st and 2nd Divisions left the Tyrol to assume responsibility for the defence of Linz.

Napoleon's long line of communications from Vienna (entered by his army on 13 May) through the Danube valley was vulnerable at many points and he posted the two Bavarian divisions at Linz to ensure uninterrupted contact with France and to hold in check various Austrian forces north of the river. The 7th Infantry was involved in a skirmish on 4 June that cost it 12 men wounded and there were occasional Austrian probes to repulse, but otherwise its sojourn around Linz was a story of poor provisions and the dull drudgery of guard duty. However, the 7th did finally receive a new commander. On 27 June Colonel Nikolas Baron von Maillot de la Traille transferred from the 2nd Infantry to take over from Lieutenant Colonel Wilhelm Rodt who had led the 7th since Colonel von Thurn und Taxis' death in April. Maillot arrived just in time, for three days later, Wrede's Division, as a mark of particular Imperial favour, was called to Vienna to participate in Napoleon's second attempt to cross the Danube and destroy the Austrian Main Army.

Wagram and Znaim

While the Bavarians had been struggling with the Tyrolean rebels, Napoleon, hoping to locate and defeat Archduke Charles and his army, had endeavoured to throw his principal force across the Danube at Vienna. This bold stroke led to the costly Battle of Aspern-Essling on 21 and 22 May, in which Charles succeeded in repulsing Napoleon's thrust and in forcing the French to withdraw to an island near the north bank of the river. An operational pause then ensued during which the Austrians vacillated while Napoleon carefully strengthened himself for a second attempt to drive across the Danube.

By late June Napoleon's preparations were nearing completion and on the 30th, Wrede at Linz received instructions to take his division to Vienna to join the army for the coming battle. Wrede responded with alacrity and by 2.30 a.m. on 1 July, the 2nd Division, reinforced by twelve guns from the Crown Prince's Division, was on the road toward the Austrian capital. Writing to Berthier from Enns that day, Wrede assured the French marshal that, after a month of 'very fatiguing outpost duty' at Linz, 'there is not a soldier who does not show a great ardour to conduct forced marches in order to have the pleasure of fighting under the eyes of His Majesty the Emperor.'[12]

Franz's diary gives a vivid sense of the daily effort Wrede expected of his men. Marching an average of 25 miles per day, the division reached St Pölten on the evening of 3 July. Here a courier arrived with a new message from Berthier, 'My dear General, if you desire to participate in the affair before us, you must arrive on the Isle of Lobau, near Ebersdorf at 5 a.m. on the 5th.'[13] Wrede thus set his weary men on another long march on 4 July (30 miles), bringing them to Purkersdorf just outside Vienna. Here again, new orders changed his plans. He was now to rest his division at Schönbrunn on the 5th after marching another 6 miles. In all, the Bavarian 2nd Division had covered more than 112 miles in slightly more than four days – a remarkable feat of marching by any standard.[14]

Nor did the division's exertions cease with its arrival near Vienna. On the contrary, to the demands of marching there were now added the dangers of combat as the Bavarians awaited the moment to play their part in the titanic Battle of Wagram.[15] Completely exhausted and soaked through from the tremendous thunderstorm that had swept over the Austrian capital on the night of 4/5 July, the men waited at Schönbrunn while Wrede went in search of orders. These were a long time in coming and the sun was already rising on 6 July when Wrede returned to his men and led them, dressed in their parade uniforms, across the Danube to stand next to the French Imperial Guard in reserve. The veteran

Guardsmen greeted them with hearty cheers, and Napoleon himself spoke a few words to them, praising their courage and emphasising the importance he attached to their arrival on the battlefield. Indeed, when Général de Division (soon to be Marshal) Étienne MacDonald's attack against the Austrian centre began to falter under the weight of pitiless artillery fire, the Emperor sent for Wrede. Napoleon's orders were brief, 'Now I unleash you. You see MacDonald's awkward position. March! Relieve his corps; attack the enemy; in short, act as you think best!'[16]

With his guns in the first line, infantry in the second and cavalry following, Wrede moved forward at about 2 p.m. By that hour, however, Archduke Charles had already ordered his army to withdraw. The Bavarians thus pursued a retreating enemy, but cautiously, endeavouring to inflict as much damage as possible through artillery fire. With its active part in the battle mostly limited to bombardment and a few brief cavalry skirmishes, the 2nd Division's losses for the day only amounted to 32 men. Franz's 7th Line and the other infantry units came through the battle entirely unscathed. One of the few casualties was Wrede himself, wounded by a cannon ball during the attack. Minucci took his place, and Napoleon, on learning of the change, replied 'Let him command as Wrede did and he will enjoy my complete confidence.'[17]

If the Bavarians had suffered few losses through the brutality of Wagram, the subsequent clash at Znaim would cost them dearly. As one of Napoleon's few relatively fresh units, the 2nd Division was in the forefront of the pursuit as the French slowly sought after the retreating Austrians. The troops were thus up and moving by 5 a.m. on the 7th for a relatively short (8 miles) but difficult march. Attached to Général de Division Auguste Marmont's Army of Dalmatia that night, the division continued north at 2 a.m. on the 8th. For the next two days, Marmont's command chased after the enemy, finally stumbling unexpectedly upon the Austrian Main Army near Znaim at about noon on the 10th.

While the French infantry and cavalry deployed to the right to engage what Marmont thought was a mere rear-guard, the Bavarians advanced against the village of Tesswitz on the left of Marmont's line. The 6th Infantry, led by Major General Beckers, succeeded in taking the town, but could not hold in the face of a heavy Austrian counterattack. The determined Beckers, however, gathered up the I/7th and some other troops (two companies of the 13th Infantry and two companies of French voltigeurs) and stormed into Tesswitz again. This attack was met by fresh Austrian reinforcements and the struggle raged back and forth through the streets with great ferocity until late in the afternoon as each side committed new units to the fight.

Most of Minucci's division was drawn into the vicious maelstrom as the hot day wore on. The only troops left were several companies covering the artillery on the heights south of Tesswitz and the II/7th, which crossed to the south side of the River Thaya late in the afternoon to clear out Austrian skirmishers. Finally, as darkness began to fall, the Austrians retired and left the burning village to the Bavarians. Relieved in the town by two French regiments, Minucci took his exhausted division some distance to the rear and counted his losses. These amounted to more than 900 men (184 of these from the 7th Infantry), making 10 July the most costly day experienced by any Bavarian division during the entire war.[18]

The battle around Znaim continued on 11 July, but the Bavarians, with the exception of some Schützen and the artillery, were held in reserve and saw no further active combat. Indeed, 11 July was the last day of the regular campaign and staff officers rode between the two armies that evening to announce that an armistice had been signed. Although peace was not yet assured, Napoleon ordered Minucci to return to Linz and, with Napoleon's and Marmont's praise in their ears, the 2nd Division left Znaim on the 13th. All of its units had reached their destination ten days later.[19]

Ces Misérables Tyroliens

While the 2nd Division was marching to glory at Wagram and Znaim, and the 1st was passing tedious days at Linz, Deroy's 3rd Division was committed against the Tyrolean insurgents. The region had appeared pacified in early May when Wrede and the Crown Prince had marched off to Linz, but the rebellion broke out anew at the end of the month. Heartened by news of the Austrian success at Aspern-Essling and by re-invigorated patriotic appeals, the Tyrolean militias took up arms again in great numbers and converged on Innsbruck. Although a battle fought outside the city on the 29th was a tactical draw, Deroy knew he could not linger in the Inn valley and accordingly withdrew to more secure positions along the southern border of Bavaria proper. As May closed, therefore, the rebels could celebrate their second 'liberation' in as many months.

With Napoleon's attention and most of his force concentrated on arranging the defeat of the Austrian Main Army, the situation in the Tyrol stagnated. Deroy and other local Bavarian commanders tried to repel insurgent raids while the Bavarian kingdom raised new forces to prosecute the war. Among the new units called into existence were 12 reserve battalions created by an Army Order of 25 June. Each line infantry regiment (with the exception of the 11th) was now to have its own reserve battalion, and it was to the 7th's reserve unit that Franz was posted in August as a newly-promoted second lieutenant.[20] Serving as the battalion adjutant, Franz would thus spend the remainder of the war in south-western Bavaria, taking part in the effort to subdue a rebellion in the Vorarlberg district, where unrest had flared into open insurrection as in the neighbouring Tyrol.

Determined to remove this annoyance in his rear while he conducted peace talks with the Habsburg court, Napoleon directed Lefebvre to launch a second offensive into the Tyrol. The 1st and 3rd Divisions, bolstered by a division of other *Rheinbund* troops under Général de Division Marie-François Rouyer, thus marched up the Inn valley for a second time at the end of July. Other French and German troops moved against the Vorarlberg. But the grand effort was again in vain. Although Innsbruck fell to the advancing Bavarians, Rouyer's men were badly handled when caught in a trap on 1 August, and a Bavarian attempt to push further up the Inn was thrown back with heavy losses. After another drawn battle outside Innsbruck, Lefebvre withdrew his corps and, by 20 August, the Bavarians and their German allies had once again evacuated the Tyrol.

The failure of the second offensive generated tension between the Bavarians and the French as each tried to lay the blame for defeat upon the other. While the army settled into the business of protecting the monarchy's long southern borders, therefore, Lefebvre bickered with his Bavarian subordinates and morale sank. By October the friction had reached crisis proportions, highlighted by Lefebvre's accusations that the former commander of the 7th Infantry, Major General von Stengel, had failed in his duties and unnecessarily retreated in the face of the enemy. Stengel's exoneration by a military tribunal did nothing to dispel the poisonous atmosphere and Napoleon, whose central interest was the repression of the insurgency, finally stepped in and relieved Lefebvre of his command. General Drouet, the VII Corps Chief of Staff, replaced Lefebvre and relations soon began to improve, but the bitter recriminations of late summer and early autumn 1809 left permanent scars that troubled Franco–Bavarian relations for the remainder of the Napoleonic epoch.

Under Drouet, the corps participated in the third offensive against what Napoleon termed 'these miserable Tyroleans' as soon as the peace treaty with Austria was signed on 14 October. With all three Bavarian divisions (Wrede's was brought down from the Danube valley) involved, the offensive made steady progress against sporadic and occasionally desperate resistance. There was one final battle outside Innsbruck on 1 November, but it was brief and ended in a clear Bavarian victory. By the beginning of December, the Bavarians had succeeded in making contact with French troops pushing north out of Italy. Simultaneously, French, Bavarian and other *Rheinbund* troops (including Franz and the

Reserve Battalion of the 7th Infantry) extinguished the last sparks of insurrection in the Vorarlberg. With the exception of a few isolated incidents, therefore, the rebellion was crushed as 1809 came to a close, and the Bavarian Army set about the demanding task of occupying the recalcitrant region.

Observations

In reviewing the Bavarian Army's role in the 1809 campaign, two general points stand out. In the first place, the army had honed its tactical skills to a fine edge. If not perhaps as vigorous and durable as some other German contingents or as impetuous as the French, the Bavarians proved solid, courageous and reliable soldiers. Under fine leaders, infantry, cavalry and artillery alike displayed an excellent grasp of flexible tactical manoeuvre in open, conventional combat, against an experienced foe.

Even in the dreadful struggle against the Tyrolean rebels, the Bavarians eventually learned hard lessons about mountain warfare against an insurgent population. They could never match the native cunning and local knowledge of the Tyroleans, but they learned to attack at night, to outflank or bypass difficult resistance and to control the heights with swarms of light troops. They also learned that they could not take irregular forces such as the Tyroleans for granted. The third offensive into the Tyrol was thus planned and executed with great thoroughness, the army advancing with careful reconnaissance, secure lines of communication and an eye toward pacifying, not simply suppressing, the Tyrolean people.

Secondly, this campaign highlights both sides of the Franco–Bavarian military relationship. On the one hand, the Bavarian soldiers responded with enthusiasm to Napoleon's appeals to their patriotic sentiments and to the honours he dispensed. The cheers at Abensberg were not feigned and it is clear that the men felt privileged to fight under the great Emperor's eye. Three months later, at Wagram, the eagerness to distinguish themselves before Napoleon had not diminished. The results of this attitude are evident in the determination and persistence with which the Bavarians fought at places as distant in space and time as Abensberg and Znaim.

On the other hand, when the officers and men felt slighted, their view of the French alliance shifted. It was not a sudden change, and it was probably not irreversible in 1809, but a gradual accumulation of grievances began that year that slowly eroded Bavarian tolerance and their willingness to exert themselves for the French. This friction is mostly associated with the disappointments and defeats in the campaigns against the Tyroleans, where the difficulties of coping with a tenacious insurgency were compounded by internecine quarrels between French and Bavarians.

Irritants arose from both sides, from Lefebvre unwisely insulting entire battalions, to Crown Prince Ludwig overlooking and perhaps supporting virtual insubordination. The acrimonious relationship between Napoleon and Ludwig made all these difficulties more acute and less susceptible to amelioration. Though the army still fought well, the Tyrolean war of 1809 left deep and bitter memories, and many Bavarians came to see first Lefebvre, and then Napoleon and all things French, as symbols of oppression. France's formerly willing friend slowly began to regard itself as an ally in chains.

Military Diary of
FRANZ JOSEPH HAUSMANN
for the
SECOND AUSTRIAN CAMPAIGN
From when the Regiment marched out on 17 March 1809 until the return of the Reserve Battalion on 18 June 1810.

March 1809

17 March	Neuburg on the Danube, in Bavaria. Today crossed the Danube. Marched ten hours, into cantonment.
18 March	Regensburg. Marched nine hours, into cantonment.
19 March	Pfatter the 1st Battalion; Mintraching the 2nd Battalion. Marched five hours, into cantonment.
26 March	Niederwalting near Straubing. Marched seven hours, into cantonment.
27 March	Dingolfing on the Isar the 1st Battalion; Landau the 2nd Battalion. Today crossed the Isar. Marched six hours, into cantonment.

April 1809

2 April	Neufahrn the 1st Battalion; Geiselhöring the 2nd Battalion. Today crossed back over the Isar. Marched

eight hours, into cantonment. After word was received on 9 April that the Austrians had crossed the Inn near Braunau and invaded Royal Bavarian territory, and that thereby Austria had officially declared hostilities, the 2nd Brigade of the 2nd Division therefore assembled on the heights of Neufahrn and in the night marched out to Vohburg, where it joined up with the division.

10 April
: Vohburg. Marched all night. Marched 14 hours, into cantonment.

12 April
: Langquaid. Marched eight hours, into cantonment.

14 April
: Sünching. Marched all night. Marched six hours, into cantonment.

15 April
: Back to Langquaid. Marched six hours, into cantonment.

16 April
: Bachl, at 8 o'clock in the evening into camp. Marched two hours, into bivouac.

17 April
: Near Abensberg. Marched three hours, into bivouac.

18 April
: Near Neustadt. Marched one hour, into bivouac. Here Marshal Bessières reviewed the Bavarian 2nd Division, and a proclamation from General Wrede was also announced. On that same evening at 4 o'clock the 2nd Division marched out along the Landshut road as far as Siegenburg. Near the village of Mühlhausen the enemy was attacked with a strong cannonade and forced back.

19 April
: Allersdorf near Abensberg. Marched one hour, into bivouac. Today His Majesty Emperor Napoleon arrived at the army. On this day the Royal Bavarian 1st and 2nd Divisions marched out in battle order. The 7th Regiment stood on the heights by the Biburg monastery; close to the monastery there was an artillery battery. At 11 o'clock in the morning the Austrians were seen in full retreat from Regensburg, and a heavy cannonade could be heard coming from the village of Thann. Marshal Davout followed hard behind the enemy, coming from Regensburg toward us. At 3 o'clock in the afternoon the enemy began heavily cannonading the Royal Bavarian battery that was positioned near the Biburg monastery, and his fire was sharply returned.

20 April
: Ludmannsdorf near Pfeffenhausen. Marched ten hours, into bivouac. On this day the enemy was attacked near Abensberg. The 7th Regiment stormed across the bridge near Biburg. The 2nd Division thereupon advanced in battle order, closely pursuing the enemy to Pfeffenhausen.

Near the village of Ludmannsdorf the enemy wanted to remain in place in bivouac, but at 9 o'clock in the evening he was chased out of the village by two battalion volleys, and he set out in retreat toward Landshut later that night.

21 April	Mariburg, a farm near Landshut. Marched ten hours, into bivouac. Today crossed the Isar. On this day the Austrians were again attacked near Landshut, and a large number were closed off in that city. The enemy was attacked in such haste, that he did not have time to burn down all of the bridge; he was pursued by storm across the bridge while it was still burning.
22 April	Frontenhausen on the Vils. Marched ten hours. Here the 2nd Brigade of the 2nd Division, along with a squadron of French cavalry, was ordered to march downstream along the River Vils to Frontenhausen, to which place several scattered members of the Austrian Landwehr had retreated, and to take them prisoner.[21] The enemy retreated without stopping, however.
23 April	Neumarkt on the Rott. Marched eight hours, into bivouac.
24 April	Vilsbiburg. Marched four hours, into bivouac. On this day at 10 o'clock we were supposed to march out again from Neumarkt on the Rott. One hour from Neumarkt, however, the 2nd Division was unexpectedly attacked by a much superior enemy force. The fighting was heavy, neither side wanting to give in, until finally the division received the order to retreat back to Vilsbiburg. Our regiment covered the retreat. Our regiment's loss of prisoners, missing and dead was considerable. According to the admission of our enemy prisoners, their loss was also very great, as could not be otherwise from such a scene of murder, where neither side wants to give in.[22]
26 April	Mühldorf on the Inn. Marched eight hours, into bivouac.
28 April	Tittmoning. Marched all night. Twelve hours, into bivouac.
29 April	Salzburg. Marched nine hours, into bivouac. Today crossed the Salzach and, after some skirmishing, Salzburg was taken by storm.
30 April	Strasswalchen. Marched six hours, into bivouac.

May 1809

3 May	Timelkam. Marched seven hours, into cantonment.
8 May	Strasswalchen. Marched seven hours, into cantonment. On this day the 2nd Division was ordered to march back out of Austria and to the Tyrol. The 2nd Brigade had to set out at midnight from near the town of Oberrain in order to cross over the mountains to Lofer, which was a very difficult march for the troops.
9 May	Wieshausen near Salzburg. Marched eight hours, into cantonment.
10 May	Oberrain near Lofer. Marched eight hours, into bivouac.
11 May	Lofer. Marched one hour, into bivouac. The two mountain passes near Lofer were taken on this day.
12 May	At Going near St Johann, in the Tyrol. Marched nine hours, into bivouac.
13 May	At the Kleiner Zoll [toll house], near the Gratenbrück [bridge]. Marched eight hours, into bivouac. On this day we attacked the Austrians and Tyrolean insurgents at the Kleiner Zoll near the Gratenbrück.
14 May	We attacked near Rattenberg, and the city, which was defended by the Austrians and insurgents, was taken by storm.
15 May	Schwaz was entirely devastated today, and today we also crossed the River Ziller and attacked the insurgents near the Ziller bridge. Also, after several howitzer salvos, they had to abandon the St Christoph chapel, which sits on one of the mountains. Marched ten hours, into bivouac.
16 May	Heavy attack in and around Schwaz. In Schwaz there was shooting at the division from the houses and windows; nevertheless, the city and bridge over the Inn were taken by storm. In general, the Tyrolean insurgents here demonstrated the greatest persistence, after having been abandoned by the Austrians right at the start of the fighting. Their persistence was poorly recompensed, however, for the peasants had to give way everywhere, and wherever the slightest resistance was encountered, everything was devastated and burned down. The fate that befell the city of Schwaz and several villages can be seen today in the ruins that are still standing there.
18 May	The insurgents began negotiations, after Austrian troops had withdrawn to Innsbruck and from there to Styria.

19 May	Innsbruck. Today crossed the Inn. Today a deputation with a trumpeter came from Hall and asked for mercy. The peasants also returned home quietly. The division marched to Innsbruck. Marched six hours, into bivouac.
22 May	The 2nd Division was relieved by the 3rd, in order to march to Linz. Marched six hours.
23 May	Rattenberg. Today crossed back over the Inn. Marched ten hours.
24 May	St Johann. Marched ten hours, into cantonment.
25 May	Unken near Lofer. Marched ten hours, into cantonment.
26 May	Salzburg. Marched eight hours, into cantonment.
27 May	There was a public religious service, to celebrate the birthday of His Majesty the King of Bavaria. The division along with the Salzburg city guard paraded before Marshal Lefebvre.
28 May	Strasswalchen, in Upper Austria. Marched six hours, into cantonment.
29 May	Vöcklabruck. Marched eight hours, into cantonment.
30 May	Kremsmünster. Today crossed the River Traun. Marched ten hours, into cantonment.
31 May	Outside of Linz. Today crossed the Danube. Marched seven hours, into bivouac.

[There are no diary entries for June 1809.]

July 1809

1 July	Strengberg, in Lower Austria. Today crossed the Danube. Marched ten hours, into bivouac.
2 July	Kemmelbach. Marched ten hours, into bivouac.
3 July	St Pölten. Marched twelve hours, into bivouac.
4 July	Purkersdorf. Marched twelve hours, into bivouac.
5 July	Vienna. Marched four hours, into bivouac.
6 July	Gerasdorf on the battlefield of Wagram. Today crossed the Danube. Marched ten hours, into bivouac.
7 July	Wolkersdorf. Marched eight hours, into bivouac.
8 July	Schwabenthal. Marched ten hours, into bivouac.[23]
9 July	Near a large mill close to Laa. Marched eight hours, into bivouac.
10 July	Tesswitz near Znaim, in Moravia. Marched eight hours, into bivouac. On this day and the following days the

regiment participated in an important battle. On the 11th an armistice was concluded.

11 July	Zarandl. Today the River Thaya was crossed. Marched one hour, into bivouac.[24]
13 July	Obermakersdorf. Marched six hours, into cantonment.
14 July	Breitenelch near Horn, in Lower Austria. Marched five hours, into cantonment.
15 July	Altpölla near Steupils. Marched five hours, into cantonment.[25]
16 July	Zwettl. Marched 7 hours, into cantonment.
17 July	Arbesbach. Marched six hours, into cantonment.
18 July	Zell. Marched eight hours, into cantonment.
19 July	Steyregg. Marched six hours, into cantonment.
20 July	Linz. Here crossed the Danube.

August 1809

8 August	To the regiment at Ottensheim. Marched two hours, into cantonment.
12 August	Here crossed the Danube and marched via Eferding to Peuerbach. Marched nine hours, into cantonment.
13 August	To Passau, in Bavaria. Crossed the Inn. Marched six hours, into cantonment.
14 August	To Eggenfelden. Marched six hours, into cantonment.
15 August	To Ampfing. Marched six hours, into cantonment.
16 August	Via Haag to Parsdorf. Marched nine hours, into cantonment.
17 August	Munich. Crossed the Isar. Marched four hours, into cantonment.
19 August	Holzkirchen. Marched six hours, into cantonment.
20 August	To Tegernsee, where I encountered the Reserve Battalion. Marched eight hours, into cantonment. Here the battalion, together with the Mountain Rifle Corps, faced the insurgents.[26]
26 August	The 4th Bavarian Infantry Regiment arrived from the Tyrol, and our Reserve Battalion marched to Tölz.
27 August	Wolfratshausen. Marched five hours. In cantonment here until

September 1809

5 September	Seefeld. Marched four hours, into cantonment.
6 September	Greifenberg. Marched five hours, into cantonment.

7 September	Landsberg. Marched three hours. Garrisoned here until
15 September	to Mindelheim. On this day crossed the Lech. Marched four hours, into cantonment.
16 September	Memmingen. Marched four hours, into cantonment.
17 September	Leutkirch. Marched four hours, into cantonment.
18 September	Wangen. Marched four hours, into cantonment.
19 September	Lindau. Marched four hours. Garrisoned here.

November 1809

29 November	Hohenems. Marched five hours, into cantonment.
30 November	Altenstadt near Feldkirch. Marched five hours, into cantonment.

December 1809

1 December	Feldkirch. Marched one hour, into cantonment.

January 1810

11 January	Bregenz. Marched nine hours, into cantonment.

March 1810

20 March	Weiler. Marched five hours, into cantonment.
21 March	Immenstadt. Marched four hours, into cantonment.
22 March	Kempten. Marched three hours. Garrisoned here.

June 1810

12 June	Kaufbeuren. Marched six hours, into cantonment.
13 June	Buchloe. Marched five hours, into cantonment.
14 June	Schwabmünchen. Marched four hours, into cantonment.
15 June	Göggingen. Marched three hours, into cantonment.
16 June	Through Augsburg and crossed the Lech, to Affing. Marched four hours, into cantonment.
17 June	Pöttmes. Marched five hours, into cantonment.
18 June	Neuburg on the Danube, garrisoned. Marched four hours.

Notes to Chapter Four

[1] Letter of 25 July 1808 from Toulouse, *Correspondance*, no. 14230.

[2] Paulus, pp. 98–99.

[3] See Paulus and the following unit histories: Auvera, pp. 407–08; Berg, p. 202; Prielmayer, p. 139; Zoellner, p. 53; Joseph Dauer, *Das Königlich Bayerische 10. Infanterie-Regiments*, Ingolstadt: Ganghofer, 1901, vol. IV, p. 217; Oberstlieutenant Döderlein, *Geschichte des Königlich Bayerischen 8. Infanterie-Regiments*, Landshut: Rietsch, 1898, vol. II, p. 106; Max Ruith and Emil Ball, *Kurze Geschichte des K. B. 3. Infanterie-Regiments*, Ingolstadt, 1890, p. 151.

[4] This chapter is largely condensed from Chapters 2 and 7 of John H. Gill, *With Eagles to Glory*, London: Greenhill, 1992.

[5] See John H. Gill, 'What Do They Intend? Austrian War Aims in 1809', in *Selected Papers of The Consortium on Revolutionary Europe 1996*, series editor Donald D. Horward, Florida State University, 1996.

[6] The *Grande Armée* had been disbanded by Imperial decree on 12 October 1808, *Correspondance*, no. 14376. The principal French army in 1809 was thus known as 'The Army of Germany'.

[7] Napoleon to Max Joseph, 14 March 1809, *Correspondance*, no. 14901.

[8] There are several versions of this speech; this one is quoted from Junkelmann, pp. 13–14.

[9] Christian Schaller, *Fragmente aus dem Feldzuge gegen Oestreich im Jahr 1809*, Augsburg: Bürgeln, 1810, pp. 26–7.

[10] In Auvera, p. 419.

[11] Friedrich Mändler, *Erinnerungen aus meinen Feldzügen*, Franz Joseph Schneidawind, ed., Nuremberg: Lotzbeck, 1854, p. 29. Mändler was a soldier in the 6th Light Battalion.

[12] Wrede to Berthier, 1 July 1809, France, Archives de la Guerre, carton C2/93.

[13] This order is reprinted in many places, but the best is Hasso Dormann's biography of Wrede which includes French and German texts as well as a facsimile of the actual note and the bibliographic reference to the Bavarian War Archives (*Feldmarschall Fürst Wrede*, Munich: Süddeutscher Verlag, 1982, p. 65).

[14] For this march, in addition to Gill, *Eagles*, see Sauzey, pp. 158–9; and Gustav Wolf, *Der Eilmarsch Wrede's von Linz bis Wagram*, Innsbruck: Wagner, 1909.

[15] Note that these elements of Wrede's Division (including the two additional artillery batteries from the 1st Division) were the only Bavarian units present at Wagram. Some other sources erroneously place a cavalry regiment and two artillery batteries with Massena's IV Corps.

[16] Dormann, p. 67.

[17] Ibid.

[18] Auvera, pp. 435–8.

[19] Napoleon personally congratulated Lieutenant Dobl on the performance of his battery on 11 July (Rudolf Ritter von Xylander, *Geschichte des 1. Feldartillerie-Regiments*, Berlin: Mittler & Sohn, 1909, p. 187) and Marmont's 12 July Order of the Day expressed his satisfaction with 'the valour shown by the Bavarian Division in its attacks on the village of Tesswitz and with the determination shown in the defence of the same' (in Sauzey, p. 169).

[20] An earlier order had established six reserve battalions, but these had just begun to form when the new instructions doubled the number and permanently affiliated each reserve battalion with a regular regiment.

[21] The *Landwehr* was the Austrian national militia.

[22] It was during this battle that Franz's father was wounded.

[23] Schwabenthal not located; Marmont's command bivouacked near Mittelsbach on the night of the 8th.

[24] Zarandl not located; perhaps Franz meant Gnadlersdorf, about five miles south-west of Znaim.

[25] Steupils not located.

[26] The Gebirgsschützen Korps (Mountain Rifle Corps) was an irregular formation organised in times of emergency to defend the mountainous southern border of the kingdom. It proved to be of questionable value (see Gill, *Eagles*, Chapter 7).

Chapter Five

The Russian Campaign

Napoleon's Russian campaign of 1812 is one of the great epics of military history. Its general outlines are familiar. The French Emperor invaded the Tsar's domains in June with an army numbering some 450,000 to 500,000 men of all nationalities; Napoleon's initial combinations failed, however, and he could not bring the Russian Army to fight the decisive battle of destruction that he hoped for; in September, the *Grande Armée*, much diminished by fatigue, sickness and straggling, finally caught up with the Russians at Borodino but the victory was only partial and the enemy retired unpursued to fight again. There followed the hollow occupation of Moscow, the hesitation in the face of an adamant foe, and the decision to withdraw. The appalling conditions of the retreat then destroyed the army despite the heroic efforts of the army's engineers in getting what was left of it across the Berezina River. Finally, the remnants of the once-proud host, numbering perhaps 100,000, dragged themselves into Prussian and Polish towns, desperate for shelter and food.[1] It was an enterprise of astonishing magnitude and a vast defeat.

The activities of the flanking forces, however, the Austrians and Saxons on Napoleon's strategic right and the Bavarians, Prussians and French on his left, have attracted little attention from historians writing in English. Franz's letters and diary thus offer a welcome insight into this dimension of the grand canvas of war in 1812.

A Mighty Preparation

The Franco–Russian War of 1812 was a long time brewing. As early as 16 December 1811, Napoleon had issued instructions warning the *Rheinbund* princes to 'remount their cavalry and prepare their contingents'.[2] As tensions between Paris and St Petersburg continued to increase, Max Joseph signed a series of directives dated between 5 and 9 February 1812 to put his army on a war footing. Furloughed soldiers were to be recalled to their units, inspections were to be held, equipment was to be prepared and all had to be placed in readiness to march at short notice. For the king, this was another painful moment. Bavarian interests were not threatened by Russia, indeed, Max and his court had often looked to the Tsar for support in the past, and it was with the greatest reluctance that he directed the mobilisation of the army.[3] For many soldiers, however, particularly for the officer corps, the opportunity to participate in a new campaign under Napoleon was by no means unwelcome; the king's orders were thus greeted with jubilation by much of the army.[4]

Mobilisation proceeded smoothly and, by the beginning of March, the Bavarian contingent of 863 officers, 28,000 men, 5,200 horses and 60 guns was assembled on the kingdom's eastern borders.[5] They were organised into two large formations which the Bavarians initially designated the 'First and Second Army Corps' under Deroy and Wrede respectively (hence Franz's somewhat confusing use of these titles). There was apparently a political motivation behind the choice of the term 'corps', the Bavarian government hoping thereby to invest its army with greater stature than its numbers warranted (the army, after all, was no larger than it had been in 1809 when it was divided into three divisions).[6] If that was the intent, it came to naught.

Incorporated into the *Grande Armée*, the two 'corps' were renamed the 19th and 20th Divisions of the VI Corps d'Armée and placed under the command of Général de Division Laurent Gouvion St Cyr, a difficult, solitary, nearly opaque man who combined intellectual brilliance and considerable military talent with a cold, taciturn nature and a frequently vindictive self-centredness. War seemed something of a mental exercise to him, a chess game played with live figures, and, despite his skill, he never developed – or seemed interested in developing – the ability to capture the affection and devotion of his subordinates. His French troops are said to have called him 'the owl'.[7]

As for Franz and the 7th Infantry, they seem to have presented a fine picture of martial spirit and bearing as they prepared for the campaign. After a 20 February inspection of the regiment, Wrede reported to King Max that

> It would be impossible to find any regiment with greater order, better appearance and better condition as far as all its clothing and equipment is concerned... I wish the regiment could be so fortunate as to be reviewed by Your Majesty in its current condition. The cut of the men in the first rank is splendid without exception; in the second and third ranks somewhat small, but of manly and healthy appearance. The grenadier and Schützen companies are splendid and appropriately formed. The spirit of the men is said to be very good, even that of the Tyroleans in the ranks is much praised.[8]

The regiment left Neuburg on 4 March with 44 officers and 1,632 men, to join General Beckers' 2nd Brigade of Wrede's Division in the army's assembly areas.

Toward Polotsk

Embarking on its trek toward Poland on 10 March, the army was in an optimistic mood. As one veteran recalled,

> Well armed, well dressed, the cavalry well mounted, the artillery, especially the light batteries, provided with select horses, imbued with the best spirits, with confident trust in Napoleon's luck and his talents as a commander – in short, physically and mentally most perfectly equipped – the Bavarian Army Corps departed the fatherland.[9]

St Cyr agreed,

> This corps was splendid, composed of experienced soldiers, well equipped, disciplined and in good spirits.[10]

Proceeding under pleasant circumstances by well-planned stages through friendly Saxony, the corps thus reached Glogau in the early part of April (the 7th Infantry arrived on the 5th of the month), Franz jokingly complained that he had gained weight on the march. Once in Silesia, however, the friendliness ceased and provisions diminished. The situation grew worse as the corps shifted into Poland itself, spending the bulk of April around Posen [Poznan] in miserable quarters. Supplies were drawn from magazines as the impoverished countryside was incapable of sustaining the vast army now making its home between the Oder and the Vistula, 'There was not even enough straw for the troops to sleep on; they had to lie on the dirty and bare floors in the miserable, roofless huts.'[11] Oppressive heat and bad water compounded the general misery. As Franz noted, therefore, no one was reluctant to leave Poland.[12]

It was during this stay around Posen that the royal order arrived abolishing the officers' waist sash and replacing it with the gorget that caused Franz so much consternation. Indeed, if Franz's reaction is indicative of the general attitude within the officer corps, this was an unwelcome and widely-ignored directive.[13]

April also brought an organisational change. In the middle of the month, much to the dismay of the Bavarian commanders, Napoleon withdrew the 1st and 2nd Chevauxlegers Regiments from the corps and assigned them to Général de Brigade Jean-Baptiste Dommanget's 17th Light Cavalry Brigade of III Cavalry Corps along with the Saxon *Prinz Klemens* Chevauxlegers.[14] The corps was thus deprived of one third of its mounted arm before the war had even begun, and the other four regiments (3rd through 6th Chevauxlegers) would also be detached before the army encountered the enemy.

Toward the end of April, the corps moved farther to the east, settling in around Plock on both sides of the Vistula at the beginning of May. Here the men were pleased to learn that they were included in Viceroy Eugène de Beauharnais' command along with IV Corps and III Cavalry Corps. Eugène, widely liked and respected, observed Wrede's Division at manoeuvres and a formal review on 20 May. He had also inspected Major General Heinrich Justus Siebein's Brigade two days earlier, an occasion which brought the troops a double ration of bread and a round of schnapps.[15] His reports to Napoleon were full of praise and the Bavarian troops recalled this event as a 'singularly splendid day' in otherwise rather grim circumstances.

The logistical situation grew increasingly difficult, exacerbated by a 5 June order for each unit to stock a 10- to 14-day supply of provisions. The Bavarians, like most of the army, were already receiving reduced rations for man and horse, and they quickly exhausted the readily available resources of the regions where they were quartered. This additional requirement could only be met by pitiless exactions from the local populace.[16] Poland and East Prussia were stripped bare,

> Departing from one's quarters or from the estate where one had been received with complete friendliness and without the slightest mistrust, one often had to remove every head of cattle and all transportable comestibles, thus leaving the desperate owners with barely enough to get through the next week.[17]

The competition for resources in a region of scarcity (made worse by a drought the preceding year) also led to friction with neighbouring units, as each command sought to comply with Napoleon's directive.[18]

Under these conditions, with the expectation of worse to come, the Bavarians made their way by the end of June to the borders of the Tsar's realm through 'an unlovely, often completely barren region that became ever more impoverished toward the Neman'.[19]

Their move from Bavaria had lasted more than four months, but now the war had already opened, for the main body of the army had begun its crossing of the Neman at Kovno [Kaunas] on the night of 23/24 June. With some 23,500 men 'present under arms', the Bavarians used two pontoon bridges to pass over the river at Pilony ('a miserable place with poor wooden houses and thatched roofs') on 2 July.[20]

Though they marched across in good order, the rigours of campaigning in Russia were already becoming evident, 'Heaps of dead horses showed us the way that IV Corps had taken, for hunger and fatigue felled them by the hundreds'.[21] Another Bavarian officer recalled,

Immediately on the right [eastern] bank where the recent rain had made the road bottomless in places, we found dozens of overturned and plundered wagons; even the finest fourgons and baggage wagons of the Italian and French Guards lay in the field next to their piles of horses, so that one felt one was following a fleeing rather than an advancing army. Such a beginning was hardly cheery and provided occasion for considerable serious reflection.[22]

The situation, of course, did not improve in Russia,

For the French Army, the peaceful move from the Vistula to the Neman, through barren regions, was characterised by exhaustion and privation. The soldiers comforted themselves with the thought of rich compensations in enemy territory. Once there, however, they found far and wide only a wasted countryside whose inhabitants had fled. One saw hundreds of horses lying on and along the roads, killed by inadequate or absolutely nonexistent sustenance.[23]

Another Bavarian officer noted that, 'A bread shortage was already evident, even though we had hardly set foot on enemy soil.'[24] Over wretched roads, the painfully frustrating and exhausting marches to the Neman and beyond highlight the mobility and logistics difficulties that would nearly cripple the army's operations throughout the summer and autumn.

'It was truly painful to watch the marches,' remembered one observer,

Wearily and very slowly, the infantry columns dragged themselves along the rain-softened, nearly bottomless roads... The soldiers, already often poorly nourished, felt themselves oppressed by exhaustion and the weight of their packs. The rain made their clothes and equipment doubly heavy... everything was covered with mud. When these poor men came to their bivouac site after the day's march, the soaked earth served as their bed and the heavens, from which the rain still poured in rivers, as their tent.[25]

Major Ludwig Count von Seyboltstorff, commander of the II/1st Infantry in 1812, left a vivid description of the practically insurmountable logistical challenges associated with these agonising advances,

From the 13th [of June], when the corps assembled, marches were conducted in large columns, in the 19th Division, by closed columns one platoon abreast. This style of marching, difficult in itself, is in no land more tiring than in Poland, where either sand or frequent defiles and swamps present innumerable obstacles to the progress of a body of troops.

The greatest burden an army can have on the march, a large supply train, naturally contributed to increasing these obstacles. The directive to carry along ten days' worth of rations and the grim prospect of encountering nothing but privation ahead, forced the commanders, concerned as they were with the welfare of the troops, to take every measure and even to tolerate some detrimental ones in order to sustain the men as long as possible.

The 30 four-team bread wagons, which every division was apportioned, sufficed in a pinch for the transport of 30,000 rations of bread. While in the cantonments around Lipno, General Wrede, through friendly cooperation with the local prefect, managed to arrange for his division to receive 60 additional wagons above and beyond these 30, each of which was capable of holding 800 to 1,000 rations of bread, and which, equipped with lids and locks, he distributed to the battalions. But even 90 wagons were far from sufficient to transport a ten day supply of bread, brandy, and vegetables as well as forage for the officers' horses. As a result, a huge number of local vehicles and horses had to be requisitioned and tolerated for this purpose and the number of detached soldiers required to gather, drive and escort the provisions wagons soon ran into thousands.

It is difficult to picture the enormous train – beyond the already very numerous vehicle park, the official baggage and bread wagons – which the necessary transport of these provisions occasioned and which the cattle, which had to be taken along as meat on the hoof to the number of 20 or 30 head per battalion, certainly in no little way exacerbated.

It is hardly possible to depict the disorder, confusion and delay which such a monstrous train, composed of such dissimilar physical and material pieces, generated, all strictness and vigilance notwithstanding.[26]

It is no surprise, then, that two days before the declaration of hostilities (22 June), General Deroy had written to King Max expressing his concern that he could not envisage 'how the army, given the continual marches, and, in case the war takes a favourable course, the quick pursuit of the enemy and a rapid advance, will be able to live.'[27]

The march proceeded regardless, the Bavarians welcoming seven days of rest (5 to 12 July) which allowed stragglers and the slow supply trains to catch up with the rest of the corps. The men, however, had already gone nine days without bread, and when the provisions wagons finally did appear, much of the bread was already in a nearly inedible condition.[28] St Cyr also calculated that the corps had already lost 200 artillery horses, but noted that this figure was low in comparison to other commands, 'doubtless', he reasoned, 'because of the care the Germans take with their horses'.[29] Nonetheless, poor quarters, short rations, foul water and desolation remained the norm for man and beast.

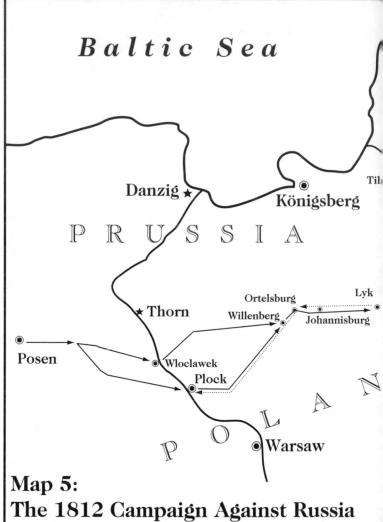

Baltic Sea

Danzig ★

Königsberg

Til

PRUSSIA

★ Thorn

Ortelsburg

Lyk

Willenberg

Johannisburg

Posen

Wloclawek

Plock

POLAN

P O

Warsaw

Map 5:
The 1812 Campaign Against Russia
The March of the Bavarian Corps to/from Polotsk

Riga

Dvina

N

RUSSIA

Daugavpils

Drissa

Kovno

Kalvarija

Pilony

Prenai

Michalischki

Kobolniki

Dunilovici

Glubokoje

Polotsk

Suwalki

Novo
Troki

Vilna

Slobodka

Wilieka

Usaci

Beresina

Lepel

Oszmiana

Molodetschno

to St
Petersburg

N

Drissa

to
Nevel

Disna

Dvina

Polota

Rudnia

Polotsk

Strunja

Operations
near
Polotsk

Usaci

Usaci

Dvina

Ulla

The corps set out again on 12 July, now removed from Eugène's command and placed directly under Napoleon's orders as part of the army reserve. Arriving at Vilna [Vilnius] on the 13th, the Bavarians established themselves in camps outside the city walls, having moved from their initially assigned location owing to the grim sight and foul stench provided by hundreds of dead horses ('more than 1,600' in the recollections of an army official).[30] At noon, General Deroy dutifully reported to Napoleon's Chief of Staff, Marshal Berthier, in the city and learned that Napoleon intended to review the Bavarian Corps the following day. On returning to his division, however, he found that Napoleon had changed his plans,

> … suddenly at 6.30 p.m., General St Cyr came to my quarters and informed me that the Emperor had just ridden into the camp. While we hastily rode after him, the Emperor came to the 1st Infantry Brigade. As the men had had no time to dress properly and appear under arms, they ordered themselves in their field caps and shirts and greeted His Majesty with "Vive l'Empereur!" The Emperor then rode to the cavalry and the 2nd and 3rd Infantry Brigades and seemed very pleased with the speed with which the troops had arranged themselves and with the manner of his reception.[31]

At 11 a.m. the next day, Napoleon held a formal review of the corps. Still some 20,000 to 25,000 strong, the Bavarians passed before their Emperor in splendid order. He 'seemed extremely satisfied with it, as it still had few sick and was well equipped.'[32] Indeed, according to a staff officer in Wrede's Division, 'Many around Napoleon expressed the opinion that VI Corps looked more splendid than the Imperial Guard.'[33]

> Our chevauxlegers regiments and light artillery battery earned his particular appreciation because they managed to present an aston-ishingly good appearance after the long and wearing marches, after all the exertions, and despite the considerable lack of provisions.[34]

Unfortunately, Napoleon's favourable impression of the Bavarian cavalry apparently led him to detach the remaining four regiments and Captain Karl von Widnmann's light artillery battery from VI Corps and reassign them to the main army. They performed brilliantly throughout the campaign, but their absence would be keenly felt when the Bavarians reached Polotsk [Polock or Polack].[35] In St Cyr's words, the loss of this cavalry 'paralysed the operations' of the corps, which was left with only a detachment of 40 chevauxlegers from the 5th Regiment for duties in the corps headquarters. Moreover, for the Bavarians, their own cavalry-men were irreplaceable, 'they had more confidence in them than in any others', and their departure discouraged the rest of the troops.[36]

That very day (14 July), the corps departed Vilna. The marches were even worse than in Poland and Franz recorded that 'we are very often twelve hours on the road but have only covered a march of four hours.' The contingent, which had held up very well thus far, now began to dwindle rapidly under the combined effects of forced marches, dreadful roads, hot days, cold nights, bad water, wretched quarters without wood or straw, a dearth of bread, and 'a new evil, the complete absence of shoes... the greater part of the corps went about with bare feet or wrapped their suffering feet in cow hides.'[37] Adding to the poignancy of the misery, an irresponsible official leading a resupply convoy decided to leave the wagons carrying the army's replacement shoes and soles behind when lack of horses forced him to abandon some of his vehicles. A dramatic increase in sickness rates and a correspondingly dramatic decline in the corps' morale was hardly surprising,

> Without paying any particular attention, let alone expending any sympathy, one frequently passed groups of 10 to 15 dead men, leaning on their rucksacks, their muskets at their sides, lying around an extinguished fire.
>
> It is not difficult to imagine the disadvantageous effect this tremendous physical exhaustion and numbness had on the morale of the troops.
>
> The singing, otherwise so common in the Bavarian Army, had long since ceased.
>
> Not a single syllable was heard all day long, not even curses. The officers still maintained their good spirits, but their encouragement and their example were insufficient to raise the morale of the men.[38]

St Cyr's comment was simple, 'Every day, the corps leaves behind a battalion's worth of men.'[39]

Ordered to support Marshal Nicolas Charles Oudinot's II Corps on the Dvina River, the Bavarians arrived at Polotsk on 7 August, but the splendid contingent Napoleon had reviewed four weeks earlier had dropped from 25,000 to 16,000 men during the march with hardly a shot being fired in anger. The 19th Division, for example, fell from a strength of 10,112 present on 25 July to a mere 6,571 present for duty on 3 August; detachments accounted for some of the reduction, but sickness and straggling were far greater problems (25 officers and 1,886 men were listed as in hospital or still missing from the ranks). Wrede's division was somewhat better off, but its strength also declined, going from 11,221 on 20 July to 10,351 on the 30th.[40]

In a joint report to Max Joseph, Generals Deroy and Wrede described the army's pathetic appearance and weakened condition, concluding that, military discipline and order are much relaxed, and in their place has come such a spirit of defeatism, pettiness, contrariness and insubordination that it is impossible to see where this will lead.

Oudinot was equally pessimistic,

I cannot assert that the Bavarians are a help to me as they are in such an appalling state of debility.[41]

Polotsk

Polotsk in 1812 was a town of some 12,000, predominantly Jewish, inhabitants. Consisting almost completely of wooden structures, the major portion of the town lay on the east (right) bank of the River Dvina, linked to the suburb of Little Polotsk on the west (left) bank by a wooden bridge. A small, meandering stream called the Polota joined the Dvina just north of town, both watercourses flowing between high, steep banks. East of Polotsk on the right bank of the Polota was the village of Spas with a massive estate and monastery in which both St Cyr and Oudinot established their headquarters. It, and the Prismenitza estate farther north, were surrounded by fences and palisades, making them formidable defensive strongpoints. A forest darkened the horizon from the Dvina to the Polota just beyond Prismenitza, arcing in a great half circle to enclose a marshy plain, relatively flat and open but dotted with ponds and cut up by numerous small brooks. The west bank of the Dvina and the southern edge of the Polota were higher than the remainder of the plain, offering a considerable tactical advantage to the Franco–Bavarian force.

This force, in addition to VI Corps, consisted of Oudinot's own II Corps of three infantry divisions (6th, 8th, 9th), two light cavalry brigades (5th, 6th) and a division of cuirassiers (3rd).[42] Like the Bavarians, II Corps had suffered significant losses from fatigue and illness en route to Polotsk and numbered only some 21,000 men in early August (from a strength of 44,000 at the outset of the campaign). The corps was of variegated composition, with soldiers from every corner of the Empire. In addition to French infantry and cavalry regiments, its order of battle included four fine Swiss regiments, several former Dutch and German regiments now incorporated into the French Army, one regiment each of Croats and Portuguese, a mixed bag light infantry regiment of Swiss, Italian and Corsican troops (the 11th Léger), not to mention Polish lancers with the cavalry. Leadership at the division and brigade level was generally of very high quality (especially the superb Claude Legrand), but Oudinot, indisputably courageous on the battlefield, had proven himself hesitant, indecisive and ineffective as an independent commander.

Now far from his Emperor's guidance, Oudinot was expected to guard Napoleon's strategic left flank and clear the Dvina for French use by attacking and containing the Russian I Corps of Lieutenant General Count Ludwig von Sayn-Wittgenstein-Berleburg[43] (approximately 25,000 men with 108 guns) while the main French Army made its way to Moscow. Although Wittgenstein had been held in check, Oudinot had been unable to mount a credible offensive despite several attempts. A week before the Bavarians arrived, a poorly managed pursuit of the Russians had brought the French a costly rebuff on 31 July which a tactical success on the following day could not redress. Oudinot had retreated hastily to Polotsk, and the two sides now faced each other in a sort of uneasy equilibrium.

Napoleon hoped that the arrival of the Bavarians would give Oudinot a decisive advantage over Wittgenstein, allowing the marshal to remove this threat to the French left rear once and for all. From 7 to 14 August, therefore, the Bavarian Corps found itself involved in a series of futile

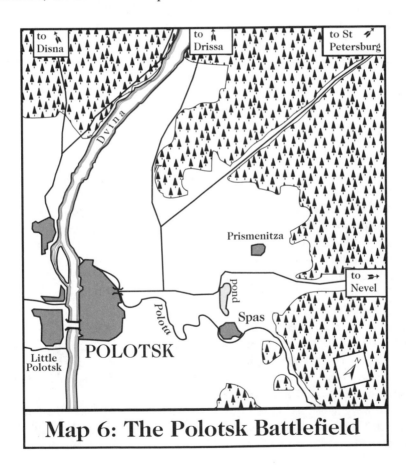

Map 6: The Polotsk Battlefield

marches and skirmishes north-west of Polotsk. By the afternoon of the 16th, II and VI Corps were back at Polotsk, the only result of the week-long offensive being the further reduction of the Bavarian contingent from 16,000 to a mere 12,500 present under arms. Wittgenstein followed closely and launched a probe at the Bavarians outside Polotsk at 2 p.m. that afternoon. The Bavarians repulsed this initial effort, and a second thrust three hours later had no better success. Thus began the first contest for Polotsk.

That evening, Oudinot called a council of war and agreed on the following dispositions for the morning of the 17th. In the first line, the French 8th Division (François Valentin) was responsible for the left flank along the Dvina and for Polotsk itself; the 6th Division (Legrand) formed the army's centre where the roads to Nevel and St Petersburg forked; Wrede's Division was behind the Polota on the right, but held the critical village of Spas with Vincenti's Brigade.[44] The 9th Division (Pierre Merle), Jean-Pierre Doumerc's 3rd Heavy Cavalry Division, Bertrand Castex's light cavalry brigade and the II Corps artillery removed to the left bank of the Dvina from which the artillery could cover the army's left across the river. Deroy's Division stood behind Wrede's on the heights above the southern bank of the Polota with Jean Corbineau's light cavalry brigade (about 400 sabres) to its right rear. The Franco–Bavarian force numbered some 22,000 to 25,500 men and thus was practically equal in numbers to the 25,000 Wittgenstein brought to the affair.[45]

Wittgenstein attacked early on the morning of the 17th. Advancing out of the woods along the St Petersburg and Nevel roads, his men pushed the Bavarian pickets out of Prismenitza and launched an assault against Spas between 7 a.m. and 8 a.m. Repulsed, the Russians tried again at 11 a.m. and this time succeeded in occupying the position with the exception of the church and monastery. The struggle swung to and fro, with the village changing hands several times during the day, but Wrede, carefully feeding in his reserves, finally established uncontested control in the late afternoon. The focus of the battle shifted to Legrand's sector around 6 p.m., but the French repelled every Russian advance and Wittgenstein withdrew his men to the wood-line at approximately 8 p.m. Of the 2,000 casualties on the allied side, the Bavarians lost 76 dead and 389 wounded. Bavarian officer casualties totalled 37 (one being Vincenti), a remarkably high number which highlights the professional dedication of these men and suggests the necessity of personal leadership example to inspire the weary troops.[46]

The weight of the battle on the Bavarian side was carried by the 1st and 3rd Brigades of Wrede's division, well supported by the artillery on the left bank of the Polota. The 2nd Brigade (with the 7th Infantry), spent the day guarding the extreme right of the Bavarian line and did not become involved in the engagement.

Among the allied wounded was Marshal Oudinot, who took a ball in the shoulder and had to be evacuated to Vilna. Though himself also wounded, Gouvion St Cyr thus assumed command of the combined force and gave the second day's struggle a much more aggressive character, 'St Cyr seized the reigns of command with a firm and capable hand, and in a few hours the aspect of things changed entirely.'[47]

While Wittgenstein expected the allies to retreat on the 18th, St Cyr was determined to strike the Russians hard with a surprise offensive and thus force them away from Polotsk. At a council of war on the evening of the 17th, he announced his intention to attack the following morning. His subordinates, however, protested that the men were physically incapable of sustaining another full day's battle, and St Cyr decided to postpone his attack until 4 p.m. to 'reduce the duration of the affair to four hours'.[48]

To lull the enemy commander, St Cyr had the army's parks and baggage moved to the left bank of the Dvina with a great deal of commotion (this was also a prudent move as it cleared the congestion and confusion in Polotsk which would have greatly hampered the army's retreat in the event of a reverse).[49] Such activity could not escape Wittgenstein's attention and it reinforced his assumption that the French would withdraw. A temporary truce declared during part of the day allowed both sides to remove their wounded and bury their dead and probably contributed to Russian complacency.[50] Wittgenstein and his officers were therefore completely surprised when the afternoon repast they were enjoying in Prismenitza was rudely broken up by the thunder of French and Bavarian artillery.

St Cyr's plan called for Wrede, forming the army's right wing, to cross the Polota and turn the Russian left, while Deroy debouched from Spas at the decisive moment to add his weight to the attack. Legrand's 6th Division was to march against the enemy centre and Prismenitza with Corbineau on his right (that is, between Legrand and Deroy), while Général de Brigade Nicolas Maison (replacing the wounded Valentin) advanced along the river with the 8th Division supported by Doumerc's and Castex's cavalry; Merle's 9th Division would form the reserve.

As the monastery clock struck 4 p.m., a shot from one of Wrede's 12-pounders signalled the attack.[51] Beckers' 2nd Brigade led the way with the attached 6th Light crossing over the Polota near the Hamernia iron works on the far right, while the 3rd and 7th Infantry Regiments filed out of Spas and hustled down into the Polota ravine to close up on its left. Deroy soon gave the order to advance as well and his 2nd Brigade made its way out of Spas, assembled, and attacked up the Nevel road. By this time, however, the Russians had recovered from their initial shock and Deroy's men got a warm greeting as they advanced. Within moments, the brigade commander and the commanders of the 10th Infantry and 3rd Light were down. Soon after, Deroy received a mortal wound in the abdomen. The 3rd Brigade, hurrying up in support, lost its commander as well. The loss of these key individuals, the heavy Russian fire and the near-simultaneous repulse of an attempt by Legrand's division to storm Prismenitza left the 19th Division badly shaken.

The Bavarian line was already recoiling when the II/7th Infantry seemed to rise up out of the earth between Deroy's men and the Polota. Led by Major Carl Albert von Merz, Ensign Carl Sartorius and Second Lieutenant Franz Hausmann, the battalion overthrew the surprised Russians to its front and pressed ahead toward the forest. According to Franz, the example provided by the 7th encouraged the retiring 4th Infantry, and it returned to the fight with renewed vigour. Perhaps even more important, Wrede arrived at exactly the right moment. With energy and decision, he inspired the faltering brigades, reordered them and stabilised the situation. Before long, the line began to advance once again, the 9th Infantry clinching the victory by throwing the Russians out of Prismenitza after a brutal struggle.

With the loss of Prismenitza, Wittgenstein knew he would have to break off the action and gave the order to withdraw. To cover his retreat, however, he sent the bulk of his cavalry against the centre of the French line. The Russian horsemen struck Corbineau's weak brigade, over-powered it, overran a battery of 20 guns and pursued the fugitives toward Polotsk. St Cyr, riding in a light carriage because of his wound, hurried over from Spas with the I/1st Infantry and a Bavarian battery to investigate, was caught up in the tumult, and narrowly escaped capture.

Now, however, the Russian troopers were in trouble. Taken under deadly fire by the Bavarian gunners and the men of the 1st Infantry led by Major General von Siebein, they were simultaneously struck by the French 4th Cuirassiers. Fleeing, the Russian cavalry abandoned the prisoners and guns they had captured and disappeared into the great woods. The battle thus came to a close between 9 p.m. and 10 p.m., darkness and exhaustion precluding any thought of pursuit. The Bavarians much regretted the absence of their cavalry regiments, however, opining that their troopers would have turned the disorderly Russian retreat into a complete rout. Wittgenstein's operations journal noted that, 'the Bavarians fought with great valour.'

Polotsk was an undeniable victory for St Cyr and his men, but the army paid a high cost for its honours during the four- or five-hour engagement. Against Russian casualties estimated to number some 5,500, the French divisions lost approximately 2,000, the Bavarians 144 dead and 1,135 wounded (14 dead, 82 wounded and 19 missing for the 7th Infantry). Casualties among the Bavarian contingent's officers had again been high: 15 killed (including two generals and two colonels) and 103 wounded (including two generals and three colonels). Napoleon was generous in rewarding the Bavarians for their service, granting 81 crosses of the Legion of Honour to the corps (Franz, Merz and Sartorius among the recipients). As a particular sign of Imperial satisfaction, Deroy was made a count of the Empire and allotted a gratuity of 30,000 francs. Unfortunately, the 'worthy and brave' old hero died on the 23rd, unable to enjoy the recognition he so richly deserved.[52] Acknowledging St Cyr's skill, Napoleon elevated him to the marshalate. With St Cyr's new status and Deroy's mortal wound, Wrede took command of the Bavarian corps.

The corps was rapidly dwindling, however, and its official situation report for 21 August listed a mere 10,276 men 'present under arms' (plus 8,284 in hospital). Given the overall weakness of the corps and the lack of senior officers, Wrede disbanded the 3rd brigades of both divisions on the 19th and divided their constituent elements between the other two brigades of their respective divisions. A reconnaissance in force out of Polotsk on the 22nd cost the corps 242 more casualties, including General von Siebein.[53] Non-battle losses were the greatest problem, however, and Bavarian strength continued to decline even in the absence of active combat, as shown by the following data[54] for the 19th Division, now commanded by Colonel Aloys Baron von Ströhl:

19th Division	*28 August*	*4 September*	*14 September*	*21 September*
Present under arms	3,953	3,793	3,282	2,170
In hospital	3,583	4,103	4,829	5,149
In the rear	1,348	1,170	1,139	1,085

The figures for the 20th Division were similar (3,687 present on 29 August), and this creeping erosion characterised the long operational pause between the first and second battles of Polotsk. St Cyr considered the Bavarian contingent 'nothing but a moving hospital', incapable of sustaining more than a few marches.[55] Jean Baptiste Marbot, then a chef d'escadron in the 23rd Chasseurs, left a curious picture of the Bavarians in September 1812,

> While the French, Croat, Swiss, and Portuguese regiments worked unceasingly at improving their position, the Bavarians alone took no steps to escape from sickness and want. In vain did General Wrede try to stimulate their energy by pointing out the activity with which the French soldiers were constructing huts, harvesting, threshing, grinding and baking; the poor Bavarians, wholly demoralised since they had ceased to receive rations, admired the intelligent work of

our troops without trying to imitate them. Thus they died like flies…
Yet these Germans, so slack when it was necessary to work, were
brave enough before the enemy, but as soon as the danger was over
they relapsed into utter apathy. Home-sickness took possession of
them; they crawled to Polotsk, and making for the hospitals which
the care of their chiefs had established, they asked for "the room
where people die", lay down in the straw and never got up again. In
this way a great number perished, and things came to such a point
that General Wrede was obliged to place in his baggage wagon the
colours of several battalions which no longer had enough men to
guard them. Yet we were in September and the weather was mild;
the other troops were in good condition and lived merrily while
awaiting further events.[56]

Franz, on the other hand, lamented that the 'situation of our troops is
very unhappy', but observed that 'the French and other allies do not fare
a whit better'. In most respects, however, his depiction of circumstances
is similar to Marbot's. He, too, noted that 'very many of our people are
dying of home-sickness'. His own regiment was down to 308 men by
1 October, but the proportion of officers to men was wildly skewed,
there being 67 officers to manage a mere 241 soldiers! In these circumstances the arrival, on 25 September, of 320 replacements for the entire
Bavarian Corps (22 only for the 7th Infantry) was utterly insignificant.[57]

While Bavarian manpower drained away, the Russians were growing
in strength. By mid-October, Wittgenstein's command numbered some
40,000 men with another 10,000 coming up in support. St Cyr, on the
other hand, could muster only 15,572 in II Corps and a pitiful 2,600
Bavarians.[58] The marshal disposed the French and other allied troops in
an arc covering Polotsk to the east. Despite their weakened condition the
Bavarians were scattered in three different locations. The 2nd Brigade of
the 2nd Division under Major General von Ströhl (promoted in
September) was on the army's far left; the 1st Division, commanded by
newly-promoted Major General Peter Delamotte, left Polotsk on
16 October for Strunja on the army's far right; and Wrede with the
remainder of the 2nd Division occupied two of the recently-constructed
redoubts outside Polotsk.

Like the first engagement at Polotsk, the second was a complex series
of fights lasting several days. While Wittgenstein's main body skirmished
with the French outside Polotsk on the 15th and 16th, a flanking column
of approximately 12,000 under Lieutenant General Thaddeus Steingell
attacked Ströhl's position at Disna on the 16th. Through good leadership
and excellent use of the terrain, Ströhl skillfully held off the vastly superior Russian force for the greater part of the day, withdrawing in the
evening to the Usaci [Uschatz] River in accordance with his instructions.

Bringing up French reinforcements, Corbineau joined Ströhl on the Usaci and took command of the small force.

Two days later, Wittgenstein made a serious attempt to take Polotsk but was unable to prevail against stout resistance by II Corps. The small remnant of Bavarians 'very valiantly' defended their redoubts. If the Bavarian role was relatively minor against the larger backdrop of the battle, Wrede's bold and judicious employment of the Bavarian artillery was instrumental in driving a Russian assault column back from the walls of the town's fortifications; prompting the French to cheer the Bavarian gunners. The contingent suffered few casualties.[59] That night, the Russians also launched an abortive attack against Delamotte's Bavarians at Strunja, but were repulsed with ease.

For the 19th, Wittgenstein decided to hold back his main force and let advances by the two flanking columns force St Cyr out of his strong position. Delamotte drove off another ineffective move against Strunja, but Steingell succeeded in crossing the Usaci and pushing back Corbineau and Ströhl. By 4 p.m., Russian troops were only two miles from Polotsk, and St Cyr's command was in serious danger of being trapped on the wrong side of the river. St Cyr recognised his peril just in time and sent Wrede with a battalion of the 19th Ligne to restore the situation.

Advancing vigorously, Wrede held the Russians in check, but, with his retreat route threatened, St Cyr decided to evacuate the city that night. The remaining elements of the Bavarian 2nd, 3rd, 6th and 7th Regiments formed the rear-guard for a time. Passing through an infernal scene of burning buildings, incessant gunfire and surging Russian attacks ('Never will I forget that terrible night in which I came to know all the horrors of war' wrote Captain Joseph Maillinger), the Bavarians reached the west bank at 2.30 a.m.[60] Despite the heavy Russian pressure, the withdrawal had been conducted with admirable orderliness, a testimony to the courage and professional competence of St Cyr's multinational command. The Swiss earned St Cyr's especial praise for their bravery and tenacity.[61]

The skillful extraction of the army from Polotsk was complemented by an equally fine feat of arms the following day, when Wrede led a mostly French force (the only Bavarians were Ströhl's small detachment of several hundred) against Steingell's numerically superior flanking column and drove it back across the Usaci with heavy losses. 'Numbers gave way before courage' wrote St Cyr.[62] It was one of finest martial achievements of Wrede's career and, while Wittgenstein paused and Steingell retreated in precipitate haste, the Bavarian general fell back to Rudnia, where he assembled the remains of his contingent on the 21st.

Retreat

Unfortunately for the French, having fought a stubborn defence and executed the daring and difficult night withdrawal under continuous attack, St Cyr's two corps now fell into a debilitating tangle of confusion and recrimination. St Cyr had been painfully wounded in the foot on the 18th and, unable to stay at his post, he relinquished command to General Legrand, the next senior French general, on the 21st. Wrede, however, held a higher rank than Legrand and refused to place himself under the Frenchman's orders. Legrand, moreover, had also been injured and was temporarily incapable of assuming responsibility for the army. The burden of command thus fell to Merle, who led II Corps off to the east toward Smolensk to help cover the retreat of Napoleon's main body.[63]

Wrede, on the other hand, commandeered Corbineau's cavalry brigade and set off on his own toward Vilna in order to take advantage of the Bavarian equipment magazines and convalescent depots that lay in that direction. He also seems to have believed he could preserve his command's order and march discipline better if he operated independently.

Military rationale aside, such behaviour was completely in character for Wrede, an independent self-willed, ambitious man, and always a difficult subordinate. Similarly, the tenacity with which he clung to Corbineau's Brigade despite repeated orders to return it to II Corps, while militarily reasonable (Napoleon, after all, had deprived the Bavarian contingent of its cavalry complement early in the campaign), did nothing to endear Wrede to his French counterparts.[64]

With the 7th Line and Corbineau's troopers forming the rear-guard, the remains of VI Corps, now numbering approximately 2,300 Bavarians, made their way west by circuitous marches.[65] The Russians pushed them continuously, and the rear-guard had several sharp fights. On the 24th, for example, the 7th and the French cavalry held off a Russian probe, and Franz's regiment, already reduced to a mere 140 men, lost another 14 in the skirmish.

The 24th also saw the loss of most of the Bavarian regimental and battalion standards. In September, with the contingent's strength rapidly dwindling, Wrede had ordered 22 of the army's precious banners to be packed up and kept with the corps' baggage train. As the retreat from Polotsk began, he sent a large convoy of ammunition caissons and artillery, including the wagon with the flags, ahead of his main body. Sadly, the wagon train was set upon by Cossacks and, after a brave but hopeless struggle, captured intact. In reporting this depressing news, Wrede, who had been advised to burn the flags, attempted to be philosophical, 'In any event, this incident, as unfortunate as it is, is finished, and we must console ourselves as best we can.'[66] Proceeding under constant battering by enemy detachments, the Bavarians halted in relative safety at Dunilovici on the 29th.

The 'corps' remained in and around Dunilovici for the next three weeks, enjoying a much improved supply of victuals and attempting to recover as best it could. By incorporating small detachments and soldiers returned to duty from the hospitals, Wrede was able to bring his strength up to nearly 4,000 combatants.[67] Given the weakness of the contingent, he organised each battalion into a single under-strength company, so that his command now consisted of 27 companies, 16 guns and a tiny cavalry detachment. In mid-November, he finally lost Corbineau's brigade (ordered back to II Corps), but gained considerable reinforcement in the form of two mixed brigades from Vilna. These changes left VI Corps with a strength of approximately 10,000 French and German troops with 28 guns; of this number, however, only 3,727 were Bavarian. The 7th Infantry mustered a meagre 157 officers and men.[68]

From 19 November to 9 December, the corps slowly made its way to Vilna, swinging to the south from Dunilovici, but generally staying just north of the main highway where the scarecrow remnants of the *Grande Armée* were struggling back toward Poland. The Bavarians had their first look at this pathetic crowd of refugees on 3 December and spent most of the 6th on the main road in its fearful company.

> That which Wrede wanted to avoid with the utmost care, the sight of the fleeing French *Grande Armée* – we had already had a tragic preview in Wileika – could no longer be prevented, as the road suddenly met with the great military highway from Oszmiana, which was covered far and wide with refugees. What a sight! For many hours, Wrede's command had to march along next to this whirling human river, which was wrapped in every sort of costume and dress, and which seemed to be composed of every race.
>
> No one can depict the astonishment, no one the impression, which the sight of so many thousand figures, lost to all discipline and order, unarmed, mostly wrapped in rags, given over to the most frightful misery, made on the morale of each and every common soldier. The officers of the VI Corps... saw, instead of a battle-ready, confident army, still powerful despite its great misfortunes, which, led by the greatest soldier of the age, only withdrew to seek new resources or to place itself nearer to its reinforcements and fortresses, only a defenceless mass of half-frozen, half-starved creatures staggering by in a wild jumble. Instead of offering protection to Wrede's weak force, Wrede would have to shield the fleeing horde from the wrath of the pursuing victors...

The Bavarian commander therefore believed that he could not

long allow his troops to witness the enormous, misery-laden procession, if he did not want to bring dissolution into his own ranks through the effect of the horror and the example of the widespread, cowardly desperation. Wrede thus led his little force on to a side road toward Slobodka.[69]

The proximity to the straggling, marauding bands destroyed much of the discipline Wrede had been at pains to instill and maintain in his corps. Of the 5,000 effectives he had under arms on the morning of the 6th, only 2,800 were still with their units by evening. During the next several days, the French infantry, denigrated by their commander as 'much inclined to desertion' in November, gradually evaporated, leaving some 1,000 Bavarians, Hessians and Westphalians, three guns and a few shivering horsemen as the core of VI Corps.

Directed to the highway east of Vilna on 9 December, Wrede's men constituted the army's rear-guard under the indomitable Marshal Michel Ney. Conducting a gallant fighting withdrawal, the tiny corps approached Vilna as the sun was setting. The city, however, was in chaos and the last bonds of discipline snapped as men slipped away to seek food, shelter, light and warmth in the deceptive haven offered by Vilna's walls. It was at this point that Franz and Second Lieutenant Franz Xaver Loe left the 'corps' ('which was already dissolving anyway') and headed west.[70]

Wrede, who had ridden into the city to report and receive orders, returned to find that his force had indeed 'dissolved'. Only late that night, and only through great exertions, was he able to collect 300 Bavarian infantry and 30 chevauxlegers. Inspired by Ney and Wrede, this last, faithful remnant of the Bavarian Army struggled west, skirmishing repeatedly with the pursuing Russians. They could not last long. The two 'divisions' were separated during the fighting on 12 December and at the morning muster on the 13th, Wrede discovered that his 'corps' now consisted of 68 men of the 2nd Division. The 1st Division had disappeared entirely, only General Delamotte and a few other officers escaping capture by Cossacks. It was the last action on Russian soil. The few remaining Bavarians crossed the Neman, united with the 1,200 men of the contingent's depot and made for Plock, the corps' designated assembly point. They saw their last Cossacks on 19 December and reached Plock two weeks later.

Moscow and Danzig

It remains to account for the Bavarian units that served detached from the main body of the contingent.

To the great regret of St Cyr and the entire Bavarian corps, all six of the chevauxlegers regiments marched to Moscow with the main army: the 1st and 2nd Regiments with III Cavalry Corps, the other four as a division under Major General Maximilian Count von Preysing-Moos in Viceroy Eugène's IV Corps. They were present but not engaged at the Battle of Smolensk in mid-August and made the march toward Borodino in continual contact with the enemy. Their conduct at Borodino on 7 September earned them high praise but cost them heavily, the 1st and 2nd Chevauxlegers suffering especially serious casualties.

When the great retreat began, they were present at the Battles of Maloyaroslavets (24 October) and Vyazma (3 November). Preysing called the latter action 'the hottest of the entire campaign... not even in the costly Battle of Borodino had the Bavarian cavalry faced such heavy and harrowing artillery fire.'[71] Vyazma diminished the regiments dramatically and left Preysing with only enough troopers to form a single squadron.

At the disastrous crossing of the Vop River near Smolensk several days later (9 November), the 'division' finally disintegrated. All Widnmann's guns were lost, and the Bavarian cavalry only continued on as individual officers and men, some with the 'sacred squadron', others entirely on their own.

As a final indignity, Preysing himself was captured by Cossacks when his horse fell through a frozen pond on 2 December. The sad, isolated remnants of the Bavarian mounted arm were cheered to see their compatriots not far from Vilna on 5 December, but weeks and months would pass before the few remaining officers and men were again fit for duty.[72]

The 13th Infantry Regiment and an artillery detachment also participated in the Russian campaign. Assigned to the garrison of Danzig in April 1811, the regiment became part of Général de Division Charles Grandjean's 7th Division in X Corps (Marshal MacDonald) as Napoleon began organising the *Grande Armée* for the great invasion.

MacDonald's Corps, the extreme left flank of the army, established itself along the Dvina and remained there from mid-July until mid-December, but its combats were few and the 13th only had one brief engagement with the enemy.[73] As X Corps withdrew towards Danzig in line with the retreat of the main French Army, however, this situation changed, and the 13th performed well in the numerous skirmishes with Cossacks during the retreat. It returned to Danzig on 17 January with flags flying, the only major Bavarian unit to escape the Russian cataclysm relatively intact.[74]

Observations

The Russian campaign destroyed the Bavarian Army. Even disregarding the prolonged misery and privation, the losses in human terms were appalling:

Original contingent (not including Danzig troops)	27,500
Subsequent replacements	5,200
Subtotal	32,700
Minus Wrede's strength on 1 Jan 1813	4,000
Total Losses	28,700

In the context of these catastrophic casualties, Franz's survival is not a little remarkable, a testimony to his own robust constitution and the significant advantage of being a member of the officer corps. As Franz notes in several of his letters, the officers, particularly those attached to a general's staff, enjoyed clothing, lodgings and victuals that were substantially superior to the lot of the common soldier,

> Praise and thanks be to God… here, with the general, I have no real privations. I live in such a way that I am not in a position to experience the conditions in which so many thousands find themselves.

Similarly, just as the army had an 'excess' of officers when it fought at Polotsk in August, the number of officers who returned from Russian captivity in 1814 (some 17 per cent of 823 returned prisoners) was notably disproportionate to the number of officers in the contingent when it departed Bavaria in March (approximately 3 per cent of 29,000 officers and men). Citing these statistics does not diminish the courage and fortitude of the Bavarian officers or disregard the difficulties and horrors they experienced during the Russian campaign. It does, however, highlight the contrast between the everyday living conditions of the officer corps and those of the common soldiers, and suggests how those conditions could influence their respective chances for survival.

Beyond the price in the broken lives and bodies of Bavaria's soldiery, however, the materiel cost of the Russian campaign was also overwhelming: 5,800 horses, 22 standards, 38 guns, 260 caissons, 300 other vehicles and all the armaments, clothing and equipment for 30,000 men disappeared in the dreadful maelstrom across the Neman.[75] Fortunately for Max Joseph, and, at least temporarily for Napoleon, the cadre that remained after the debacle was sufficient to permit the formation of a small division. Furthermore, throughout the campaign, as the contingent's overall strength had fallen, Wrede had sent small groups of excess officers back to Bavaria. These, combined with the pitiful remnants of

VI Corps, would eventually provide the foundation for a resurrected Bavarian Army.

But there was a psychological or moral cost as well, particularly as far as Napoleon's interests were concerned. For the habitual, unquestioned faith in the French Emperor's skill, genius and luck was gone, and with it went the trust and respect simultaneously accorded to his army in previous campaigns, the confidence that had helped Bavarians and other Germans overlook the often domineering behaviour of their powerful ally in the past.[76]

Curiously, Franz did not comment on Bavarian disaffection in his letters. Indeed his correspondence is remarkable for the scarcity of references to the French and their great emperor. Whether from loyalty to Napoleon, fear of censorship or, more likely, worry about the reaction back home (as he hinted on 26 August), Franz almost completely avoided discussion of Napoleon and the French. For most Bavarians, however, the Russian campaign extinguished their glowing hopes of glory, leaving behind a relentless and expanding rancour. As one of Wrede's staff officers recalled on learning that the army's flags and some of its guns had been lost on the retreat from Polotsk through, in his opinion, the confusion and panicked behaviour of the French, '[the Bavarians] could hardly hide the anger that filled their hearts toward the French, whose fault it was that the Bavarian Army lost the crowns and symbols of its honour.'[77]

But we must exercise some caution here. If the frequent confusion, the exhausting but pointless manoeuvres, the prevailing wretchedness and the ultimate catastrophe that was Napoleon's Russian campaign turned most Bavarians against the French, there remained no little apprehension that the Emperor just might recover with brilliant suddenness. A generation accustomed to the Austerlitz phenomenon, to the astonishing dethroning of empires in an afternoon, could not immediately discount a mighty and successful riposte from the general who had so often and so devastatingly surprised his foes over the past 15 years. Moreover, Napoleon personally retained a residual store of charisma. Much of the old fire was extinguished, but when conditions were right, the customary magic burned as brightly and fiercely as ever – albeit for rather shorter lengths of time.

Though they began to explore other options, to open channels to Austria and to husband their military resources more carefully, therefore, the Bavarians did not immediately abandon their Napoleonic alliance. The result was yet another campaign under French eagles.

❖ ⚜ ❖

Military Diary of
FRANZ JOSEPH HAUSMANN
for the
RUSSIAN CAMPAIGN
From when the 7th Bavarian Line Infantry Regiment
(Fürst Löwenstein) marched out
from Neuburg on the Danube on 4 March 1812.

March 1812

4 March	With the entire regiment to Ingolstadt and into quarters. Crossed the Danube.
5 March	To Kipfenberg and into quarters.
6 March	To Beilengries and into quarters.
7 March	To Neumarkt and into quarters.
8 March	Paraded through Nuremberg and into quarters in Feucht.
9 March	To Erlangen and into quarters.
10 March	To Höchstadt on the Aisch and into quarters.
11 March	To Bamberg and into quarters, and then immediately
12 March	to Zeuln [Marktzeuln] near Staffelstein.
13 March	To Kronach.
14 March	To Unter-Rodach near Steinwiesen in Bavaria. Day of rest on the 15th.
16 March	To Lobenstein.
17 March	To Schleiz.
18 March	To Auma in Saxony. Day of rest on the 19th.
20 March	To Gera in Saxony.
21 March	To Altenburg.
22 March	To Rochlitz. Day of rest on the 23rd.
24 March	To Nossen.
25 March	To Meissen near Leipzig. Here we crossed the Elbe.
26 March	To Berbisdorf near Radeberg. Day of rest on the 27th.
28 March	To Bischheim near Kamenz.
29 March	To Teichnitz near Bautzen.
30 March	To Kupritz near Löbau.
31 March	To Kieslitz near Görlitz.

April 1812

1 April	To Hennersdorf near Lauban [Luban].

2 April	To Kroschwitz near Bunzlau [Boleslawiec]. In Silesia.
3 April	To Modlau near Aslau.
4 April	To Klein-Obisch near Gross-Glogau.[78] Day of rest on the 5th.
6 April	Crossed the Oder near Gross-Glogau and to Linden.
7 April	To Maucha in Poland.
8 April	To Zielencien. Day of rest on the 9th.
10 April	To Gromblewo. Made a halt on the 11th.
12 April	To Strykowo.
13 April	Posen and crossed the Warta, then to Kopolipoli.
14 April	To Grzibobo.
15 April	To Wagrowiec and into extended cantonment.

May 1812

3 May	To Rogowo.
4 May	To Mogilno.
5 May	To Kobylniki.
6 May	To Radziejow.
7 May	To Lubranice.
8 May	To Kempka. Day of rest on the 9th.
10 May	To Chocen near Kowal into cantonment until
19 May	crossed the Vistula [Wisla] near Wloclawek, then to Ostrowit.
20 May	Passed in review for 2 hours before His Majesty and Imperial Highness the Viceroy of Italy near Lipno. Afterwards manoeuvred for a couple of hours and then marched into our former quarters in Ostrowit.
21 May	To Dobrzyn on the Vistula. Remained here until
25 May	to Sudragi.
26 May	To Glinke.
27 May	To Kowalewo near Szrensk.
28 May	To Spaki near Mlawa.
29 May	To Bokrzywnicia. In cantonment until

June 1812

3 June	to Kowalewo near Szrensk. In cantonment here until
11 June	to Slabugora. Made a halt on the 12th.
13 June	To Janowo.
14 June	To Raczin in East Prussia.
15 June	To Swietanjo.

16 June	Bivouacked in Peitschendorf [Piecki].
17 June	Quartered in barns in Woznice. Made a halt on the 18th.
19 June	Quartered in barns in Camionen. Remained there on the 20th and 21st.
22 June	Bivouac near Lyk [Elk].
23 June	To Markowsken in East Prussia.
24 June	To Cywawoda in the Duchy of Warsaw.
25 June	To Bobonice. Remained here until
28 June	to Strosdy in the afternoon.
29 June	To Krakeniki.
30 June	To Slabodki.

July 1812

1 July	To Strzelze.
2 July	Crossed the Neman near Pilony and into bivouac near Wizkini, in Lithuania.
3 July	In bivouac near Juchnani.
4 July	Bivouac near Sumieliszki.
5 July	Field camp near Hanusiszky. Both corps remained here until
12 July	bivouac near Novo Troki [Trakai].
13 July	Bivouac near Ponary.
14 July	Passed in review before His Majesty the Emperor of the French outside of Vilna, marched around this city, and went into bivouac near Minzkoy.
15 July	Bivouac near Slobodka.
16 July	Bivouac near Michalischki.
17 July	Crossed the Vilija before the above-named town and went into bivouac near Svir.
18 July	Bivouac near Rodoscham.
19 July	Bivouac near Woroniez.
20 July	Bivouac near Dunilovici.
21 July	Bivouac near Glubokoje.
22 July	Bivouac near Svila.
23 July	Bivouac near Schlo.
24 July	Bivouac near Manznin.
25 July	Bivouac near Usaci.[79] Remained here until
27 July	crossed the Usaci in the afternoon and bivouacked near Senawiene.

28 July	Bivouac near Czenzako.
29 July	Bivouac near Gurenka. Remained here until

August 1812

1 August	field camp near Biscinkowice. The army corps remained here until
5 August	downstream along the Dvina until going into bivouac near Ulla.
6 August	Bivouac near Ostrokiewe.
7 August	We crossed the Dvina near Polotsk, marched through this city, then over the Polota, and joined up with II Corps of the Grande Armée, which Marshal Oudinot was commanding. Both corps immediately went into battle order. The troops of II Corps, who were ahead of us, attacked the enemy one hour's distance from Polotsk at 9.30 in the morning, thereby forcing him back, and both corps set out on the two roads leading to Riga and Petersburg. This night we bivouacked near Gamzelewo, and also followed on
8 August	after the enemy along the Petersburg road for a few hours more, but since word was received that the enemy was withdrawing toward Riga, we also left this road and bivouacked for this night near Brutniki in the Polotsk woods.
9 August	We crossed the Drissa and camped near it, without any town to be seen near or far.
10 August	Near Walensk we again reached the road to Riga and bivouacked before the monastery of that name. On
11 August	at noon an engagement took place between the French and Swiss, who formed the outposts, and the enemy; we observed while standing to arms. Since now the Petersburg road, which was only very weakly held by cavalry detachments, was threatened by the enemy, we therefore moved on the night of the 11th
12 August	toward the Petersburg highway and marched the whole day until we bivouacked near Muschek. Here we remained on the 13th, 14th and 15th and were unremittingly harassed by the enemy. During this time II Corps, which had remained near Walensk, also withdrew almost as far as Gamzelewo on the 13th. On the night of the 15th
16 August	both corps marched back to one hour's distance before

Polotsk, where on the 16th the outposts skirmished all day with the enemy. On the night of the 16th

17 August we marched across the Polota near Polotsk and were lined up in battle order on the left bank of this river. At 6 o'clock in the morning the enemy was engaged by the French, Dutch and Swiss on the right bank of the Polota, and on the left bank by the 1st and [unclear, either 6th or 3rd] Brigades of the 2nd Division. On this day the regiment was covering two batteries and had to stand in unremitting cannon fire until 4 o'clock in the evening. A few stray musket balls also found their mark. In the evening we relieved the 1st Brigade in the outposts on the Polota. On this day there were among the wounded Marshal Oudinot, General St Cyr, General Vincenti, Lieutenant Colonel Butler, Majors Reichlin, Bach and Mann, and many others; from our regiment we had 1 dead and 5 wounded soldiers.

18 August In the morning before it was daylight we were relieved at the outposts by the 1st Brigade of the 1st Division, and we marched back almost as far as the city into bivouac. At 2 o'clock in the afternoon we received the order to break camp, crossed the Polota, and at about 3 o'clock arrived behind the Spas monastery. Now the enemy was to be turned by the 2nd Brigade of the 2nd Division advancing through defiles, while the 1st Brigade with the 3rd Brigade and II Corps attacked the enemy from the front.

Four battalions of our brigade successfully crossed through the defile, which could be traversed only one by one, but we as the fifth [battalion in the sequence] were prevented from following them by Russians who had gained a nearby hill. Therefore, in order to make place for ourselves on the plain, we were forced to take this hill by storm. This was accomplished by the 2nd Battalion of the 7th Regiment, just at the moment that one regiment on our left was in full retreat. The latter was inspired by the arrival on the hill of our battalion, and we now joined forces to drive the enemy toward the woods [see also pages 154–7 for Franz's later account of this incident]. Here we remained still for a time, until suddenly the Swiss and French positioned on our left were thrown back behind us almost to the city of Polotsk, but the 1st Brigade of the 1st Bavarian Division, which was still standing in reserve, forced the enemy back into his first position two hours' distance from Polotsk. Thereupon we bivouacked on the battlefield, though the fusillade lasted the whole night.

In this battle we lost General of the Infantry von Deroy, Colonel Wreden and Colonel Preysing; among the wounded were Colonel Comeau and Colonel Collonge, and the wounded staff officers from our regiment were Captain Leistle, who died shortly thereafter, Captain Dettenhofer, First Lieutenants Grebmer and Imhof, Sr.; wounded were Lieutenants Dufresne and Deltsch, and missing were Captain Schintling and First Lieutenant Seidel; wounded were 13 non-commissioned officers and 69 men; missing were 3 non-commissioned officers and 57 men. Thus in total 8 officers and 140 men [Franz's arithmetic is shaky; his figures give a total of 142 NCOs and men]. On this day the provisional adjutant of General Count Beckers, First Lieutenant Proesel, was wounded, and I had to take over the adjutant duties for the general, who now commanded the division.

19 August	We marched close to Polotsk into the bivouac we had left behind the day before, where the division remained until
22 August	The army again broke camp and marched off along the Petersburg road, headed by the 1st Division under the command of General Siebein, which came upon the enemy near Beloe. After a stiff struggle, during which the 1st Light Infantry Battalion and the 1st Line Infantry Regiment suffered a significant loss, our troops had to withdraw to the edge of the woods. During this General Siebein, Lieutenant Colonel von Gedoni and others lost their lives. Major Gravenreuth of the General Staff was wounded. The 2nd Division bivouacked near Gamzelewo.
23 August	General Count Beckers assumed command of the outposts; in the evening these were withdrawn to Gamzelewo.
24 August	The division command was lodged in the church at Robni, where we remained, and daily we had to ready and inspect all the outposts of the army corps. On the 26th the army corps went into camp near the city of Polotsk, until finally on

September 1812

12 September	the division quarters were moved to a house in the Polotsk suburbs. Since, during this period of rest, the

enemy was threatening the areas around the Usaci and Disna Rivers, which the army had been assigned for foraging, a brigade or rather a detachment of 400 men was sent to Disna, in order to prevent the enemy from crossing the Dvina. Therefore

October 1812

3 October
General Count Beckers left Polotsk with the 3rd Brigade of his division, crossed the Dvina there, and bivouacked near Brzdziadowice.[80]

4 October
Took Disna, and positioned the outposts outside of the city. Since the city of Disna did not offer any advantageous points for defence as a result of its location, the occupation force therefore

5 October
in the evening marched back out of the city to a half hour's distance, took up post on the heights, and held the city only with outposts. Since in the meantime

6 October
General Ströhl arrived and assumed position, General Count Beckers therefore turned over command to him, and we went back to Brzdziadowice.

7 October
Again across the Dvina to Polotsk and took up the brigade's earlier position. Now the corps remained quietly in place, while the bad weather and winter intensified so much that it would have been a sheer impossibility to let the army remain any longer in this camp without any straw.

14 October
Therefore on the 14th the order arrived to leave the breastworks that had been built and the bivouac, in order to enter into close cantonment on the other side of the Dvina.

16 October
The 1st Division moved into the suburbs of Little Polotsk and Ekimania; of the 2nd Division, the 1st Brigade into Potcotcielczi, the 2nd Brigade Plaxi, Sieradama, Sloboda and Druczani, in which latter the division command was lodged, and another detachment was removed to Uiscie across the Usaci; all of these locations lie downstream along the Dvina. Around 4 o'clock in the afternoon the 2nd Brigade under General Ströhl was attacked near Disna. This division immediately moved during the night

17 October
back to Little Polotsk, and the 3rd Brigade also held the bridge over the Usaci near Pononia. On this day the 1st Division moved three hours from Polotsk up the Dvina toward Strunja. The French outposts outside of Polotsk

were fiercely attacked, and they were forced to withdraw until close to the city. In the afternoon the 2nd Brigade of the 2nd Division occupied the two breastworks and the abatis connecting them, where we stood on outpost duty in a continuous cannonade throughout the afternoon and night. Except for minor annoyances, on this day the 1st Division remained calmly at the bridgehead in Strunja.

18 October Then today the Russians began their concerted attack on the right flank of the city of Polotsk, which was only weakly defended by the French; the Russian left wing gained a certain advantage over them and made a cavalry attack, which was repulsed from our side. As this firing on our right wing lessened somewhat, Marshal Count Gouvion St Cyr, who had stayed in one of our breastworks, rode out so that he could better observe the enemy's movements, but he returned forthwith, having been wounded in the left foot. Here he had his wound dressed and looked on for a time, but then he left, since the French of the right wing had to retreat all the way back to the trenches around the city, as well as back into the city itself.

The firing on the right wing slackened off, and it was believed, since it was already late in the day, that we would now have a respite, when all at once an unbelievable enemy horde rushed at us and at the Swiss and Croats who were on our left. We waited calmly for the enemy and let him come on with his terrible commotion and, when he seemed to be close enough, fired canister salvos at him from 18 artillery pieces located in the two breastworks, which seemed to fill him with a great deal of respect for these two entrenchments, because he then left us and turned with redoubled energy on the Swiss and Illyrians.

The latter now also retreated to behind our batteries, and the enemy had just climbed up the second rise that lay behind one of our entrenchments when His Excellency General of the Cavalry Count Wrede had two artillery pieces there removed from their mounts and turned around, while at the same time sending a small detachment into the enemy flank, and so they brought about the desired effect, again with canister fire. The huge human horde that was pouring into the valley was astounded, it seemed, at seeing cannon behind it; the enemy quickly turned around and sought his salvation in flight, but as he retreated he was so fired upon by our two batteries, which had earlier been unable to act while the enemy was in the valley and closer to the city than they were, that he had to speed up his withdrawal considerably and was unable to avoid heavy losses. As night fell we could hear the enemy drawing up many cannon aimed at our wing. It was at this time that Major van Douve from the train acted like a dilettante and lost a leg, just as many soldiers were laid low by cannonballs.

The 1st Division, which was in position at the Strunja bridgehead, was on this day only insignificantly bothered; on the other hand, the 3rd Brigade, which was standing near Pononia, was attacked around the noon hour with such force and strength that it fled back to Little Polotsk in the greatest disarray. When General Count Wrede learned of this circumstance, he placed himself at the head of two infantry regiments, two cuirassier regiments and two light cavalry regiments, in order to support the 3rd Brigade, and forced the enemy, although he was twice as strong, to withdraw with extraordinary loss back to Pononia and Druczany.

The 3rd Brigade alone, though scattered and only about 200 men strong, took some 900 prisoners during this attack. The 3rd Brigade in particular lost many officers and soldiers; Major Grossgebauer was among those wounded.

19 October Now it was generally recognised that the Russian Army was aiming for Polotsk, but that II and VI Corps of the Grande Armée were too weak to maintain this point, so it was therefore decided to leave this place, and the decision was made to relinquish the city of Polotsk on this day.

Accordingly, at nightfall the French artillery was to be moved over to the left bank of the Dvina, and after them then ours, and so both corps little by little. The French artillery park started out while it was still daylight, however, and had to pass through behind our redoubts; as naturally this withdrawing artillery was assiduously fired upon, and the enemy artillery had to shoot across our breastworks, we therefore lost very many people to this cannonade. At nightfall the French in the right wing set fire to the previously occupied bivouacs as well as to the outer houses of the suburb and withdrew,[81] but the enemy noticed this withdrawal and with his left wing attacked the French right wing between the burning camps with astounding vigour, took one entrenchment after the other, and exerted every effort to hinder our withdrawal. He did not succeed in this, however, for our artillery safely reached the left bank during the night. At 12 o'clock we ourselves fought our way to the other side of the Polota bridge, where we met up with French, but through the whole city and even on the Dvina bridge we encountered very heavy artillery fire.

After crossing the Dvina, we immediately took up position behind the suburb of Little Polotsk, where both corps gathered, except for the 3rd Brigade of the 20th, Division, which did not join the army corps until the

20 October	coming from Strunja. With the exception of the continuous cannonading from both banks, on this day everything remained quiet.
21 October	At about 3 p.m., after we had endured a terrible barrage of shell and canister shot, II Corps set out in retreat toward Usaci, and we toward Rudnia. VI Corps bivouacked near Rudnia. Several wagons and many supplies that could not be transported for lack of horses had been burned at Polotsk. Ambulances, munitions carts and other wagons were left behind on this march .
22 October	We marched into bivouac near Attikoven. Here General Ströhl and the rest of the 3rd Brigade met up with the corps. Since the march lasted until late at night, many wagons, including the ambulance of the 7th Regiment, were left behind for the enemy. On this same night a band of Cossacks fell on our flank, seized a few lead horses, and was chased off. From here on the morning of
23 October	we sent our lead horses ahead and bivouacked near Babienizky, after beforehand again suffering a significant loss of wagons.
24 October	The rear-guard was continuously chased and harassed by the enemy up to Kuplice, where we took up a position and with artillery prevented the enemy from following us.
25 October	At 1 o'clock in the morning both divisions marched through Waron to Peischna, where we bivouacked.
26 October	We bivouacked at the Berezina not far from its source.
27 October	Near Tolschitz.

28 October	Bojare. At the source of the River Vilija.
29 October	To Dunilovici. Here the Bavarian Army was about 2,500 soldiers strong. On the 31st a company was formed from each regiment; the 2nd Brigade of the 2nd Division formed 2½ companies and numbers 325 soldiers. The corps remained here, until

November 1812

1 November	when we again marched forward toward Glubokoje and bivouacked near Barille. Then we remained here until
5 November	we marched back to Dunilovici. Here the corps (at the strength of 1,937 muskets) remained quietly in bivouac.
8 November	First Lieutenant Michels again entered the service of General Beckers, and therefore on
13 November	I was ordered back to the regiment and to the staff as supernumerary.
14 November	To Humieniki near Kobolniki.
15 November	To St Svir, where there were already officers and non-commissioned officers from our regiment.
16 November	To Bolkowne near Svir. Here the staffs of all regiments remained in an area of 30 hours' distance, until on

December 1812

1 December	the command arrived to assemble, because the enemy was closing in, at Kobolniki and Svir, to which latter place we went. On this night those at Kobolniki including Captain Spizel were attacked by the Cossacks, and most of them were taken prisoner. We marched on the morning of
5 December	through Michalischki; there we crossed the Vilija and went to Worone.
6 December	Via Lawariszki without stopping, and then on to
7 December	enter Vilna at 7 o'clock in the morning. Here the retreating Grande Armée was passing through in a constant stream, until on
9 December	the rear-guard, which had the remaining best organised corps of ours, came through Vilna and had one more stiff engagement outside of the city but continued retreating down the road. The entire 2nd Brigade of the 2nd Division formed one line. We went to Novo Troki, since the whole corps was dissolving in any case.
10 December	To Mustinian, where it was already every man for himself. Lieutenant Loe and I went our own way.

11 December   To Koronie.

12 December   Into Bokrone, after on this day having first crossed over the ice of the Neman and then through Prenn [Prenai].

13 December   To Wornopie, where I came down with a nerve infection.[82]

14 December   To Kalvarija.[83]

15 December   To Sidory.

16 December   To Wulka [Suwalki].

17 December   To Kleszczewo.

18 December   To Lyk.

19 December   To Arys [Orzysz].

20 December   To Mikolajki.

21 December   To Crawink.

22 December   To Willenberg [Wielbark]. Here I made a day of rest, because we both [Franz and Lieutenant Loe] had such a bad case of nerve fever.

24 December   To Mlawa.

25 December   To Szrensk.

26 December   To Sierpc.

27 December   To Plock on the Vistula.

28 December   To Biala, where all the scattered members of the 7th Regiment assembled, and from them, and also from the replacement detachment,[84] a battalion was formed on 4 January 1813. The staff was at Srebno, where I arrived on the 13th. On the 12th or a day earlier all supernumerary officers returned to their peace garrisons, thus those of our regiment went to Neuburg on the Danube.

LETTERS FROM
THE RUSSIAN CAMPAIGN
1812-1813

Letter No. 1

Dearest Parents,

We, the staff of the 2nd Battalion, have just arrived here safe and sound and without mishap. I shall therefore not fail to let you know this at once.

Pluto [Franz's dog] was not able to take these marches on foot. He was hardly able to make it to Ingolstadt, because it was impossible for him to walk on the paw that had already been sore in Neuburg. The poor creature was very sick yesterday in Erlangen. Today, however, it is as if there had never been anything the matter with him.

I have met several people here who still remember you and me well. The son at the mill by the bridge has been dead for some time, and there have been many other changes. Mr Gmeiner sends his regards to you both. He has sold his house and lives all by himself. His sons and daughters all got married a long time ago.

Our cantonment here is of short duration, for tomorrow we shall surely march on. I have not yet received today's regimental orders, but I shall be able to add in a postscript the route that we shall take to the cantonment quarters in Silesia. I do know that this cantonment goes as far as Sagan in Silesia.

Werner is also in good health, and today I had to have him transferred to the regiment, as all the staff officers are having to do without their junior fouriers.

My horse is still fine and is getting along well.

When you write, the lieutenant colonel would probably be so kind as to enclose your letter with his mail.[85]

There is no special news of the regiment to report. In Nuremberg I was sorry to learn from First Lieutenant Rogenhofer that First Lieutenant Widnmann is said to have died. In case it should not be true, I beg you not to mention it to anyone.

Lieutenant Deltsch will therefore probably soon be sent to join the regiment, and, since my junior fourier must now also be armed and mounted, I beg you to be good enough to send us his helmet and coat, which you presumably have, through the kindness of Lieutenant Deltsch, who, I am sure, will be so kind as to take them along.

Continued on the 11th.

Today we are already in Bamberg. Tomorrow the quarters of the 2nd

Brigade will be in Staffelstein, on the 13th in Kronach, and on the 14th in Steinwiesen, where on the 15th there will be a day of rest. I shall send you the subsequent route, which we already have in the orders of the day, as soon as I can get hold of it.

It is common rumour that the Saxons have set out pickets and outposts along the Prussian border.

According to reliable letters, Napoleon passed through Frankfurt on the Main on the 8th of this month.

Please pay my respects not only to Lieutenants Loe and Predel but also to all the others, as well as to all our friends. I had promised Lieutenant Predel to write when we moved into cantonment, but since this did not take place, and besides I have really not had the time, please make my apologies to him for this and give him my best regards.

Since my time is very limited, I can only tell you in haste and until a further opportunity presents itself that I shall always remain,

My dear parents' most grateful son,

Franz

<hr />

Letter No. 2

Unter-Rodach near Kronach
15 March 1812

Dearest Father and Mother,

I still cannot let an idle half-hour pass without writing to you, because we are still not very far away.

In my last letter I promised to send you the marching route as far as Silesia:

On the 12th we marched to Zeuln, ten hours, the 13th to Kronach, four hours, and the 14th to Unter-Rodach, 1½ hours away. Here we have a day of rest today, and the brigade staff arrives. On the 16th to Lobenstein, the 17th to Schleiz, the 18th to Auma, the 19th day of rest, the 20th to Gera, the 21st to Altenburg, the 22nd to Rochlitz, the 23rd day of rest, the 24th to Nossen, the 25th to Meissen near Leipzig, the 26th to Radeberg, the 27th to Kamenz, the 28th to Hoyerswerda, the 29th to Spremberg, the 30th to Muskau, the 31st to Sorau, from where the cantonment quarters will extend through Silesia as far as Sagan.

Since I wish I had a cap like the ones our soldiers wear – to give an example of the kind I mean – I would like, if possible, to have one made out of cornflower blue cloth, cut the same way but a little more nicely finished, and the gold tassel from my dark blue hat could be used on it.[86] On no account should it cost very much. It should have only one fairly wide half-galloon [braid trim] of about one and a half inches, and a second of only one inch in width, and then it should be decorated with a gold cord. Only in the event that you have some cornflower blue cloth, or can easily get it, should you send this to me with Lieutenant Deltsch. If, however, you cannot get the cornflower blue cloth or have the entire cap made cheaply, then I would like to have the lieutenant bring me only the above-mentioned tassel, since in that case it might be easier for me to get such a cap.

The fouriers and sergeants have just arrived and given me your package, together with the letter inside it. I shall therefore answer it in haste.

I already regretfully learned of the death of First Lieutenant Widnmann on the 9th, when I was in Nuremberg.

I have often thought that I could use the maps, so I thank you very much for them, as well as for the socks, and I am also grateful for the chocolate and the watch chain.

I shall give the receipt to First Lieutenant Ebner and the note to Lieutenant Hergoth. I kiss your hand for the news that you sent, and, since I must hurry to close this letter in order to make the pouch for the Reserve Battalion, I can thus say no more except farewell, and may God keep for me my dear parents and keep for you,

Your ever grateful son,

Franz

Werner and Pluto are very well, but tomorrow's march of eight hours will be another warm one for my little horse. My respects to all who know me, especially to Mrs Wisner, Mrs Siegert, etc. – and to Captain Fortis and family.

I shall write again when I have some free time. I wrote from Bamberg by post – I trust the letter has already arrived. In greatest haste.

Please put the letter to Kempten in the mail, and if a return letter should come from there please send it to me through battalion channels or otherwise.

Franz Joseph Hausmann.
This undated portrait shows Franz in uniform as a first lieutenant,
with two bars on his collar, and wearing his cross of the Legion of Honour.
[*Cynthia Joy Hausmann*]

1806

Oberleutnant

	1809		1814	
Korporal	Tambour	Füsilier	Unterleutnant	Schütze

Anton HOFFMANN · MÜNCHEN. 1905.

Top left: Johann Wilhelm Hausmann (1759–1841). A veteran sergeant, Wilhelm expected his son to provide detailed accounts of the 7th Infantry's marches and combats. [*Cynthia Joy Hausmann*]

Left: Theresia Hausmann, née Nüllen, (1769–1831). Wilhelm's wife, she made the 53-day march from Essen to Bavaria with her husband and the young Franz in 1799. [*Cynthia Joy Hausmann*]

Above: Bavarian Infantry 1806–14. The first lieutenant at left wears the blue and silver sash and the double-breasted uniform coat with the regimental colour shown on the lapels (pink for the 7th Infantry). The second lieutenant on the right shows the officer's gorget introduced to replace the sash in 1812. At the far right is a *Schütze* (light infantryman) with his distinguishing green plume and tassels. [*Anne S. K. Brown Collection, Brown University*]

Far left: First lieutenant, 7th Line Infantry, 1805. Franz would have looked much like this officer, but with only one bar on his collar, on his promotion to second lieutenant in 1805. [*Anne S. K. Brown Collection, Brown University*]

Left: Maximilian I Joseph, King of Bavaria. [*John H. Gill*]

Bottom left: Bavarian Infantry on the march 1813–14. [*John H. Gill*]

Right: Field Marshal Carl Philipp Prince von Wrede (1767–1838). Though a difficult subordinate, Wrede was a tough disciplinarian and a good battlefield commander. [*John H. Gill*]

Below: General of the Infantry Bernhard Erasmus von Deroy (1743–1812). A solid, competent professional, Deroy was much loved by his men. [*Anne S. K. Brown Collection, Brown University*]

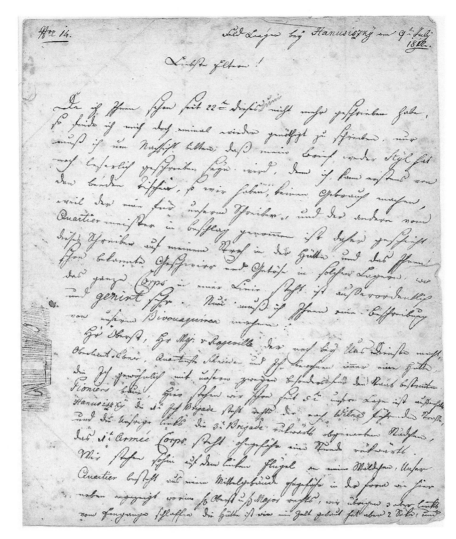

Top left: Marshal Laurent Gouvion Saint Cyr (1764–1830). A cold man but an officer with superior tactical and operational skills, St Cyr commanded the Bavarian VI Corps in 1812. [*John H. Gill*]

Left: French troops on the march in Russia, August 1812. This eyewitness sketch by Bavarian war artist Albrecht Adam depicts the confusion that was evident even early in the campaign as the French and their allies swarmed across the landscape in search of the principal Russian armies. Note the improvised vehicles and the rather small and underfed horses. [*John H. Gill*]

Above: Franz's letter of 9 July 1812, showing the hutment Franz and his colleagues inhabited, 'Our quarters consist of a central building roughly in the shape I have shown in the [left] margin…'
[*Cynthia Joy Hausmann*]

Marshal Nicholas Charles Oudinot, Duke of Reggio (1767–1847). A tough warhorse who eventually accumulated over 20 wounds, Oudinot initially led the combined II and VI Corps at Polotsk, but was badly wounded on 17 August and had to hand over command to St Cyr. Although competent enough under Napoleon's supervision, he proved inadequate when given independent command. [*John H. Gill*]

General Ludwig Adolf Peter von Wittgenstein (1769–1843). Son of a Prussian general, Wittgenstein took service under the Tsar and participated in the 1805 campaign in Austria. As commander of the Russian forces around Polotsk, he fought against the Bavarians in 1812, but found himself campaigning with them against Napoleon in France two years later. He was made a field marshal in 1825. [*John H. Gill*]

Provisional Notification of Membership in the Legion of Honour for
Franz Joseph Hausmann, issued in Moscow, 25 September 1812.
Signed by Marshal Alexandre Berthier, Napoleon's chief of staff.
[*Cynthia Joy Hausmann*]

Bavarian infantry attack Russian grenadiers at Polotsk in this sketch
by Franz Adam, son of the renowned Albrecht Adam,
who accompanied the Viceroy of Italy,
Eugène de Beauharnais, on the Russian Campaign.
[*Anne S. K. Brown Collection, Brown University*]

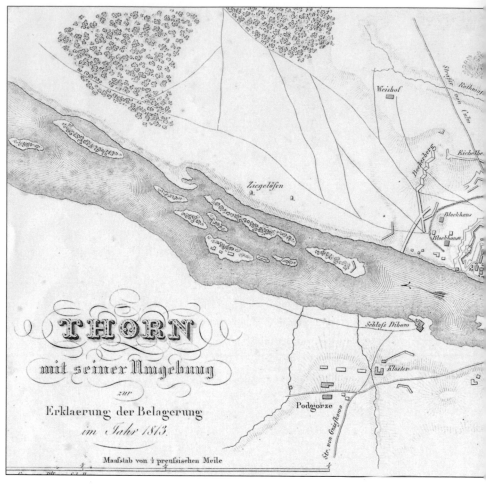

Above: The fortress of Thorn in 1813 showing the Russo–Prussian approach trenches (saps and parallels on the Beckerberg and Eichelberg), the weak Bavarian bridgehead on the south (left) bank of the Vistula (spelt Weichsel here), the fortified island between Thorn and the bridgehead, and Schloss Dybow (Dibow) on the south bank where Captain Savary and his sturdy Franco–Bavarian garrison held out against superior numbers.
[*Bavarian Army Museum, Ingolstadt*]

Right: The Battle of Bar-sur-Aube. The Bavarian 10th Infantry Regiment storms into Bar late on the afternoon of 27 February 1814. General Wrede wrote to King Max, 'It is only thanks to the outstanding courage of the 10th Line Infantry Regiment that we captured the city.' The Bavarians, including Franz and the 7th Infantry, were involved in similar brutal street fighting at Torcy-le-Grand during the Battle of Arcis-sur-Aube several weeks later (20 March).
[*John H. Gill*]

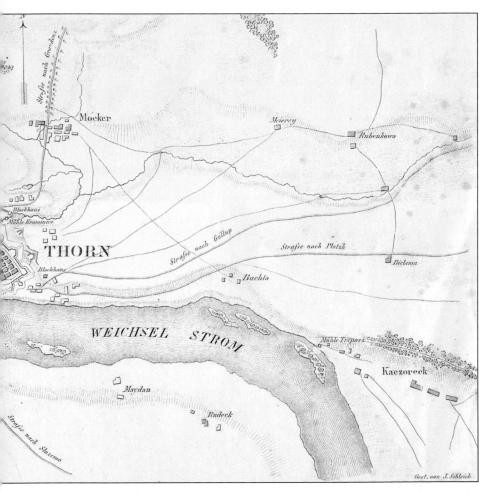

Previous page: The Battle of La Rothière. Wrede gives orders as a Bavarian infantry column advances on the snowy afternoon of 1 February 1814. The village visible beyond Wrede is probably Chaumesnil. The capture of this village by the 7th Line and the Austrian 1st *Szekler* Infantry weakened Napoleon's left flank and made a key contribution to the Allied success.
[*Bavarian Army Museum, Ingolstadt*]

Above right: Franz Joseph Hausmann as a civil official. Though he had left the army several years before this portrait was painted, Franz's memories of his military service remained vivid and he proudly displayed the red ribbon and white cross of his Legion of Honour.
[*Cynthia Joy Hausmann*]

Right: Antonia Hausmann, née Adolay, (1817–92). Franz's second wife and mother of Julius Hausmann; she and Franz were married in 1837. There is no known portrait of Franz's first wife, Otto's mother, Catharina Hausmann, née Chandon, (1793–1834).
[*Cynthia Joy Hausmann*]

Letter No. 3

Kupritz near Löbau
30 March 1812

Dearest Parents,

Since Captain von Xylander is returning to the Reserve Battalion tomorrow, I shall not fail to write to you at once, in order not to neglect any opportunity.

The day before yesterday we received the orders that the sashes for staff officers and superior officers of the infantry are to be discarded and replaced by gorgets.[87] For this reason I am, by courtesy of our captain, at once sending you my sash with the box that belongs to it. I ask you, however, not to get rid of the sash, since the adjutants of the commanding officers as well as others must still wear one, but also, when you have an opportunity, to buy a gorget according to regulation specifications. The latter, however, is of no great urgency.

Up to now we have still had no relaxation except for the rest days, on which we were up to our necks in work anyway. As soon as we have any free time, though, I shall allot some money to you, but I shall let you know when I do.

The imminent departure of Captain von Xylander is responsible for this letter being written so poorly and incoherently.

Except for the 20th of this month, today has been the first fine day of our entire march. Palm Sunday, the 22nd, was especially noteworthy for its bad weather.

I did inform you in my last letter of our marching route, but this was changed in that we went from Meissen to Berbisdorf near Radeberg on the 26th, to Bischheim near Kamenz on the 28th, to Teichnitz near Bautzen on the 29th, and arrived here today. Tomorrow will be a day of rest again, and on April 1st the brigade staff will go to Görlitz, and on the 2nd to Luban, where further instructions will be given to us.

Today we are a quarter of an hour from Hochheim, where old Frederick of Prussia lost the great battle on the 14 October, 1758. I have seen the grave of Field Marshal Keith, as well as the battlefield.[88] You might want to read about the life and deeds of Old Fritz in the officers' private library, which Loe has. Then you will be able to imagine yourself right here and to find all the places that I visited today. The title of the book is 'Lives and Deeds of the Greatest Army Commanders of Modern Times'.

Not only all the various staff and other officers but also I and all your friends are still healthy and well. Werner and Pluto are fine. The latter now has a brass collar.

There is little political news to report. I have given Major von

Werndle my sash and the box, which you will receive from his wife. Please pay my respects to her when you do.

I am in very good health. I hope that you are also well. Be assured that I shall always remain,

In haste, my dear parents' ever grateful son,

Franz

Lieutenant Deltsch should bring my spurs with him.

Letter No. 6[89]

Cantonment quarters Wagrowiec
27 April 1812

Dearest Father and Best of Mothers,

On the 24th of this month I went to the Supreme War Commissariat [Ober-Kriegskommissariat] at Murawana Goslina in order personally to pick up the package that Mr Wisner brought with him, which I indeed received on that day. I immediately turned over to Franz Lindemeyer of the 1st Fusilier Company the 5 francs, 48 kreuzer and the letter. The helmet, coat and one pair of leggings for my orderly were contained in the package.

Yesterday evening we received orders that the entire corps was immediately to resume its march toward the Vistula. We shall cross the Vistula near Plock, and it really seems that things will now become serious. We have been here in cantonment for almost two weeks. The day and hour have not yet been set, but it is practically certain that we shall have left here by the 29th.

Werner, my horse, Pluto and I are in very good health. Up to now every officer has had his orderly, as usual, so I do not need a private servant. I have now taken Betz, who was with the major, as my regular aide.

Since Major von Fortis really has come up for his pension and will leave for the Reserve Battalion the day after tomorrow, I hasten to give him this letter before we march on.

Up to now I have consistently lived very well. I have even become so fat that almost everything is too tight for me.

Two weeks ago I wrote you that I had sent you an allotment of 20 francs per month beginning April 1st. I shall go by my circumstances and on that basis decide how long I shall keep sending this and whether I shall perhaps decrease it later. I did this mainly so that, in case we no longer received our pay, I would at least find something at home. For, if money is short, then everyone will be given a reduction in pay. We have received our pay for April.

I bought a horse from Major Fortis, the small brown one. I had all the more reason to do this, since we may now soon be in a situation where I will greatly need a second horse and where my safety may depend on this. Here in the entire vicinity, as you know, there is no usable horse to be had, and even if one could be procured, it might be too late. Therefore I bought it (because I also know it is very healthy and sound) for 105 francs with saddle and harness. The saddle and bridle, etc. are worth at least 3 louis d'or, so the horse costs me but 6½ louis d'or. If I can easily obtain another one I shall take it, too, just in case.

For the moment I have paid the major 25 francs, because I could not spare any more, and I ask you to pay the remaining 80 gulden from my monthly allotments.

If we should receive supplementary pay, I shall allot some of this in addition; how much, I shall write to you later, however.

Then Major von Fortis gave me a cooking pot, which is arranged very handily with a cover that serves as a soup dish, two small plates, a cup to cook something else in and for lather, then ladles, also a coffee set, all made of tin. Since, however, he had no idea what the cost should be, I told him just to tell you in Neuburg what it costs and you would pay him. So I ask you to do this, too, and then write me soon how much it cost, so that I also may know.

According to the Order of the Day of the 19th, our First Corps is the 19th Division of the Grand Army, and the Second Corps is the 20th Division. The Cavalry Brigade of the First Corps is the 21st, and that of the Second Corps is the 22nd Light Cavalry Brigade. We all belong to the VI Corps of the Army.

I have written Major von Fortis a receipt for the 80 francs that will be coming to you and have assured him in it that you will make monthly payments on this debt, in such a way that this sum will be paid off in eight months at the latest, and that, should supplementary pay be given out, I would turn over a certain amount of it to you.

Therefore be so kind as to pay off only as much of this as you can spare, for I am convinced that the major also does not expect any more. But please, dear parents, do not be angry that I overwhelm you with so many requests. I shall certainly seek to make it up to you, at least as far as that is possible for me.

Furthermore, I hope you both remain in the best of health. For this I pray earnestly to God, and He will surely preserve for you,
    Your eternally grateful and most obedient,

Franz

P.S. When I was at the War Commissariat I did not see Wisner, because he was still in Posen with the commander in chief. He and I send regards to Lieutenant Strunz and to the whole group.

Since a pouch is just leaving, I am sending this letter with it. As yet – it is now six o'clock – we still do not have a marching route.

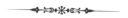

Letter No. 7

Wagrowiec
30 April 1812

Most Precious Dearest Parents,

The arrival of Dr Knittelmeier and also the departure of Major von Fortis make it necessary that I send you in haste another little note.

As I said, Dr Knittelmeier arrived here at four o'clock this evening and gave me not only your dear letter Letter No. 5 of the 12th of this month but also a box in which were a cap and three bars of chocolate. The cap is beautiful and has turned out beyond my expectations. It arouses all sorts of attention and is admired by all. The colonel immediately put it in a piece of paper and sent it to a local tailor. He wanted to have one made for himself, but no one was able to produce a similar one (which is to be expected in Poland). As mentioned above, I cannot tell you enough how well I like it. My dearest thanks for this I would whisper daily to you, if it were possible.

You have probably received my six earlier letters as, to keep them safe, I enclosed them in the pouch to the Reserve Battalion.

I have so far received all your letters, all of which, thank God, assure me of your continued good health. For my part I can assure you that I have never known myself to be in better health than I am now. Please God that you both are also so, and then I am consoled. Werner, my two horses and little Pluto are very well.

I also learned that Lieutenant Deltsch has been replaced at Eichstädt, so he will surely soon be here.

I would like to know why Reichmann and Pfordten left the regiment, especially whether there was any unpleasantness or not.

Please give my thanks and respectful return greetings to Mrs and Miss von Fortis, Miss von Auer, Captains von Hardungh and Fortis, also to the lieutenants, etc. (Incidentally, in connection with the belt for hanging a sword on the wall, I have often thought of Miss von Auer.)

Our colonel is not to be moved in letting Lieutenant Loe come up until von Ebner gets to be captain. I have already gone to great pains in this matter, but there is nothing to be done. At any rate, he should not have thoughts of golden days in this present war, for there is surely no one here who would not like to be in his place. In short, Major von Fortis will make him aware of the pleasantries of the present campaign.

With regard to the [...] money, I would suggest asking the lieutenant colonel to have a letter written from the battalion about it. In the same way you should turn to him also in the matter of Lieutenant Heilmann, for the latter is well aware that the payments sent every quarter are to be used for that purpose. Furthermore, in this respect I would not be too polite but would inform the lieutenant colonel of these debts (without accusing the officer) and ask him to have them paid off.

You write that you have not paid for the cornflower blue cloth for the hat. I would therefore like to know whether it should be taken from my pay or how it might otherwise be paid in the most expeditious manner. If I know, then I can allow for it, so that it is not paid for twice.

Major Werndle, Captain Wagner, etc. will soon also be coming. The lieutenants will therefore soon be able to experience the happy life of their dreams and judge for themselves. I was very upset over Reigersberg's death, for I did not yet know of it, nor did anyone in the regiment.

Major von Fortis will tell you the marching route from here to Plock, since I do not have the time to add it here. It still does not look dangerous, because we have had our marching route since the 28th and are not leaving until May 3rd.

In my last letter I wrote you that I had bought a horse from Major von Fortis and still owed 80 francs on it. The major is leaving on 1 May at 3 a.m., so I must hasten to close and venture to sign myself as always,

My dearest parents' eternally faithful and obedient,

Franz

Pluto has been half-shaved, but he does not like it at all, for he is always scratching.

My respects to all who know me.

Letter No. 8

Dearest Parents,

Since Captain Wagner is leaving here tomorrow, I shall not neglect the opportunity to give him a note.

I do not doubt that you all continue to be in good health. I, at least, am quite satisfied. I have again become so accustomed to marching that I do not feel quite right when we rest!

Following Major von Werndle's request (to be transferred to the Reserve Battalion), the Supreme Command decided that, as soon as another staff officer replaces Major von Fortis with the regiment, Major von Werndle can begin his return journey without further ado. Now we are very curious to see what sort of a staff officer will come here.

Captain Seyda will also, as I learned in confidence, receive his pension.

Our marching route was: on the 3rd from our cantonment at Wagrowiec to Rogowo, the 4th to Mogilno, the 5th to Kobylniki and today here. For tomorrow we know only that we shall spend the night near Brzesc, and the day after tomorrow we shall again go into cantonment near Kowal. How long this will last remains to be seen.

I have packed the cap into my travel bag so that it will not be ruined.

Now it is finally beginning to get warm. The sun has been burning down on us for three days, and for this reason we always break camp between 4 and 5 in the morning. Until now the weather has been dreadfully raw and cold, and we even had snow as recently as two weeks ago. But the days are already long, and one can see without a light from 3.30 in the morning until 9 in the evening. And in general, this is a beautiful, blessed stretch of country.

Our practising regimental doctor, Dr Blume, came to us today.

Now surely an army order will have come out in Neuburg. We have great hopes, for here First Lieutenants Schmeckenbecher, Saint-Sauveur and Grebmer are already in command of companies.

Since I know of no news, the only reason for writing is to tell you once again that I am, thank God, still in good health, and I hope to learn of the same from you. Your letters I have already answered.

Deltsch has probably left already, and Reichmann must be leaving soon. Therefore Predel also has hopes. Likewise the lieutenant colonel will also probably follow.

While I entrust you, dearest Parents, and myself to the protection of God, I mention that our colonel and all the rest are well, and I beg you to pay my respects to Major Fortis' wife and all the officers, and also to Miss von Auer.

Furthermore, I shall ever remain, my dearest parents' most loyal and obedient,

Franz.

Werner, Betz, both horses and Pluto are well and send greetings.

Letter No. 9

Chocen near Kowal, Poland
14 May 1812

Best of Parents,

Since Captain Baron Seyda now has received permission to return to the Reserve Battalion, I shall therefore not miss the opportunity to direct a note to you through him.

Captain Lahsberg is no longer here, since he departed the day before yesterday, and he left too quickly for me to be able to give him a letter. Seyda is still here, however, and I have asked him not only to take this letter along but also personally to convince you of my good health when he delivers it.

This time, as I have so often said, I find Poland much changed. Major von Werndle, I, Captain Leistle and Dr Faust are quartered here at the home of a baron who has a large estate. His favourite son among three died the day before yesterday, and the family is almost inconsolable over the loss. We are nicely situated, only we miss our daily wine. I have made up to these people a little, and I get wine quite often, as does the major.

By now you have probably received my Letter No. 8 of the 6th through Captain Wagner. Our further marching route from Radziejow is as follows: the 7th Lubranice, the 8th Kempka, the 10th here, where we have been in cantonment since then. The army orders of 15 April did not reach us until the 8th.

Major Werndle sends greetings to you and is daily expecting to return to the Reserve Battalion.

There is a strong rumour that all the guard and grenadier companies will soon march to Warsaw for the coronation of the King of

Poland, and then the troops are to return to their homes. Fine, but I cannot believe the latter.

When you receive the money that I have allotted, please notify me. Stay well and happy, for that is the heartfelt wish of,

Your eternally obedient son,

Franz

P.S. Lieutenant Deltsch has not arrived yet. I have already duly acknowledged receipt of the cap.

◆ ᐳ◍◆᙮◆᠅ᐸ ◆

Letter No. 10

Spaki near Mlawa
28 May 1812
The Feast of Corpus Christi

Best of Parents,

Since Major von Werndle is leaving here very early tomorrow and returning to Neuburg, I shall not miss the chance to write to you at once.

Captain Seyda must have already brought you my last letter. Our continued marching route was as follows. We broke camp on the 19th, crossed the Vistula near Wloclawek and marched to Ostrowit. On the 20th the entire corps had to pass in review near Lipno before His Imperial Majesty the Viceroy of Italy [Eugène de Beauharnais], who is the supreme commander of all the troops stationed here. After that we manoeuvred for a few hours and then moved back into our old quarters. The 21st we marched to Dobrzyn, where we stayed until the 24th. The 25th to Sudragi, the 26th to Glinke, the 27th to Kowalewo, and today here. Tomorrow we shall camp near Janowiec, and so it now appears that we are headed for Königsberg [Kaliningrad]. I am well satisfied, especially since the day after tomorrow we shall be in Prussia, where we can again talk to the people, as Janowiec lies on the Polish border.

I have no doubts that you are both in good health. Major von Werndle will tell you himself how I am.

Up to now no one here has any other news either.

I send my greetings not only to Major von Fortis but also to Lieutenant Loe and the other gentlemen.

Since I had to snatch a half hour from the night and the major is departing immediately, I must close, and I entrust both of you and myself to God's care. For the rest, I am in greatest haste, and I remain,

My dear parents' most obedient,

Franz

P.S. Major von Werndle will tell you how we are doing. The last letter I received from you was No. 5.

Letter No. 11

Kowalewo near Szrensk in the
District of Mlawa and Department of Plock
4 June 1812

Most Precious Parents,

Now surely, I believe, you will soon be receiving letters from me often enough, for every other moment there is an opportunity to have letters taken home, only it is lamentable that one must always hurry so much in writing, for, in the first place, we of the 2nd Battalion staff are far away from the 1st Battalion, and, secondly, he who has permission to return sees to it that he gets out of Poland quickly, as one can readily imagine. On the 28th of last month I wrote to you through Major von Werndle, and tomorrow First Lieutenant Rainprechter is also returning to the Reserve Battalion, so I shall give him this letter.

I hope and pray earnestly that you both may be in as good health as I am, only I still cannot comprehend how it is that since your fifth letter of the 12th of April, which I received on the 30th of the same month through Knittelmeier, I have not received any more.

Major von Werndle left Spaki on the 29th of last month, so I shall add only the following marching route: the 29th to Bokrzywnicia near Janowiec on the Prussian border. There we camped until the 3rd of this month, and then we returned here covering two days' march in one, and we shall stay in cantonment here for a while. I saw Wisner once recently, but only on the march. He is very well and sends greetings to you both and to his mother.

There is no news here at all. Many things are mentioned, but one may not and cannot repeat them. This much is a fact, that at the Polish border a few hundred Cossacks came into Polish territory to forage, and when this was perceived by the Poles, they chased the intruders back across the border and made prisoners of about 200 of them. Shortly thereafter, the Russians withdrew entirely from the border and retreated about ten miles into their country. However, they devastated and ruined this stretch along the border completely and took their subjects with them into the interior of the land, where, it is said, they will be recompensed for their losses. Such is the common talk here, but actually I have not seen it.

Up to now no officer has yet come from the Reserve Battalion, but Lieutenant Deltsch has been appointed to the 6th Fusilier Company, Reichmann to the 7th and Predel to the 2nd. Lieutenant Lutz will therefore have to follow for First Lieutenant Rainprechter. At present we have Major von Rogeville of the 3rd Regiment assigned to us. I suspect, however, that the lieutenant colonel and Major Merz will soon show up, so that once again we shall have some of our own men in the 2nd Battalion.

Our colonel and all the rest of the regiment are still in good health. At first we had very few sick, but the poor drinking water and the raging heat, which has been prevalent for some days, are causing a number of cases of sickness again.

Now we shall soon be at the point, as six years ago at Pultusk, where there is no more night, for it is light now until after 11 o'clock. At Spaki we were not far from Lisno and Przaznitz, where we were encamped in 1807. You were at that time with the Leibkompanie on a hill in a village where Maier deserted with that woman.[90] I visited this village again.

We have already received the Army Order No. 4 of 18 May, which turned out miserably for our regiment, but this does not satisfy me, for I believe that by the time this letter reaches you another will have come out that will serve us better.

Please let me know what the kettle and mess kit from Major Fortis cost.

Please pay my respects to Miss von Auer as well as to all the officers and Mrs and Miss von Fortis.

May you be healthy, well and happy. Do not be concerned about me, for I am lacking nothing but the presence of my dearest parents, and be assured that I shall always remain,

My dearest parents' most obedient son,

Franz

Letter No. 12

Kowalewo
9 June 1812

Dearest Father and Mother,

Lieutenant Deltsch arrived here on the 7th and immediately sent me everything from Kowalewko, where he and Captain Schmitz are in cantonment and which is a quarter of an hour away from here. This was all correct as stated in the letter, for which I am very indebted, and I mention only that I have not used up the coffee, sugar and chocolate that I already had, since there has not been need so far. I do, however, thank you very much for all this. The ham and mustard will serve me especially well. I would only wish that I could keep it for when I will need it. Now to answer your letter No. 7 of the 11th of last month.

It is certainly amazing that Major von Fortis covered this trip in ten days, but Lieutenant Deltsch likewise made good time, because he was only on the road 21 days to here, and it is considerably more difficult to come in this direction, because the constant troop movements cause very great delay.

I still have not received Letter No. 6, which dates, as you write, from the 4th of last month. I would like to know whether it was to come by itself in the mail or was included in a pouch to the regiment.

We received the French decree the day before yesterday, sent to the regiment via the brigade. As our colonel insists, however, and as I myself realise, it can have no reference to those who were born to servicemen.

I have sold Lieutenant Predel my sword for 5 francs, 30 kreuzer or, rather, for a ducat. Therefore, in case he does not agree to the 5½ francs, then he will surely remember the ducat, which is the same to me, if he pays the latter in gold. At present, thank God, I still do not need money, for I have always got along on the balance of my pay, and my 5 louis d'or are still a nest-egg, and so I have need of nothing.

We have now been authorised the two bonus payments but have not yet been paid in cash. I shall allot you a round sum, which will amount to about one and a half times my regular pay, and keep a half payment here. Only I am not yet positive what I shall receive, and therefore I cannot make a definite decision. We have also been put on a wartime pay scale since 1 April, but there will hardly be any pay increase for me, because an adjutant even in peacetime draws an additional allowance for his horse, while a company officer receives only six francs for that. Besides, there is no longer any allowance for the junior fouriers. My two lads, Werner and Betz, my two horses and my little Pluto are in fine health.

Lieutenant Deltsch tells me that the colonel has received a cap like mine from Major von Fortis, only the tassel of his is much more elegant. These are therefore the only two of this kind that exist. In your letter you write the following: 'Upon receipt of it (the money from Heilmann) I shall pay in cash for the cornflower blue cloth, which comes to only f. 44 kr.' Since I cannot work out how many gulden this amounts to, please mention this in a letter.

N.B. The following is not to be broadcast around: I can readily believe that the wife of M[ajor] v. W. was not happy that her husband returned to the Reserve Battalion, for he had not announced his intention to her beforehand and received her permission. The good man is to be pitied.

In my humble opinion you should not procure too much for me, unless it is something that you happen to get very cheaply, and send me very little or even nothing at all, for the situation could now develop that we might be very far away, and that very soon, and then something that does not keep well might spoil and could moreover get lost because of the great distance. I thank you very kindly, furthermore, that you have paid off Major von Fortis and others so promptly, and I therefore ask you to cover the debts with the money that is gradually to be paid to you in allotments and to keep any balance for yourself as recompense. The more so, because I shall get money from the colonel if I should need it for any reason, and this then can be repaid upon my return.

The mustard container probably became somewhat soft from the heat, but all it did was to spot the three enclosed letters a little. Nothing leaked out of it, however, and the can itself was still tightly closed.

What an infamous lie that Corporal Fink is dead! He is now just as lively and healthy as before. He became sick in Wagrowiec and had a serious haemorrhage, but he has long since been back with the company, for I just recently saw him lying sick along the road, when we marched from 5 in the morning until 10 at night on the way here. So it is a lie, as many another thing.

When we get to eat the ham, etc., which can only take place in bivouac, then Deltsch will certainly not be forgotten. Anyway, I am greatly looking forward to our first day in camp.

The room that you have moved into sounds very pleasant, and I presume that you are living in it by yourselves. Should, contrary to expectation, the request be made that you take in others, of course nothing could be done about it then, but I beg you to inform me of this at once, so that I might see the commander about possibly making other arrangements.

I have never doubted that you of the Reserve Battalion would have plenty to do, but I ask only that you yourself not do too much.

It is indeed strange that we are so unlucky with canaries. Surely

Isabel and the males that were hanging in my room are still alive.

You wrote that by the time Lieutenant Deltsch arrived here I would know more. Today I told Lieutenant Deltsch: Ha! More? On the contrary, we know less. Back there you at least know a 'perhaps' that might be reasonable, but we, we know nothing at all now, except that we are lying here and shall soon have nothing more to eat. For the first time in more than three weeks it rained today, but this will do little good unless more rain follows, for in this constantly dry, sandy soil it could rain every day. If the weather had been good we should have had hay long ago, but now the grass has dried up. In addition, many a man has the misfortune that his horses do not eat grass, but mine like it. I let them graze for three hours every day. At first there was a good stand of grain and all crops, but because of the continuous heat, which increased so in one day, nearly all the seeds dried up. We were anticipating a long-deferred harvest as last year, but if today's rain keeps up, things may still turn out all right. On the 24th of last month we still had snow in Dobrzyn, but on the 25th the march to Sudragi was scarcely bearable because of the heat; thus on the night of the 24th to the 25th winter departed into summer, without thought of any spring, and since then we have been living with the heat.

There is much talk here, but much of it is not true. I therefore sell you the rumours as I have purchased them, as follows:

His Majesty Emperor Napoleon is said to have toured all the borders of Poland incognito; however, it is not known if this is true. He takes along a few hundred windmills, an equal number of wagons with soup or bouillon tablets, fire fighting equipment, several hundred labourers of all sorts.[91] From this it is concluded that he will march through Russia to India ['Ostindien', 'East India' in original]. Russia may or may not satisfy his desires; he will go through quietly or by force. The trip from here to India would take at least a year. The reason for taking possession of India can reportedly be guessed by taking England into account. But enough of this.[92]

According to all appearances we are waiting here until all the French have passed, for they frequently march ahead. It could probably be true that we and the Poles will form a reserve corps.

Incidentally, thank you for the good advice in regard to my health and my deportment. I assure you that I will follow it.

Sergeant Höblinger is going to the Reserve Battalion, and therefore I am sending this letter to the regimental staff at Szrensk, so that he can take it with him. By the way, I am going to stop writing by the ordinary mail because of security.

I have the rank list of the officers in my possession, because I intend to keep it up to date and will make a note of all promotions and other items.

I am happy that all payments are still coming in regularly to you. With us, at least, such is not the case, for we have not yet received our pay for May.

The major's assurance that we have so far suffered no need is true. But I fear that we might soon feel the pinch.

We are very comfortably situated at the home of a pensioned Polish colonel, but the men are no longer getting all the necessities. For example, the bad drinking water is notorious. Brandy is now also lacking, and, as I said before, there has been a dearth of straw for a considerable time, and most of the buildings have been stripped of their thatch.

Now I have answered your 11-page letter, and I only regret that it was not longer, for you know that I much prefer reading letters to writing them. Therefore I beg you to forgive me for stopping now, but time – since I do not know whether Sergeant Höblinger might not leave early tomorrow – and the uncertainty of several items of news cause me to close and to beg of you to keep him in constant memory who dares to call himself,

My dear parents' eternally obedient son,

Franz

Please do not forget to give my regards to Majors von Fortis and von Werndle, to the lieutenant colonel, and to all other friends.

The latest news that is making the rounds is that at the first cannon shot the Austrians will rush to our support from Galicia with 160,000 men.

The day before yesterday the following order allegedly appeared here: His Imperial Majesty the King of Italy has commanded that in future no proclamations or appeals shall any longer be printed. Moreover, everyone is to continue talking about peace; nevertheless, no one may pass the outposts without a pass from the minister of foreign affairs, von Posso (or whatever his name is),[93] except for couriers and liaison officers, who must legitimise themselves by means of their dispatches. All foreigners entering at these outposts are to be taken to the nearest corps commander. It is correct that this was in an order of the day, but I ask you not to let it be spread around that I told you about it.

Letter No. 13

Dearest Parents,

Since Captain Baumann is going to return now, I hasten simply to assure you of my good health and to acknowledge that your Letter No. 6 finally arrived today.

Today the army orders came in with the news that now the campaign shall begin, and that from now on we shall be loading up in earnest.

Today we had a hot day and marched for seven hours. I wrote on the 9th, and you know the route up to that day. On the 11th we marched from Kowalewo to Slabugora, the 13th to Janowo, the 14th to Raczin, the 15th to Swietajno, the 16th to Peitschendorf, where we bivouacked for the first time, the 17th to Woznice, the 19th to Camionen and today, the 22nd, to this place. Here our gypsy life begins, but no one knows anything of actions for now.

Since no more time is left at my disposal, I must close in haste and assure you that in any case, according to your advice, I shall certainly be careful, and therefore you need not cause yourselves any anxiety.

I am in haste, as always, your most obedient,

Franz

❧ ⋅≫✿≪⋅ ❧

Letter No. 14

Dearest Parents,

As I have not written to you since the 22nd of last month, I feel compelled to write to you again, but I must ask your consideration in that my letter neither has any style nor is legibly written, in the first place because I cannot make use of the two tables that we have, because the one has been commandeered for our clerk and the other by the quartermaster. Therefore this writing is taking place on the straw in my hut, and you well know that the confusion and tumult in such camps, where the entire corps is in one line, are extraordinary and cause great annoyance. Now I must give you a description of our encampment.

The colonel, Major von Rogeville, who is still in service with us, First Lieutenant von Ebner, Quartermaster Schneider and I are still living in a hut that I usually put up with the aid of our two pioneers who have been especially appointed for the staff.[94] We have been here since the 5th; our camp is outside of Hanusiszky. The 1st Infantry Brigade is on the right of the road leading to Vilna, and ours on the left. The 3rd Brigade is behind the above-mentioned town [Vilna]. The 1st [Bavarian] Army Corps [i.e. 19th Division] is about an hour behind us. We are thus on the left flank in a small wood. Our quarters consist of a central building roughly in the shape I have shown in the margin, in which the colonel and the major sleep at the left and the other three of us at the right of the entrance. The hut is built like a tent but has two pockets, and the entrance is on one side, which is covered with branches, as are the pockets; the other side, which is entirely closed in, is covered with thatch. Since the heat was unbearable in this house, I built two wings to the right and left of our palace, one of which was designated as a dining room and the other as a boudoir in which one can dress or undress without being seen and can also wash. Our horses are quartered in the woods.

The army is faring miserably. Yesterday was the sixth day on which we received no bread, but today we received a three-day supply. We have, however, suffered no real need, so far.

One cannot occupy one's time with political matters, for one knows absolutely nothing. Emperor Napoleon has been in Vilna for over two weeks, and the outposts are already said to be at the Dvina, and yet no shot has been fired, even though war has been declared, according to army orders of the 22nd of last month. In haste I shall quote as much as I can recall from memory.

His Excellency Count Wrede, General of the Cavalry, says in his Order of the Day of June 26th as follows: 'His Majesty the Emperor and King [Napoleon was also King of Italy] in the general orders of the 22nd speaks as follows to the Grand Army. "Soldiers! The second war in Poland has now begun; the first ended at Friedland and Tilsit. At Tilsit Russia swore eternal friendship for France and war against England. Today she broke her oath. Russia does not intend to give an explanation for her strange behaviour until the French eagles have crossed the Rhine, whereby France would have to leave her allies exposed to the caprice of Russia. She lets us choose between honour and contempt. We shall not hesitate in our choice. The time has come for Russia's fate to take its course. The second campaign in Poland will be as rich in honour for us as the first. We shall cross the Neman and carry on war in her country."'

My last letter was from camp near Lyk, from where we marched on the 23rd to Markowsken in East Prussia, the 24th to Cywawoda in the Duchy of Warsaw, the 25th to Boboince, encamped here until the 28th, and on that afternoon we broke camp and spent the night at Strosdi, the 29th at Krakeniki, the 30th at Slabodky, and July 1st at Strzelze. On July 2nd we crossed the Neman or Memel near Pilony and encamped in Russian Poland near Wizkini, the 3rd near Juchnani, the 4th near Sumieliszki, and came here on the 5th.

How difficult the marches are in the present heat is easy to imagine when I tell you that every day we break camp only at 7, 8 or 9 o'clock in the morning.

Since I mess with the colonel, the major and others, and the cooking utensils from Major Fortis were somewhat too large for me, I turned them over today to Captain Fortis of the 4th Light Battalion, as I had half promised his brother, for 4 francs, 3 kreuzer, because I kept one pot for making coffee.

Coffee and sugar each cost 1 franc, 30 kreuzer a pound in our money, or so we are told, for wherever we go the inhabitants have all fled. If we only came to a city I would buy some anyway. By the way, I have just used up what I brought along. I am only now beginning to use what Lieutenant Deltsch brought me. I have drunk chocolate only once, because one bar got wet.

I have already written you that I received your Letter No. 6 on the 22nd of last month. Otherwise nothing new has developed with us. Captain Baumann has probably already delivered my 13th letter of the 22nd of last month. Captain Wallraff was sent to the hospital sick a few days ago, but otherwise all are well and healthy.

Since the two active service pay bonuses have been approved and these amount to 65 francs, I shall allot 50 francs of this to you.

Because the colonel wants to close up the pouch at once, in my haste I can only wish that you are faring well, and I remain, as always,

Your most obedient,

Franz

Letter No. 15

Usaci in Podolia
26 July 1812

Best of Parents,

Since the pouch that I spoke of in my last letter of the 9th of this month was not closed in camp near Hanuschyschky but could only be taken to the mail here, where we shall enjoy a few days of rest, so I shall add this little note as a postscript to my Letter No. 14. I can only mention that not the slightest thing has happened since that time. According to certain reports, Marshal Davout is said to have fought some successful skirmishes against the Russians at the Dvina, which is still six miles away from us, and among other things to have captured 36 cannon. Furthermore, Smolensk, we are told, has already been occupied by the French, although the princely pancratic corps has not yet entirely left the Dvina.[95]

In order to acquaint you with our further march, I add herewith that we moved on the 12th from Hanusiszky to camp near Novo Troki [Trakai], on the 13th to near Ponary, and encamped near Minzkoy on the 14th. On that day the entire Bavarian Army paraded before His Majesty the Emperor of France and marched around the city of Vilna, because all the streets of the city were teeming with prisoners. Before Vilna we saw our first dead people, because the French had wrung this city from the Cossacks. At least 8,000 dead horses lay on the road from Hanuschyschky to Vilna. In short, the roads were almost impassable, and the marches too fatiguing. On the 15th we bivouacked near Slobodka, the 16th at Michalischki, where we crossed the Vilija, the 17th near Svir, the 18th near Rodoscham, the 19th near Woroniez, the 20th near Dunilovici, the 21st near Glubokoje, the 22nd near Svila, the 23rd near Schlo, the 24th near Manznin, and the 25th to this place.

On this whole march the troops received almost no bread. Once two companies got five small loaves, the second time each company one and a half loaves, and the third time a piece from a large, poor loaf of oatmeal bread. Therefore one cannot be surprised when I say that on many a day of march companies in the regiment had 12 or 13 dead, that the sick mounted up day by day so that, even with the addition of the stragglers who are now back, our numbers are down to 350, and that on account of the wretched roads we are very often 12 hours on the road but have only covered a march of four hours.

I would really be telling a lie, however, if I should complain about shortages, for one can well imagine that we take care of ourselves first.

In Vilna I bought a pound of coffee for 6 Polish gulden and the same amount of sugar for 5½. Now one must accept the fact that because of the crowds of people these victuals must be paid for at three times the ordinary cost. For some days we have been marching along with the Imperial Guard, since we are now directly under the command of the Emperor.

It is strange that we have no recent news at all, except what was brought by Lieutenant Deltsch. No letters, no army orders, in short nothing has come in. To be sure we are now about 500 hours away from Bavaria. You wrote to me several times in your letters that I should write if I needed money. For this I thank you heartily at this time, but I still have a few gulden in silver and the 5 louis d'or in gold, so it would still be unnecessary. Should I get into any embarrassment you know that I can turn to our colonel. I have already received one advance of 10 francs on my pay, which, however, has already been paid back.

The Reserve Battalion has already been informed in today's report that I have allotted you 50 francs out of my supplementary payments.

Wisner is now here, too. He is in good health and sends many greetings not only to you but also to his mother. Please pass this on to her and inform her that Wisner wrote to her from Vilna.

On the 27th.

This afternoon at 5 o'clock we broke camp and marched to Senawiene, the 28th, today, to Czenzako, where I am adding this note. The Russians have taken position between the Dvina and the Dnepr, whither we shall probably make our way. For the rest, may you stay well and be assured that I am always,

Your forever most obedient,

Franz

◆◆◆◆◆◆

Letter No. 16

Bivouac near Polotsk
18 August 1812

Best of Parents,

Since my last letter from Usaci on the 26th of last month, various new events have taken place, which I shall endeavour to reconstruct in compressed form herewith. On the afternoon of the 27th we received the command to follow the Emperor's Grande Armée on the road to Vitebsk, and then on this same day we marched to Senawiene, the 28th to Czenzako, the 29th to Gurenka. Up to this point we had been camping in the villages, but on the morning of the 30th in Gurenka a fire broke out next to the pigsty where the staff was quartered and quickly spread. Accordingly, we not only had to vacate the village immediately, but also had to camp in the open fields on all the following days. We came into camp near Biscinkowice along the Dvina on 1 August. On the 5th news arrived that the French under Marshal Oudinot (Duke of Reggio) had been defeated near Polotsk and compelled to retreat to the Dvina. We immediately broke camp and marched to Ulla and on the 6th to Ostrokiewe, from where at 8.30 on the morning of the 7th we crossed the Dvina, and on the outskirts of Polotsk we joined with Marshal Oudinot's Corps, which consisted of two divisions of French and one division of Dutch and Swiss and which had just reoccupied Polotsk.

At exactly 9.30 the outposts attacked the Russians and overthrew them, whereupon the entire corps, 60,000 strong, moved left on the road toward Petersburg. After an hour, one division of the French and our First Army Corps [19th Division] left this road and turned into the one leading to Riga. We camped in the Polotsk wood, which is 12 hours march long and lies two hours from Polotsk. On the 8th we also left the Petersburg highway and made our way over country and logging roads back to the road to Riga and spent the night near Brutniki. Here it should be mentioned that on this afternoon such a storm of hurricane proportions arose, that our poor men, who for over three weeks had not received two rations of bread and many of whom had a violent diarrhoea, which saps the strength so extraordinarily and goes over into dysentery, had to wade in water and bog up over the knees for more than three hours, for which reason very many men collapsed on the way and died miserably from exhaustion and also because they received neither help nor relief from anyone. But I am straying from my subject and must therefore get back on course.

On the 9th we crossed the Drissa and camped in front of it. On the 10th we reunited near Walensk on the road to Riga with the two divisions that had become separated from us. Since now the very weakly held Petersburg road was threatened by the enemy, we returned there in one day and spent the night of the 12th near Muschek. On the 13th the French who were on the Riga road had to retreat again. We were disturbed continuously day and night by the enemy on the 14th and 15th, and, since the terrain was not favourable to us here, we retreated up to Polotsk on the night of the 15th. On the 16th we again had to turn back several small skirmishes, which task, however, was accomplished by the outposts alone. We had to stand to arms every few moments, but not until yesterday, the 17th, at 1 o'clock at night did we move out of our bivouac and draw up in battle formation to the right of Polotsk across the Polota.

At about 6 o'clock a few 6-pounders were directed at a Russian picket, and towards 8 o'clock the affair began. It was our task to cover two batteries behind the Polota. Now it is easy to imagine that all the enemy artillery, of which to be sure they had only about 20 pieces, was concentrated upon these two batteries, which caused very much damage in the Russian army because of their excellent location, and we therefore endured a stiff cannonading that lasted until 4 o'clock.

The brigade had extraordinarily good luck in this place, for we counted only six wounded, while the 6th Regiment had 17 officers and over 200 men wounded, and the 2nd Regiment about five officers and 190 men. Captain Pierron of the 6th Regiment was killed on the spot. Marshal Oudinot, General St Cyr, General Vincenti, Lieutenant Colonel Butler, Majors Reichlin, Bach and Mann are among the wounded. In this affair, in which the firing continued with great force until 8 o'clock in the evening, the Russians have likewise lost very many men, for all day today their wounded, who were not found on the field of battle until today, have been brought past us to [...].[96]

Nothing happened to any officer of our regiment. The first cannonball shattered the right leg of the orderly or light [...] (as the fouriers are now called). Of the [...], five men were slightly wounded by musketry. [...] the Carl Regiment [3rd Infantry] has a very insignificant loss.

We did not get to fire our muskets; we had only to stand still the entire time exposed to the enemy fire. A spent bullet struck the rein of my horse quite sharply. The horse can now stand the firing quite well. I lost Pluto in a forest on the 28th of last month on the march, and poor Werner got the Polish sickness (diarrhoea) three weeks ago, and it got so bad that I had to have him taken to the hospital in Polotsk on the 16th. However, I expect his recovery in the immediate future.

Since we are marching off at 2 o'clock, I must hasten to close. We have many sick in the regiment, among others Captain Wallraff, First Lieutenants Saint-Sauveur and Weinberger, Senning, Lechleitner, Pirkner and Lieutenant Schönner. All the rest are hale and hearty. Major Merz has arrived and brought the map and pipe ribbon, for which I thank you. Your letter will soon be answered by,

Your eternally most obedient son,

Franz

In greatest haste I am writing at once, since you asked me to in one of your letters. Give my greetings to Loe and tell him that his brother is a corporal in a Swiss regiment, which is here, and he was slightly wounded yesterday. Or at least so I have been told, for I did not see it.

I do not know where we are marching. Farewell.

Letter No. 17

**Camp near Polotsk
19 August 1812**

Dearest Parents,

In the conclusion of my letter of yesterday I said that we were marching at 2 o'clock. This was the reason why I could not write any more and had to finish today.[97]

We did break camp yesterday at 3 o'clock in the afternoon, and the 2nd Brigade under General Count Beckers went behind a church on the little River Polota, in order to turn the flank of the enemy by defiling past. However, at 4 o'clock, when, under the thunder of cannon, the brigade was about to finish defiling past one man after the other and reach a wood, it happened that after our 1st Battalion had passed this valley and Major Merz with the 2nd Battalion was likewise about to go through, when the enemy seized a hill that was on our left. Now it became a question of first clearing this hill again. Our battalion stood in an unspeakable rain of shot and musket balls, but by much encouragement and cries and blows we brought our men to storm this hill, and so we drove the enemy back in the greatest disorder and with much loss and followed them as far as the woods.[98]

On our left a few battalions retreated, but we were ordered to force our way through. This we did, but we thereby drew upon ourselves fire from in front, from the left and from three batteries. It is not possible to take the time to describe this in detail, for I shall tell you about it orally. I only mention that in this really heated battle among many others General of the Infantry von Deroy, General Raglovich, Colonel Comeau, Colonel Colonge and Colonel Wreden were very seriously wounded and perhaps will not survive. Very many are lightly wounded.

However, in our regiment we have only Sergeant Filchner, Corporal Sterner and eight men who we know are dead. Seriously wounded are Captain Leistle through the head, but he will survive, Lieutenant Deltsch in the groin, and Lieutenant Dufresne through the chest; lightly wounded are Captain Dettenhofer in the shin, First Lieutenant Imhoff,

Sr., in the lower leg, First Lieutenant Grebmer a ricochet on the arm, and also Ensign Sartorius in the foot, but not seriously. Sergeants Zenger and Hintermeyer died of their wounds yesterday. Sergeant Kegler and Sergeant Sichler are also wounded. In all, the regiment has 13 non-commissioned officers and 59 men wounded. Three non-commissioned officers and 57 men, as well as Captain Schintling and First Lieutenant Steidl, are missing and have not yet made an appearance. Our entire loss thus amounts to eight officers and 140 men [once again Franz's arithmetic is at fault; the listing above comes to 9 officers and 144 men]; the exact number is not yet known today. Lieutenant Engler is severely wounded, Lieutenant Weller is sick, and Major Tausch also died in this way. Lieutenant Michels, who is brigade adjutant with General Beckers, has been ill for four weeks, and therefore the adjutant of the 4th Light Infantry Battalion was performing his duties. Since this officer, however, was also seriously wounded, I was appointed today as adjutant to General Beckers.

According to today's orders, the General of the Cavalry [Wrede] has command of both divisions, while Major General Siebein commands the 19th and Major General Beckers the 20th Division. In our division, Colonel Spaun commands the 1st Brigade, Maillot the 2nd and Habermann the 3rd. In the other division, three colonels likewise command the three brigades.

Since the courier who takes the letters with him is about to leave and I have my many duties, I must close.

To sum it up, the enemy has been completely overthrown, and we now have nothing more to fear. They are also talking about peace negotiations that are to take place.

I did not have my horse with me, because all the staff officers and adjutants of the brigade had to defile through on foot.

Finally, your sincere son, in very good health, thank God, wishes you continued prosperity.

Franz

Greetings to all.

FRANZ'S 'RELATION' OF
THE FIRST BATTLE OF POLOTSK

The following, extracted from the published history of the 7th Infantry, is a supplement to Franz's accounts of the First Battle of Polotsk in his letters and military diary.[99] He composed this in 1829 or shortly thereafter in response to what he perceived as a misrepresentation of the action on 18 August 1812 as delivered by officer turned historian Eduard Baron von Völderndorff und Waradein in his magisterial work *Kriegsgeschichte von Bayern unter König Maximilian Joseph I.* In his version, Völderndorff credits the 4th Infantry with halting the Russian advance against the Bavarians with well-delivered musketry and then inspiring their countrymen by a determined attack that turned the tide in this portion of the battlefield.[100] Franz, on the other hand, gives most of glory to the 7th Infantry.

Individual perceptions of combat events can vary tremendously and controversies such as this exist in all armies for almost any battle, but Franz's is particularly convincing because this is almost the only spot in his known writings where he specifically describes himself performing an heroic deed. While we may never know with certainty which regiment truly 'saved the day' for the Bavarian Army on that August evening in 1812, Franz's detailed account enhances our picture of the battle and provides a wonderful vignette of tactical realities in the Napoleonic age.

Account [101]

At 4 p.m. on the afternoon of 18 August, when the 12-pounder battery posted on the left bank of the Polota began to fire and thereby gave the signal for the entire line to attack, the 2nd Brigade of the 20th Division of the Grande Armée (the 3rd and 7th Line Infantry Regiments), which had been awaiting this moment concealed in the shrubs of the estate[102] gardens and arrayed en colonne[103] under General Count von Beckers' command with staff officers and adjutants on foot, set itself in motion in such a way that it broke through those shrubs and the thorn hedge that enclosed the gardens by files to the right of the estate and village of Spas and descended into a wide ditch that surrounded the estate and which was connected to the stream bed of the Polota, and marched ahead in a ravine which formed the narrow space between this little stream and its very high and steep bank in order to reach the Gromewo Forest and thereby to get around the enemy's left wing, which lay between this forest and the village of Spas in what was for us a very uncomfortable proximity. The difficulties presented to the brigade by the penetration of the thorn hedge and the descent into the aforementioned ravine without any prepared path had the most uncomfortable result that the leading elements [of the column] had almost reached the edge of the forest before the tail – the 2nd Battalion of the 7th Regiment – had completely departed the starting point. This delay created significant intervals between the various units of the brigade.

As Beckers' brigade was advancing in the manner described, the 19th Division had likewise begun its advance with the aforementioned attack signal, and Raglovich's brigade had attacked the enemy on the road to Newel [Nevel] and pushed him back toward that renowned forest, which seems to be the reason that the enemy, thus occupied, at first failed to notice the movement of Beckers' brigade through the ravine 500 or 600 paces farther to the left. However, after the enemy commander had sent substantial reinforcements to his hard-pressed left wing, and from them [the reinforcements] had shoved a strong force into the gap which had been left open on the plateau between the right wing of Raglovich's brigade and the much-mentioned ravine, these reinforcements effected both the discovery of Beckers' brigade filing up the ravine and the retreat of Raglovich's brigade, as well as a break in Beckers' brigade, from which the last company of the 1st Battalion of Löwenstein and the 2nd Battalion of the same regiment, in part still in the process of descending from the aforementioned gardens, were cut off when the enemy attacked them from the plateau above. The isolated seven companies of the regiment had no choice but to withdraw into the previously mentioned broad ditch that encircled the Spas Estate, in order to reform themselves when possible, as a retreat out of this ravine in any other direction was impossible owing to the Polota flowing on the right and the steep, enemy-occupied heights on the left.

Arriving in this ditch, or cauldron, I quickly convinced myself that the battalion would be a defenceless target for the enemy's fire and would certainly suffer greater losses than it would in an attack across open ground. As a retreat into the estate gardens (our initial position) was unfeasible owing to the rugged terrain described above and the impassable route, I allowed myself, in this most desperate situation, to ask the battalion commander, Major von Merz, to order the battalion to climb the steep height before us at once, in order to get out of the enemy's line of fire as we climbed and to take part in the mightily raging battle once we were on the plateau.

At a wave of his [Merz's] hand, the entire command scaled the height, and, behind a sort of natural breastwork there, found the time to form itself hastily and hold at bay the pursuing enemy troops, who had thrown themselves into one of the many ditches on this plateau. At the moment of our arrival on this height, however, it did not escape my notice that one of our units with yellow lapels and cuffs was retreating at a distance of approximately 500 paces to our left and had already come very close to the village of Spas. It seemed to me that this was the 4th Infantry Regiment of Raglovich's brigade. I only allowed myself a moment to consider that, if this unit continued its retreat into the village or indeed beyond it, our battalion, for which, as just mentioned, there was no open route of retreat, was probably destined for captivity, and would be thrown, in any event, either back into the cauldron we had just left or into the Polota. I then turned to Ensign Sartorius (then serving as a sergeant-major) standing next to me on my right and to a sergeant on my left and called on them to leap atop the breastwork with me and to attack the enemy with the bayonet, assuring them that the battalion certainly would follow if we set the example. In no time, this occurred and just as rapidly the battalion was up and running toward the ditch in which the enemy had thrown himself, driving him thence from ditch to ditch up to the forest without respite.

At the time that the battalion of the 7th Regiment stepped on to the plateau of the battlefield and attacked the enemy with the bayonet, the withdrawing battalion or regiment mentioned earlier (apparently the 4th) halted, turned about and, aligned with us, joined us in pursuing the Russians up to the forest, by which time it had become dark.

Shortly thereafter in this wood, the battalion met with the 1st Battalion of the 7th Regiment under Colonel von Maillot, which had followed the original route with the rest of Beckers' brigade.

Furthermore, there is no doubt that the hand of fate which caused this episode, and which threw the 2nd Battalion of the Regiment Löwenstein into the line of battle without orders from above, is to be considered fortunate for the outcome of the battle; because at the moment that the enemy commander was reinforcing his defensive line and pushing an infantry detachment into the open gap between the right flank of our attacking line and the right bank of the Polota (that is, Beckers' brigade), the former [the attacking line] was forced to withdraw for fear of being outflanked and the latter [Beckers'] was completely isolated in the Gromewo Forest and condemned to inactivity. These movements by the Russians would have had decisive disadvantages and incalculable consequences for the two [Bavarian] detachments just mentioned had not those seven companies of the 7th Infantry Regiment crossed supposedly impassable terrain, surprised the enemy at just the right moment and, by their impetuous bayonet attack, forced the enemy into hasty flight, which haste was probably caused because the boldness of the attack by such a weak force of infantry would have led the enemy to conclude that strong supporting troops were at hand that could have been hidden in the hollow behind us. Through the rapid repulse of the infantry column which had forced its way into the gap, the retreating right wing of our 19th Division lost its concern about a flanking attack and could return to the attack with us, whereby the balance of the battle was restored and, much more, the decision of the entire day's business was promoted.

As Major von Merz, Ensign Sartorius and I received the order of the French Legion of Honour shortly thereafter, I do not doubt but that the 7th Regiment brought this episode in the Battle of Polotsk to the attention of the commander; but how astonished was I in 1829 at Pirmasens on the outermost borders of the realm, when Volume III of Baron von Völderndorff's Bavarian military history fell into my hands, in which, in addition to a number of other errors, I found the facts described above recounted in totally incorrect fashion on pages 115 and 116, and the 7th Infantry Regiment not mentioned at all. It now seems probable to me that an account of this spontaneous action by the 2nd Battalion of the 7th Regiment, operating on its own initiative and completely cut off, was never submitted. This could well have happened because Major von Merz was transferred to command the 2nd Light Infantry Battalion shortly thereafter and because I was called to be General von Beckers' adjutant the following day, the 19th of August, so that we both had to leave the battalion.

Now that I have put down on paper the facts described above, I believe I have repaired as much as possible my previous neglect, committed when I was adjutant of this battalion, and I leave to fate and the future whether and in what manner the 7th Infantry Regiment, in whose ranks I spent the happiest years of my youth, with which I participated in all the campaigns of this century up to the year 1818 with the exception of the military promenade to France in the year 1815, and to which love and gratitude bind me with equally strong ties, maintains or vindicates this leaf in its crown of laurels.

Letter No. 18

**Bivouac near Robni,
two hours past Polotsk
on the Petersburg road
26 August 1812**

Most Precious Parents,

By now you have probably received my letter of the 19th of this month, Letter No. 17. I should have written to you again on the 22nd, because I had news again, but I considered it unnecessary, for we did not take part in this action. I have already told you that on the 17th and 18th we had a tough battle, and so I shall continue. On the 19th, 20th and 21st we remained in our position near Polotsk and were always ready to break camp, but not until the 22nd at 1 o'clock in the afternoon did we get the command to march, and we started out on the Petersburg road. The First Division [19th Division] led by General von Siebein formed the advance guard, then a French cavalry brigade followed, and then the Second Division [20th Division] under the command of General Count von Beckers. Except for two batteries that went with us, all the artillery and the baggage were to go along the left bank of the Dvina, but we were to go along the right bank toward Disna. Thus we marched quietly along for three hours.

Then our division received the command to halt, but the First continued another half hour farther, where they met the enemy outposts and forced them back. (Here I must call attention to the fact that the road to Petersburg is straight as a ramrod and so wide that from a hill one can at any time see for a distance of almost two hours, and thus one can always shatter everything on the road with cannon shot. At the right and left there are only woods and swamps.) These outposts then allowed themselves to be forced back to Beloe, but our men had hardly arrived there in columns when a cannonade started from one piece by which six to eight or more men were severely wounded with every shot. Nevertheless, this division [the 19th] went on and in this way came close to this cannon, which suddenly let loose a horrible fire of canister. Now, therefore, all had to leave the road, and the enemy was attacked on a plain that was here, and the village of Beloe was taken, but we had to withdraw again just as quickly, because the enemy pressed our men severely. The position outside of the woods a half or quarter hour from Beloe was maintained, however, and here our outposts and those of the enemy were only a stone's throw from each other. We remained here on the 23rd, and General Beckers was put in charge of the outposts, so we two reconnoitred the enemy, who kept very quiet, just as we did. One could talk with the enemy here, so close were we, and we saw quite well how he had taken possession of the entire hill.

On the evening of the 23rd we withdrew our outposts one hour's march to Gamlzelewo, where the road to Riga separates off from the one to Petersburg, and here the 1st Brigade of the Second Division took a position. They were relieved on the 24th at noon by the 2nd and 3rd Brigades, and also at this time the enemy's outpost appeared at a quarter hour's distance before ours on the highway. Command of the outposts was turned over to Colonel von Maillot, who is in charge of the 2nd Brigade, and General Beckers and I with the entire divisional staff found quarters here in the church. I get along very well with the general.

Lieutenant Strunz is acting as brigade adjutant for Colonel von Maillot.

At the affair on the 22nd, the following misfortunes took place: General Siebein was wounded and died on the 24th; Lieutenant Colonel von Gedoni was killed on the field of battle; Major Gravenreuth of the General Staff was shot through the foot, and it was amputated the day before yesterday; likewise Captain Pelz of Laroche's [6th Light Battalion]. First Lieutenant von Xylander of Gedoni's [1st Light Battalion] was severely wounded; First Lieutenant Haake of the Leibregiment [1st Infantry Regiment] remained dead on the road.[104] Besides this, about eight more officers were wounded and a few were left behind dead; also several were captured. The battalion of von Gedoni has only four or five officers and 60 men left, the battalion Laroche likewise, and the 1st Infantry Regiment suffered greatly in this engagement. The following died of their wounds of the 18th: General of the Infantry von Deroy, Colonel von Wreden, and on the evening of the 24th Captain Leistle, of those whom you know, but many more in addition. Colonel Count Preysing was also badly wounded on the 18th. Senior War Commissar Böhm died of exhaustion. I visited Lieutenant Deltsch yesterday. He will recover completely and is already quite cheerful.

The situation with our troops is very unhappy. Rations are poor; meat and water, with a 16-pound loaf [sic] of bread about once every two weeks, are all that a soldier gets. Disease is rife. On all roads one finds dead men who had been sent to the hospital but could not reach it for exhaustion and therefore died in a most pitiable manner. The French and the other allies do not fare a whit better, and that is what lets me hope, as is rumoured, for an armistice very soon and peace thereafter.

The following tells plainly of our weakness. The effective strength of the division excluding the cavalry is 12,507 men. Of these, 990 are on special detail, 4,221 sick, then 811 missing and prisoners, so that the loss is 6,022. According to report, then, there are 6,485 available for duty, and from this are to be taken those who remained weary and sick along the marches, also those in the train and those who were put on special duty as junior fouriers or with the baggage and in other regimental service, who amount to about 730 men. Therefore, of the above-mentioned effective strength of the division, there are under arms 13 staff officers, 203 officers, 581 non-commissioned officers, 103 musicians and then 4,855 shadow-men, for such are our soldiers as they wander around here. I can guarantee that this number would not show up, if we were today lined up in formation. So now you can get a good idea of our condition when I add to this that our division is significantly stronger than the First. But please, dear Father, keep this to yourself, for it might cause an undesirable mood in the country if the pitiable fate of the army became known.

Praise and thanks be to God, nothing has really happened to me so far, and here with the general I have no real privations. I live in such a way that I am not in a position to experience the conditions in which so many thousands find themselves.

One can truly not thank one's God enough, if one is always so fortunately preserved, and it is a miracle to have come out so luckily, especially after the battle of the 18th. It seems to me that now the war will also soon be coming to an end. Our victory on the 18th cost us many brave men, but the Russians were also thoroughly beaten, even though under the command of Prince von Wittgenstein they were at least twice as strong as we, and they lost 1,500 men who fell into our hands as prisoners, and 21 cannon. The battlefield was sown with wounded and dead to such an extent that even by the evening of the 21st not all the wounded and dead had been removed from the scene. Their loss in wounded and dead is comparatively four times as large as ours. In short, the carnage was terrible right up to nightfall. I myself took one prisoner, who was at the point of stabbing me.

Yesterday also news came from the Emperor that Smolensk had been captured by storm by the French, 100 cannons won and 12,000 prisoners taken. The Russians are completely routed and are being pursued by the Emperor with much success. A decisive battle has not yet taken place, however.

I have already told you that Werner went to the hospital. He was sick a long time while still with me. I had him taken care of and he did not take duty, but at the end he got so weak and could no longer stand without aid, so I had to have him taken to the field hospital, especially since the dangerous days were at our very door. I have frequently had people look for him since then, but no one can find him.

On our march on the 12th of this month our forage wagon remained behind and only caught up with us on the 14th, but it had lost almost everything that we had in it. In this way I lost my overcoat, a pair of boots and other things of this kind. Today on the 30th of August as I close, we are still located at the place mentioned above, without having learned anything more.

I am, you may be sure, now as always, my dear parents' faithful and most obedient son,

Franz

Letter No. 19

Dearest, Most Precious Parents,

Your letters sent to me arrived in the following manner. Your Letter No. 9 without date was, as I have already written you, duly turned over to me by Major von Merz, together with the map and little ribbon, on the 11th of August just as we had the thunder of cannons and musketry very close, for the French and Swiss were having an affair at this time half an hour away. And on the 16th of this month we had a lucky day when for the first time in some while the post arrived again. Here I received in the enclosures to Major Merz, who now is in command of the regiment, your dear missives No. 8 of the 29th of May, No. 10 of the 8th of June and No. 12 of the 13th of July. I am therefore writing in reply according to the numerical sequence, and I call attention to the fact that I could not possibly find time on the 18th, 19th and 20th to reply to Letter No. 9, which I had already received earlier, because, as is known to you, on such days after battles and at the outposts one has very little peace and quiet in which to write letters.

So to Letter No. 8. It is easy to imagine that the captains who have been transferred to the Reserve Battalion take their duties and drill very seriously, because in the first place they are all diligent, and because in the second place they hope thereby to remain with the battalion in active service, although I doubt that it will help any, for it is said that all those officers that have returned will be pensioned. The death of Secretary Marx has affected his son greatly; he is now also sick.

I have already written you that I have allotted 50 francs to you from my supplementary pay, and likewise I shall continue with the monthly 20 francs. The spending of it, how much and how, I leave entirely to your good judgment. So Quartermaster Burger has after a long wait got into bookkeeping after all.

I am well aware that the said Mr von Wagner can be a thorn in people's sides. I also know that he has nevertheless had the longest reign. Therefore, just let the fools run along with their dunce caps. Millach's daughter will be very saddened at the loss of her husband. Sterner's wife left here on 20 or 21 August. She has probably made a lot of noise, but, I beg of you, do not believe any such wailing, for we know, of course, that these people always believe that they have seen more than a prudent man can see. You may rest assured that I shall write to you at once at the conclusion of even the smallest conflict and shall always stick [...] to the truth, for it is a fact that since the affair near Beloe on the 22nd of last month we have not fired a shot at the Russians, excepting the skirmishes of the patrols, and the latter have not fired on us, and [...] reason that we shall not fire again. I heard that my cousin went to the Light Horse, and he will surely like that better than in the infantry. Captain Wallraff returned from the hospital a few weeks ago, and in the last Army Order No. 6 he received the First Class Medal, and he is also acting major now. Therefore I do not believe that he will go back so soon.

Army Order No. 5 never did arrive here, and therefore no one knows whether Saint-Sauveur and Thannhausen have been promoted or not. Regarding your request for a settlement, I can do nothing but wish you good success, only I believe that now is not the right time, for you know well what decision was made on your request at the Reserve Battalion three years ago with respect to detached service. To be sure, the lieutenant colonel will support your request, but what will acting Company Commander Wagner do for you? Furthermore, I do not know whether you still suffer pains in your foot, in which case you must be very thoughtful of your rest. Finally, I am convinced that you want to do everything and yet are not able to, and the lieutenant colonel has told not only me but told you as well, that you should spare yourself and not exert yourself too much. There are surely other sergeants in the company; leave something for them to do, too.

All regards that you receive for me, please return in my name.

The gorgets for the division have been here for some time but have not been given out. The General of the Cavalry [Wrede] did not want to do it, and we can get along all right without them. We can wait until we get the epaulettes, and then both things can be done at the same time.

To Letter No. 9. As I have already said, in Russia I duly received the map of Poland as well as the little ribbon, through Major Merz himself. I thank you very much for these items, and the ribbon is already adorning my silver-chased pipe bowl. With regard to the withdrawal and payment of my debts, I have already told you that I leave that entirely to your discretion.

To Letter No. 10. From this letter I see, then, that Lieutenant Loe has been permitted to resign his position as adjutant. Neither he nor any of the other officers, viz. Reichmann, Predl, Lutz, etc., have arrived here as yet. On 1 July two of these marched out of Bayreuth, so one can see what a tremendously long journey it is from Bavaria to Russia.

It is not at all necessary that I procure my own victuals, because I always eat at the regiment with the staff officers and now with the general, but I always have something on hand, which is especially advantageous for me if the need arises, as is often the case here. But I suffer no privation. For example, I was not feeling well a few days ago, so I immediately sent for a quart of wine, even though it cost 2½ taler, or 4 francs 30 kreuzer, and was about half a Bavarian measure. In general provisions are very scarce here and only to be had at exorbitant prices. For example, beer is not to be had at all. A pound of butter costs one rouble or about 2 francs in our money. A little loaf of commissary bread only three weeks ago cost four 24-kreuzer pieces. When I get two shirts, two cloths and two pairs of socks washed by someone in town, I am very fortunate, and if I really am so lucky I must give the washerwoman the soap myself. My orderly must stand beside her all day, and I must pay four 24-kreuzer pieces in advance. They try to get money out of you for everything here. In short, in Polotsk they do not know any different but to demand two, three and four 20-kreuzer pieces for the slightest thing. In this respect our poor wounded and sick officers are to be pitied, for if one of them wants to have some soup made he must pay almost 3 francs, because a handful of flour costs 48 kreuzer, two potatoes cost a penny ['groschen' in original] – in short, everything is like this.

I do not know if I have already written you that on the march from Walensk to Muschen on the 12th of last month I lost my overcoat, my jacket, a pair of boots and other minor items from our transport wagon. Therefore I was faced with the necessity of procuring another overcoat, and so I bought one of the deceased Major Baron Gravenreuth's for 11 francs. My ready cash has shrunk considerably as a result.

I wrote to you immediately each time after the affair of the 17th and 18th and after the battle on the 18th and 19th. Then I wrote on the 26th of last month after the affair at Beloe on the 22nd, although we took no part at all in the latter.

I am very sorry that you have had so much bad luck with your birds, but perhaps next year will be better. By then I can feed them sometimes, or forget to do so, as has happened so often.

That my dear mother is suffering from a cold causes me much concern, and I hope that it will soon have passed, and please give me news of this in the near future. From my heart I wish her a speedy recovery. I am only sorry that I cannot give her part of my good health, for I have no ailments of any kind at the moment.

Now I shall answer the last letter, No. 12. I have already said at the beginning that Lieutenant Lutz has not yet arrived. He will then bring along Letter No. 11, which I have not yet received, and I am very anxious to see the regulations. That the good fellow thought he would join us in 24 days will […], for today it is already 74 days […] more […] perhaps, and he surely will not come this month. Lieutenants Reichmann and Loe are also not here yet. I cannot understand why Predl is still at the Reserve Battalion, since Lutz has already left; however, he may have started this happy journey by now. I would have paid Sergeant Sichler the 10 francs by now, if he were not in some unknown hospital, lightly wounded. I do not dare say anything about your credit, for there is not a single farthing ['heller' in original] in the coffers of the corps paymaster, much less in the regiment, which has much less than nothing. I have, to be sure, not much more left now, but I can get money any time. You need not worry about me, for I have not used any of my gold. Only my silver has melted away, and we have not received much yet, so I am not used to having any. Money is being expected daily anyway.

Captain Frank and Professor Plager are the most uncouth bums in the city of Neuburg. Therefore it is easy for me to believe that they are quarrelling with each other. For the one will never admit that the other is more uncouth than he.

About Lieutenant Voltolini I am also not surprised, because, just between us, he is a loudmouth. [...] has not yet been hushed up enough, so he has to get still more [...].

I have noticed from the newspapers, which we have from as late as the 29th of August, that storms have caused much damage in Bavaria. One may conclude that this is the reason for the prevailing high prices. General Beckers has the Nürnberger Correspondent, and on the 16th of this month he received the issue of the 29th of August and many earlier ones.

Now to news. You surely already know that Captain Leistle and First Lieutenant Senning are dead. Lieutenants Deltsch and Dufresne are better. Deltsch was shot through the left side with damage to his ribs, and Dufresne through the left chest and from the right through the right chest and through the right shoulder. Dufresne will probably have a permanently disabled arm. First Lieutenants Ebner, Lechleitner, Imhoff, Sr., Pirkner, Weinberger, Thannhausen and Schönner are still very ill. Captain Dettenhofer went back with his wound, God knows where. All the rest of the officers are hale and hearty.

Sergeant Baldauf and Corporal Oberfrank from the 1st Light Infantry died a few days ago, just as many of the non-commissioned officers and soldiers of the regiment have already started on this journey to eternity. My orderly Werner is also said to be dead, but I am not yet sure of this. You probably already know that Sergeants Hintermeyer and Zenger are dead.

Our army has really suffered greatly already, for the First Division has only 1,709, [and the Second Division according to] report only 1,958 including privates still in the ranks. Therefore the entire army has 3,667 muskets [in readiness]. The 7th Infantry Regiment of the Line, according to this report, consists of one staff officer, 17 officers and 48 non-commissioned officers, then 11 drummers, 204 men [...], so the entire regiment is 303 men strong. Now just imagine this beautiful regiment of 1,615 men in former times [...]. In the hospital at Polotsk 50 to 60 men are dying every day, and likewise the number of sick increases. All

[move] around like shadows. This campaign will truly be a costly one for Bavaria.

On the very day of the battle of the 18th here near Polotsk, [...] von Cetto of the 10th Line Infantry Regiment, ordnance officer with General Count Gouvion St Cyr, was sent with our news to the Emperor.[105] He came back on the 2nd with rewards. In the first place, General Count Gouvion St Cyr was made a marshal, and secondly [...] Infantry von Deroy was raised to the Imperial French peerage as a count with a stipend of 60,000 francs annually. Deroy did not survive to learn this. In the third place, all officers, non-commissioned officers and soldiers who [lost] an arm or a foot in this battle [are to] enjoy the same pension as the French in such a case. In the fourth place, all the widows and orphans [...] of the officers, non-commissioned officers and soldiers who died in this battle are to be treated and receive the same pension as those of the French. In the fifth place, His Majesty bestowed upon the two army corps 80 Legion of Honour crosses for officers and 40 for non-commissioned officers and privates.

Furthermore, a few days ago a salute of 50 cannon was given here, at which time the victory of the Emperor at Mozhaysk, 22 hours' march this side of Moscow, was disclosed.[106] This battle took place on the 7th of this month, and the victory consisted of 1,500 prisoners and 60 captured cannon. In addition, 40,000 men and 9,000 horses succumbed on the field on the Russian side, and only 20,000 men on the French side. This is said to have been a terrible battle.

The courier who brought this news did not travel very quickly because of lack of horses, wagon, bread and everything. He said that a courier from another corps had overtaken him near Vitebsk who was bringing the news that the French were on this side and the Russians on the other side of Moscow, that the city had been vacated by both sides and could not be entered, as negotiations had indeed begun there. Also that the senate in Moscow had declared that if Russia did not make peace then Moscow would do so, because they did not want to see the city surrendered to the enemy.

This courier also said that on the 7th before the battle the Emperor had inspired courage and bravery in his troops by promising them that in the space of four weeks he would procure peace and good winter quarters for them.

The news has also just come in that the reinforcements will arrive here on the 25th, [which is probably where] Reichmann and Loe are. Today, the 23rd, our regiment is again 17 men weaker.

Lieutenant Colonel Baron Zweibrücken of the General Staff is returning [to] Bavaria tomorrow as courier. He will take this letter along and [post] it in Munich.

Ensign Sartorius and Sergeant Kugler, who was left behind wounded, will be decorated with the Legion of Honour.

I hope that we shall see each other soon, and I am, as always, My dearest parents' son, most obedient unto death,

Franz

For this time my letter will be a good, long one, and you will have enough to read.

I am well situated with General Count von Beckers. We have, as is well known, a good mess, but there is nothing to drink, although it is just for the present, and we must be satisfied with nothing but water. General Vincenti is in command of the First, and General Count Beckers the Second Division.

Lieutenant Colonel Deuxponts [i.e., Zweibrücken] is leaving this afternoon, the 24th, at 2 o'clock, and the news has just come in that the Emperor of France entered Moscow on the 14th of this month.

Lieutenant Schönner is said to have died yesterday.
Farewell.

Letter No. 20

Polotsk
10 October 1812

Dearest Parents,

On 25 September I received your second Letter No. 10 of 19 June. The two bottles with the crate for the colonel arrived on the 28th, and I received Letter No. 13 of 21 July on the 7th of this month.

Lieutenants Reichmann and Loe reported in on 25 September, and Predl on the 5th of this month. All arrived in good health, but of 47 soldiers who were to join us only 23 reached the regiment; the rest remained behind in hospitals on the march.

On 27 September Lieutenant Loe immediately became very sick and is still in Polotsk. Now to answer your two letters.

It was correct that Letter No. 10 did not reach me through the two lieutenants until September, as you wrote, but that there would be peace or we would be in Petersburg was not the case, for we are still 60 miles away and also do not yet have peace, although we do have hopes.

One should think that food products ought to be very cheap here, but because of the tremendous usury of the Jews it is not so, for coffee as well as sugar costs eight Polish gulden per pound, or one Bavarian taler. In Disna, where we were recently, one could in the beginning get a pound for six Polish gulden, but no longer at the end, and all products, as I have already written, are at very high prices. For the bottle of arrack as well as the vinegar I am much obliged to you. Both arrived safely. I am especially grateful for the arrack, since one cannot get it here, much less the vinegar.

It would be nice if Colonel von Maillot became a general. Besides, since he is the senior colonel, his chances are good.

Yesterday Colonel Rodt should have left with the first reinforcement column, and three others will follow him in the near future.[107] The regiment has received 250 men, but there is no talk of activating the Reserve Battalion.

From here it is 80 hours to Vilna; from there, by way of Breslau and Prague, 416 hours to Munich. So one can easily say that we are over 500 hours away from you. This is certainly too far to send anything, yet it is amazing that none of the bottles sent to the colonel and me were broken. [...] six bottles were sent to the colonel through Lieutenant Colonel Merz, of which only one remained intact, and all the others were broken. I have not yet received Letter No. 11, because Lieutenant Lutz lies sick in Ebing, and, therefore, I have not yet received the training regulations either.

You write that our situation must have improved, since all the rivers are in our power. I cannot see this at all, for almost all waterways are useless to us. For the Dvina is only navigable after Daugavpils [Dünaburg or Dinabourgh], and, moreover, its mouth, Riga, is in the hands of the enemy. The Disna, Usaci, Ulina, etc. are nothing but brooks, the Neman as well as the Vistula are too far back, and the roads from there are too risky for merchants, on account of the huge amount of army transport. The Dnepr, which the Grand Army has at its back, flows from the interior of the country, where there is nothing, and it is also unnavigable upstream as far as Smolensk, and so all waterways are useless to us except the seaports, which are too far away.

According to my calculations I owe you money, which you must be sure to take from my allotted pay: for merchant de Crignis 11 francs, 15 kreuzer; for saddler Haunschild 8 francs, 48 kreuzer; for the bridle maker 7 francs, 20 kreuzer; for tailor Hellfritz 11 francs, 54 kreuzer; the 24 francs borrowed from the racecourse; for Major Fortis 80 francs for his horse, and for him also 4 francs, 30 kreuzer for cooking utensils. Since you have already paid these expenses, which amount to 147 francs, 47 kreuzer, it is of course only right that you take this sum from the money

I have allotted to you. This amounts to: from April through October, 20 francs per month or 140 francs in all, plus 50 francs from the supplementary pay, thus making a total of 190 francs. Therefore there is only a balance of 42 francs, 13 kreuzer left, from which you should first take out the cost of the cap, 18 francs, 22 kreuzer. With the remaining 23 francs, 51 kreuzer I have not by any means paid up the 54 francs I owe you for board for the six months from September to last February. And therefore I would like it very much if you would consider yourself somewhat reimbursed, for it will surely never be possible for me to repay the entire debt that I have already contracted with you.

Your ill health, dear Father, causes me great concern, and only the assurance of Lieutenant Predl that it has cleared up entirely and that you both look very well again has made me easy again. Please write me soon to let me know how you both are.

I am sure the newspapers are the first to bring most of the news to Neuburg. Right now the latest reports of the Grande Armée tell us only that Moscow was half burned down through mishap.

I have already written a few times by post, because it was news of the battles, but I sent my last letter with a courier, and this one I shall give to Major Tausch, who is also going to Munich as a courier. Both of these will be posted in Munich. Since there is no important news in this letter, I have written everything in a jumble, but in the future I shall give consideration to your remarks. Colonel Maillot is so well that everyone is amazed, and his appearance tells nothing of Poland or Russia. There is not the slightest thing wrong with him. Dear Father, please be so kind, besides paying my respects to the colonel's wife, to give her my especial thanks for her kindness in including the two bottles, with the observation that a shipment of wine and other beverages is always welcome to the colonel for the reason that these products are absolutely not to be had here.

Sergeant Sichler is in the hospital. As soon as he can be located, I shall pay him the 10 francs. Bimsner's son is not well. I am with the regiment very little and cannot do much for him for this reason. If he should want for anything, I would spring to his aid wherever possible.

Lieutenant Voltolini has surely left already, so it would be useless for me to write.

Now I want to add a word about the marching. After the enemy patrols in the districts of the Usaci and Disna Rivers, which the army had been assigned for foraging, had caused much damage and even made the region unsafe, one brigade, or rather a detachment of 400 men, was sent to Disna in order to prevent the enemy's crossing the Dvina. This detachment was led there by General Count Beckers. We came on the 3rd of this month to Brzdziadowice, and on the 4th, my saint's day, to

Disna. The enemy withdrew, and not a shot was fired. Since it was not possible to take a position in Disna on account of the disadvantageous situation of the city, the detachment came out again on the evening of the 5th and took a position half an hour behind Disna.

On the 6th General [...], who now is in command of the 3rd Brigade, arrived, and, after all had been put into readiness, General [Count Beckers] and I went back to Brzdziadowice and on the 7th back to Polotsk. Here we are again in [camp].

When we returned, Army Order No. 7 had just come in, and a letter with the following contents [was] presented to me by Lieutenant Colonel von Merz:

Moscow,
25 September 1812

To Monsieur Hausmann (François),
Lieutenant with the 7th Bavarian Regiment of the Line.

I advise you, Sir, that the Emperor by a decree of this day has named you Chevalier of the Legion of Honour.

His Majesty authorises me to give you this provisional notice, while waiting for the one [that] you will receive officially from the Grand Chancellor.

Prince of Wagram and Major General
Alexandre[108]

I am therefore sending you this pleasant news and note that from our regiment there were also named as knights, no longer [...] members, of the Legion of Honour First Lieutenants von Imhoff, Jr., and Zinn, then Ensign Sartorius, now Lieutenant, Sergeant Kugler and a lance corporal of the regiment by the name of Eisenhofer, as well as Major (now Lieutenant Colonel) Merz. In all there are 80 officers and 40 non-commissioned officers and soldiers [of the] Bavarian Army who received this decoration. There is no ribbon to be had here, so I beg you to send me a couple [...] of such ribbons enclosed in a letter. We have not yet received the decorations.

Our names will appear in the next army orders.

I congratulate my dear mother on her saint's day but, to be sure, somewhat late, for my letter might even arrive so late that the saint's day of my dear father might also be approaching at the same time.

Meanwhile I wish you all blessings at all times, and I do not except a single day on which I do not wish that I could impart to you by word of mouth that which I feel for you both in renewed form.

May God keep us all. This is the pious wish that accompanies my prayer to God Almighty that He may soon lead me back into the arms of my best of parents.

Very many of our people are dying of homesickness. Thank God it

has not come to me. My respects to all acquaintances who enquire about me and assurance to all of my very good health – this is the request of,
My dear parents' most obedient son, thankful unto the grave,

Franz

Letter No. 21

Dearest Parents,

Today on the first day of rest after two weeks of danger I hasten to give you the details as briefly as possible of the events and the abandonment of the city of Polotsk. It was on 14 October when we received orders to leave our camp and the two epoulements, or small redoubts, that had been built by our men in the vicinity of the same and to occupy a narrow cantonment on the left bank along the Dvina downstream as far as the confluence of the Usaci with the Dvina. Now since this cantonment could not be cleared so quickly owing to the small number of houses and its being a great distance away, the occupation of it did not take place until the 16th, when we marched off at 6 o'clock in the morning. The First Division occupied the suburb of Little Polotsk and the village of Ekimania. Of the Second Division, the 1st Brigade went to Potcotcielczi; the 2nd Brigade, with its right wing, the 3rd Regiment, occupied Plaxi and Sieradama, with the 7th Regiment Sloboda, and the general with the 4th Battalion occupied Druczani and sent a part of the battalion to Uiscie, where the Usaci flows into the Dvina.

After we had moved into position, at about 3.30 we heard a lively cannonade coming from Disna, which continued until about 6 o'clock. Soon thereafter we learned that the brigade stationed at Disna under General Ströhl had been attacked by a strong detachment, and at the same time we received the command to go to Polotsk immediately, because the division had a new assignment.

Therefore the 3rd Brigade withdrew to Pononia during the night of the 16th. The Second Division marched into the suburb of Little Polotsk, and the First Division went on the 17th to Strunja, three hours upstream on the Dvina, toward which the Russians were also moving. On the 17th heavy skirmishing began at the outposts near Polotsk, which continued into the night and forced the French to withdraw their outposts to the level ground near Polotsk. On the afternoon of the 17th we received orders to occupy with the two brigades of the Second Division the two ramparts and the abatis set up between the two for the purpose of communication, at which place we were visited a few times on this day by shells and 18-pounders, which, however, caused us no harm.

On the 18th there took place the formal attack on the right wing of Polotsk, which was occupied, but also very weakly, by the French. The Russian left wing gained a few advantages over them and made a few cavalry attacks, which were only with difficulty turned back by our side. When the firing on this wing became somewhat weaker, Marshal Count Gouvion St Cyr, who the whole time had been keeping to one of our redoubts, rode there in order to see the movements of the enemy better, but he had hardly arrived when he was immediately wounded in the front part of his left foot by a musket ball. He came back, had himself bandaged with us and looked on for a time, but after the fighting of the Russian left wing became heavier and heavier and the French had to withdraw back to the trenches by the city, he did go back into the city.

We believed that the situation would then remain calm, because the firing had suddenly ceased entirely, but we were wrong, for all at once an unbelievable number of the enemy rushed upon us and upon the Swiss and Croats standing to our left. We let them come on, waiting quietly, and when they were close enough we gave them a few canister salvos from 18 pieces that had been placed in the two ramparts, which inspired a great deal of respect on the part of the enemy toward our two ramparts, but now the enemy threw themselves with even greater strength upon the Swiss, who then withdrew to a position behind our batteries.

The enemy had already captured the second hill, which lay behind one of our ramparts, when His Excellency the General of the Cavalry [Wrede] had two pieces taken from their position and turned around, and he sent a small detachment against the enemy's flank. This then brought about the desired effect. The immense horde of men that was just rushing into the valley was thrown into consternation, as it seemed, by seeing cannons behind them. Therefore they turned around quickly to seek safety in retreat and withdrew completely, but on their way back the enemy were so greatly fired upon by our batteries, which had not been able to come into action while the fighting was closer to the town than they were, that the enemy had to hasten their retreat. This attack cost the enemy a huge number of men. On our side only Major von Douve of the train and two soldiers had their legs shattered by cannonballs, while several artillery men and a few soldiers in the ramparts were wounded by musket balls.

Night had fallen and put an end to the affair for the 18th. The enemy now, as one could hear, brought up a large amount of cannon against us since they seemed to have found a hair in their soup, as the saying goes, in the attack on this side. It can therefore be imagined that, although we had a strong cannonading to endure in our ramparts on the 18th, it was nothing compared to that which we were to get on the 19th. Well, back to my story.

When day broke on the 19th we saw many movements of the enemy directed toward our weak side, that is toward the right side of the city, but everything remained quiet until toward noon, except for some cannonading on our redoubts.

I shall now quickly also touch upon the happenings on the left bank of the Dvina. The First Division stood quietly on the 17th at the bridgehead in Strunja, and on the 18th it was only insignificantly troubled. The 3rd Brigade stood on the 17th near Pononia, without being especially attacked, but on the 18th General Ströhl was again attacked and defeated after a half-hour fight, and he retired in very great disorder to Polotsk. General Count von Wrede, when he learned of this setback, set out on the march with two French regiments of infantry, two regiments of cuirassiers and two regiments of light cavalry in order to support the 3rd Brigade. Although now the enemy were more than twice as strong as that corps under the command of the General of the Cavalry [Wrede], nevertheless they were driven back to Druczani and Pononia with extraordinary losses. The men of the 3rd Brigade, having reassembled and now numbering about 300, took 900 prisoners in this second attack. With the exception of minor harassment, this corps remained quietly in position on the 18th and 19th.

After it had become evident to everyone that the Russian Army was in earnest about Polotsk, and that II and VI Corps were too weak to maintain this position, it was decided to leave this place. Therefore arrangements were made to vacate the city of Polotsk on the evening of the 19th. According to this plan, at nightfall the French artillery was to be moved to the left bank of the Dvina, then ours, and so gradually the two corps, but the French artillery park began this move when it was still light and went past [our] trenches and on into the city. The Russians began again to fire upon this artillery with all their pieces. Now it can be imagined how things went with us in the trenches over which they had to fire. We considered ourselves entirely lost, but nightfall put something of a damper on it. Hereupon the French set fire to the camp they still occupied and to the outer houses of the suburb and withdrew, but the enemy noticed this and furiously attacked the French with their left wing. They took one bastion after the other and summoned all efforts to make our withdrawal difficult and to gain the bridge before we did, but in this they were not successful. We sent our artillery across and at about

12 o'clock withdrew fighting under continuous cannon and small arms' fire up to the Polota bridge, where the French relieved us, while we continued our way very slowly through the city and across the Dvina. Even on the bridge we were not yet out of range. On this side of the Dvina we drew up behind the suburb.

On the 20th the First Division left Strunja and moved likewise toward Polotsk. Except for that, things remained quiet for the time. On both shores there was occasional shooting, but without result.

On the 21st the two corps began to withdraw at approximately 3 o'clock in the afternoon, after we had sustained another terrible hail of shell and some canister fire. The [French] II Corps moved toward Usaci, and we [the Bavarians] on this day went to Rudnia. Even at Polotsk our artillery had burned several wagons and many supplies, which could not be brought away on account of the lack of horses. On the first march the ambulances and a few munitions wagons as well as other ones had got stuck.

On the 22nd to Attikoven. Here General Ströhl coming from Pononia came upon us. Also on this march several heavily laden wagons fell into the hands of the enemy, and, since this march took place at night, a hostile cavalry patrol fell from the left side upon our baggage, but they did not get much booty, for we came up immediately.

On the 23rd to Babienizky. Since, on orders, on the morning of the 23rd all extra horses had to be sent ahead, General Beckers and I sent our horses on, except for one to ride, but they have not yet come back to us, although we do have news that they are in safety. On the 24th the rear-guard was constantly pursued and provoked by the enemy, and so we marched to Kuplice and let the hostile cavalry bump their noses against our artillery. We considered it wise, however, to go an hour farther to the Usaci River during the night. From Babienitzky the baggage of the war commissary was sent via Usaci to Glubokoje under the direction of War Commissioner Amman, but on the evening of the 24th we received news that this had all been captured near Usaci. Wisner was not with them, and on the 25th our baggage went to Lepel, from where we have no news up to now. It is almost impossible, however, that it is lost. On the morning of the 25th we marched to Peischna by way of Waron, on the 26th to a large village on a little stream whose name I do not know, on the 27th to Tolschitz, on the 28th seven hours into another village whose name I did not learn, and on the 29th finally to this place.

We are sitting here today, the 31st, wavering between fear and hope and cheerfully waiting for whatever may come. It is not likely that the enemy have followed us here. Among the property captured with Commissioner Amman near Usaci were all the flags of the Bavarian Army, all of which were deposited with the baggage in Polotsk because the regiments were too weak to protect the flags. In addition, the war chest with 6,000 francs in gold. It is also said that Captain Weishaupt of the artillery along with the 12-pounder battery of the First Division has been captured by the enemy in this same region; it is said, however, that he did not surrender until his last round had been fired.

The following are the results, then, as far as is known. The Russians may have captured about 300 of our corps including men of the train, stragglers, wounded, etc. On the other hand, 2,100 of the enemy were taken prisoner by us and II Corps. Only the threefold superiority of the enemy and other special circumstances compelled us to retreat. Our corps may still have 2,500 soldiers under arms. What a force?! Just now the news has come that Marshal Victor[109] with his corps, coming from Vitebsk, has moved into Polotsk and joined with II Corps, and tomorrow we shall march forward again to Glubokoje. Perhaps we are headed for Disna now. I do not want to vouch for this news yet, but it is very probable.

The conclusion in the enclosure.

Now, in closing, dearest, most precious Parents, I want to tell you something funny. As I said in my letter, on the 21st my second orderly by the name of Kindle from the 1st Grenadiers ran ahead from Polotsk on the road to Usaci. (I am mistaken; I did not mention this in my letter). He was carrying my most necessary small, personal items with him. On the 23rd my first orderly, Betz by name, was riding ahead of us on the road to Plissa and Glubokoje with my brown mare and my small travel bag, in which my most indispensable linen was kept. Of these I have seen nothing since then, and likewise since the 25th our baggage that was sent via Lepel has been separated from us, so that I am therefore stripped of all linen, etc. We learned that Kindle went with the artillery to Michalischki, while Betz went with the general's orderly toward Vilna, but the baggage of the General of the Cavalry [Wrede] and of General Beckers (with which mine is) has been attached to the II Army Corps, and therefore everything is said to be safe. But it has been 16 days now that I and all of us have not been able to undress, much less put on fresh linen, because we do not have any. Therefore it can be imagined that unbidden guests have settled in with us. Therefore yesterday I put on a rough Polish farmer's shirt, took off my underwear, all kerchiefs, etc., and had them all washed. After this had taken place, I darned my stockings myself, hemmed for myself a little piece of cloth that I had bought and cut into two pieces, fashioned a towel for myself, and so I am entirely clean again, and I thank my dear mother that she let me see such operations in my youth and, as I remember, do it myself. No tailor is doing any work. There are almost no women here any more. Those that are here can themselves do nothing and are full of dirt and filth like the soldiers, for you can picture to yourself that the 7th Regiment in the Anzing Forest was nothing compared to our present grimy coal miners, and thievery is the order of the day.[110]

I am, praise be to God, extraordinarily hale and hearty. Colonel von Maillot enjoys the best of health, and neither of us has any need, except to go to Neuburg. Until further notice, the 3rd Regiment forms one company, the 7th one company, and the 4th Light Battalion a weak company, for the entire brigade has 325 soldiers today. Therefore only one captain, one first lieutenant and two second lieutenants are assigned to each regiment, and all the rest are going to Michalischki to gather up all the soldiers following behind, form companies and catch up in this fashion.

The gorgets have been issued but there were too few and therefore I did not get one, with which I am very satisfied. Therefore be so kind as to send me one when you have an opportunity, for as long as I have none I do not need to wear it.

From the 2nd Regiment, 5th Regiment and 5th Battalion, about 20 officers were captured and 16 wounded. Captain Zobel of the 5th Regiment and Lieutenant Imhoff of the Gen[darmerie] Corps remained in Pononia. Major Grosgebauer was also wounded.[111]

Dear Father and Mother, I wish both of you a good life and hope to see you soon, for the war cannot last much longer. After the end of the campaign, however, a reunion will be an immeasurable joy to,

Your eternally true and most obedient son,

Franz

My respects to all acquaintances. I received your last letter through Lieutenant Predl. Lutz has not yet shown up. It is true that our corps will march off from here tomorrow for Glubokoje.

[Letter No. 22] [112]

[Biala December 1812]

[…]

By the time the recruits are trained, they will have to come back here, unless we go to meet them. I still have hope that we shall see each other soon. I shall send off a package of red cloth that I had a chance to buy from a Frenchman for two Bavarian talers. It comes to about two lengths, if not more, so at any rate I shall get the money out. If we had not come to rest camp I would, without further ado, have had a pair of trousers or something else made out of it, because our entire baggage has been lost. I still had my baggage with General Beckers and this was still in Dunilovici, while in Kobolniki everything had already been captured. This is therefore irrevocably lost, and all my good things were in my travel bag, but I was wearing the poor things. I still do not have a whole pair of trousers. My drawers are torn, and my old blue drawers are also full of holes. I am still supplied with about three ragged shirts, two poor pairs of drawers, four miserable pairs of socks, three handkerchiefs and four scarves, for I had this much with me for my immediate use. I still have my shaving kit and my bordered headdress. But all else is lost.

If blue cloth from the Netherlands should be available in Neuburg, I beg you to have a pair of trousers made for me, or if one is still there, that will be fine, too. I must also ask for some underwear, but not too much. We shall probably soon have an opportunity for you to send me something. My watch was also stolen in Mikolajki during my illness. [Added in the margin:] N.B. Since I have just bought a pair of trousers from Captain Schmitz, you need not send me any, for I do not want to have much more.

Now to answer your letters. To Letter No. 11. I have not yet been able to pay the 10 francs to Sergeant Sichler, because since the battle of August 18th he has been in some hospital, lightly wounded. Should he turn up, I shall pay him these 10 francs against receipt (N.B., if I have any money). With regard to the credit that you have with the 1st Grenadiers in the amount of 6 francs, I can do nothing about it, because Captain Wallraff is dead. I have also received the copy of the training regulations. I do not see Wisner any more, nor do I know where he is.

Now to Letter No. 15. Captain (now Major) von Fortis has correctly paid me for the coffee set with 4 francs, 3 kreuzer. I understand how you have formulated your request. It seems better to me this way, for, as is rumoured, the gendarmerie takes only men who are completely fit for field service.

Letter No. 16. I am happy that my letter from the battle of the 18th of August arrived so promptly. Good Werner is dead. Lieutenant Deltsch will now also return to Neuburg. Dufresne will probably be there soon. The wounds of Imhoff and Grebmer were very slight.

Colonel Rodt, as well as Rummel and Hausmann have already arrived with their columns.[113] The three pairs of new shoes of the new reinforcement were of no use to us, for the regiment was hardly 30 men strong, and there were 200 youngsters who arrived here.

I thank you kindly for your good wishes for my saint's day, and at the same time I add my congratulations for the saint's day of my dear father with the wish that the dear Lord may keep him for me for a long time. May God hear my prayer and keep my dearest parents for many more years. My fortunate fellow officers may be in Neuburg by 10 February. Oh, how I wish I were with them, so that I could personally bring you my congratulations.

I still have the two letters for Blos with me. I cannot catch sight of him, for since Polotsk he is presumed missing, like many fouriers. For Colonel von Maillot to become a general would be desirable, and also for Colonel Rodt to return to the regiment. Colonel von Maillot is the senior-most, and we are already short one general, and Raglovich will probably go to the gendarmerie, so then it surely will not take long.

I am pleased that my allotments have been duly paid. The colonel will probably see to it now that the coming months will also be paid out, for I have continued to have 20 francs deducted per month.

Fourier Geist is also missing. Quartermaster Schneider, Actuary Burger and several fouriers are captured. Private Michl Kopp was still present when I left the regiment at Dunilovici. Since we are too far apart now, however, and all the companies are thoroughly mixed up, I can find out nothing about him now. It is hardly possible that anything has happened to him since this time, however.

As Ströbel was still with the general's baggage and since my departure from the general this has not yet arrived, I therefore do not know where he may now be. He will probably, however, come with the general to Neuburg, as will Joseph and Mrs Koch. I have seen neither of these two since Polotsk, because they were also with the baggage.

My horses are both well, thank God. The fat brown one was somewhat pressed by my orderly during my illness and the stout march, but it did not bother him.

Betz stayed behind back at Prenn and has a small leather pouch with him in which my most necessary articles were, such as towel, mirror, boot-jack, nightcap, sword belt, arrack, raspberry vinegar, etc. He has probably been captured, and my things are gone.

My second orderly, Kindle, was sick and went to the hospital at Plock. After that I had another one, who also had to be taken to the field hospital in Plock, as he was very sick. Now I have one of those men who came with Colonel von Rodt. For your congratulations on the red ribbon, as well as for the ribbon itself that you sent me, I thank you most kindly.

Sergeant Bimsner's son is well and is still with the regiment. I have frequently asked him how he was, and he gave me good assurance each time.

With regard to transferring money through me, it looks risky. I have no cash reserve and have spent a lot myself, especially during my illness.

If you directed a transfer through me, I would run the risk of not being able to pay it out. Therefore it is better not to enter into such an arrangement. I am glad to help, but in doing so I must not myself be embarrassed. As I have already said, I have not seen Wisner since September.

Now to the final letter, No. 17, which I just received on the 2nd of this month. I am only surprised that Mrs Sterner has not related more. Mrs Altmann and the wife of Sergeant Bauer died on this retreat. Sergeant Sonleitner and Sergeant Taugner brought their wives very ill to the Sisters of Mercy in Vilna. I would like to know at once what resolution is made on your request.

I cannot quite fathom the contradiction that you write me, namely, 'I suffer pains again, and with your mother I am as healthy as a bird.' When I have pains, it is impossible for me to be as healthy as a bird. At any rate, I hope the pains have all gone and that you are well again, for this I wish with all my heart.

I am very astonished at the congratulations that have poured in. One could hardly believe that one could find even a small corner in the memory of these ladies and gentlemen. It is really beyond all expectation, and I only ask that if I ever get back to Neuburg you will again enumerate to me these ladies and gentlemen who have remembered me, so that I shall be in a position to give them my thanks orally.

I still do not have a gorget and do not need one until I am compelled to have it. My feet still hurt because of weakness from my illness. I am not doing any duty until I am entirely well, but otherwise I am not depriving myself of anything. You say, to be sure, that I should go into a private house if I should become sick. I have done that, but I found it advisable to go to a different house each night, as the circumstances here altered the case.

I am sure that I am not bothered too much by home-sickness. I am heartily glad that Grandmother is still alive. When you answer, please send her many greetings and regards from me. The army orders in regard to the establishment of the gendarmerie have been here for a long time.

In my letter of 30 October I already reported to you on the affairs of 18, 19, 20 and 21 October near Polotsk and the retreat following thereupon.

I am eagerly awaiting the articles that Ensign Gundlfingen is bringing with him, because I can now really use them.

Mittel is out of the hospital again and is in good health with the regiment. It is indeed strange that Captain Dettenhofer is being given such a run-around. He is already listed in the government records, but no army orders release him from the military. Colonel von Maillot asked me to give you his regards when I wrote. Now he is bringing them himself.

On account of my French decoration it will probably be necessary for me to furnish my baptismal certificate. If this should be the case, you will learn of it at the Reserve Battalion.

[...]

Letter No. 24[114]

Dearest, Best of Parents,

Now for once I have time to answer your letter of 26 November, No. 18, brought to me on 14 January of this year by Corporal (now Ensign) von Staader. Bloody indeed were the many affairs that we had at the beginning of the past winter, especially those of 18, 19, 20 and 21 October, but the retreat back to the Vistula that followed thereupon in the bitterest cold was indescribably worse, and I shall never be able to picture it to you as it really was. We were fortunate, to be sure, that we were thrown into the fortress of Thorn, for there we could, at least in the first days, recover from the hardships we had endured. It is true that many hundred German sons found their graves there, but it was advantageous for me, for I recovered completely from the nerve fever (or typhoid) that I had an advanced case of, and I became as healthy as I could ever wish.

You correctly guessed that we have lost our entire baggage. It was the greatest luck that on my horse I had the things I needed most in two saddle bags, namely, my small travel bag in one and coffee and cooking utensils in the other, and in this way I did at least save these things.

In Plock I managed to purchase several new things, but we had to send these with Sergeant Schnapauf to Grossglogau, from where they have probably gone to Neuburg.

If these articles have not arrived and Sergeant Schnapauf should be there, then please question him about it. My travel bag is marked with my initials and is inside a pack that is labelled Major von Greis on the outside.

The package that you were so kind as to give to Ensign Staader has been duly received with all that was contained in the letter and in the list, and I express my very grateful thanks for it.

I wrote my Letter No. 22 at Biala, and you have probably duly received it, together with a small package, through Major Golsen, as well as Letter No. 23 of 31 May from Stangerback in Bohemia. (I mailed the latter at Reichenberg and paid postage as far as the border.)

From Biala I came on 13 January to the staff at Srebno, likewise near Plock. On the 17th we marched near Dobrzyn over the ice of the Vistula to Kowal, the 18th to Wloclawek, the 19th to Nieszawa, both on the Vistula, and on 20 January again across the same into the fortress of Thorn. This we defended, as you know, until 18 April, whereupon we marched until now according to the attached marching route.[115]

What we endured in the past campaign, on the retreat and during the siege of Thorn I shall tell you orally. It is impossible to describe here, so I shall not even try.

If my baggage has not arrived through Sergeant Schnapauf, then I shall be very embarrassed, for not only my present two shirts and two pairs of drawers but even my socks and kerchiefs are in miserable condition. It is pitiful the way we look now, not one whole coat and torn boots and trousers; in short, we re-entered Bavaria clad in rags, and this is how we had to appear before the eyes of the people.

I have no doubt that you have been receiving the 20 francs per month that were allotted by me. At least I had them correctly deducted from my pay.

It gives me great regret that Colonel Maillot again had to take the field as a colonel and brevet brigadier and has still not become a general. Taken all in all, this is really unjust. Therefore I also cannot believe than any promotions have taken place among the subalterns.

Although I have often searched among the Russian troops, I have so far been unable to obtain any medals. If, therefore, you should find one for sale, please buy it, if feasible. During our retreat, the Cossacks pinned on themselves those [medals] that were destined for us. If any of the French cloth should be available in Neuburg at the Economic Commission, it would be a good idea if you would secure enough for a dress coat and at least one pair of trousers for me, since by our arrival perhaps it may have all been bought up.

As I started writing this present letter at Berbiswalda and was planning to mail it there, everything herein is written under the assumption that you would still be in Neuburg. But today on the 16th I learned at Hof that you have been appointed lieutenant and adjutant of the Mobile Legion of the Rezat District at Nuremberg, so this is my first opportunity to extend my congratulations for this, and of course I must now cancel all those things that I have asked you to do in this letter in case you were in Neuburg, since you are, I presume, in Nuremberg. But it is also said that there are some mobile legions in camp near Munich, so again it is also possible that you might be there. Now I do not know where I shall meet you. We shall probably enter Nuremberg on the 21st or 22nd and will definitely be in Bayreuth on the 18th. I beg of you to inform me by letter of your present whereabouts and that of my dear mother.

From the Army Order of 18 May I see that I am a first lieutenant, to my greatest astonishment.

If you can or must keep a horse, please let me know about it, because then I want to give you one that will be just right for you, of course with saddle and bridle, etc.

Dearest Father, write to me very soon, and be assured that as long as I live I shall be in all sincerity,

Your and my dear mother's most obedient son,

Franz

Notes to Chapter Five

[1] The number of soldiers involved in the Russian campaign is always in dispute. These figures are taken from Leyh; see also Vincent J. Esposito and John R. Elting, *A Military History and Atlas of the Napoleonic Wars*, New York: Praeger, 1968.

[2] Napoleon to Maret, 16 December 1811, *Correspondance*, no. 18,334.

[3] Leyh, pp. 193–4; Uebe, pp. 82–3.

[4] This is Leyh's reasonable assessment (pp. 193–4); Uebe makes no mention of any enthusiasm on the part of the army, but his often tendentious approach vitiates his arguments (he seems intent on highlighting every instance of Franco–Bavarian friction regardless of true salience), and I suspect, in this case, that he simply decided to ignore the evidence Leyh found.

[5] Note that Bavaria had already sent one regiment (14th Infantry) and an artillery battery to Danzig in April 1811 as part of that crucial city's garrison. The 14th Infantry was soon renumbered as the 13th, when the 13th took the designation 11th (while the old 11th Infantry Regiment was disbanded).

[6] Leyh, p. 259.

[7] Bavarian Captain Joseph Maillinger, who was headquarters commandant during the campaign and whose company (1st Fusilier Company, 1st

Infantry Regiment) provided St Cyr's escort on the retreat, left a distinctly negative impression of the Frenchman in his memoirs, echoed and reinforced by the editor of those memoirs, the German military historian Paul Holzhausen (Maillinger, Joseph. 'Tagebuch des Hauptmanns Joseph Maillinger im Feldzuge nach Russland 1812', Paul Holzhausen, ed., *Darstellungen aus der Bayerischen Kriegs- und Heeresgeschichte*, Heft 21, Munich: 1912., pp. 58–9). See also Elting, *Swords*, pp. 148–9: 'He was never the man to seize a flag and rally a broken line.' The 'owl' nickname is from Jean Baptiste Marbot, *The Memoirs of Baron de Marbot*, London: Longmans, Green and Co., 1905, vol. II, p. 541.

[8] Auvera, pp. 462–4.

[9] Colonel Ludwig Count von Seyboltstorff's manuscript account quoted in Auvera, p. 469.

[10] 'Although the Bavarian nation did not enter into the war which was now commencing with the same perspective as it had had in preceding conflicts, the memory of the glory acquired in fighting under our banners, the favourable and marked advantages it had already attained, meant that it sent its army forth to remote climes and for utterly foreign interests with a profound calm, one may even say with satisfaction...' Laurent Gouvion St Cyr, *Mémoires pour Servir a l'Histoire Militaire sous le Directoire, le Consulat et l'Empire*, Paris: Anselin, 1831, vol. III, pp. 24–5.

[11] Seyboltstorff , in Auvera, p. 470.

[12] Franz, Letters 7, 11 and 12.

[13] At least Franz gives no hint that he was under pressure from his superiors to acquire a gorget.

[14] These two regiments had been the 1st and 2nd Dragoons respectively; all of the cavalry regiments were renumbered as part of their conversion to chevauxlegers in 1811 (the 1st through 4th Chevauxlegers became the 3rd through 6th respectively).

[15] Maillinger, p. 68.

[16] Printed in Sauzey are several complaints about the exactions demanded by the Bavarian contingent (Sauzey, pp. 203–7). See pp. 208–11 for orders relating to the additional transport.

[17] Seyboltstorff in Auvera, p. 470. Franz used the German expression 'eight days', translated as a week.

[18] Sauzey prints a number of interesting pieces of correspondence in this regard: one from Wrede angered by other troops (French and other Germans) emptying magazines or stripping supplies from near his cantonments; as well as two from Wrede in which he complains about Deroy's men removing victuals from his district (Sauzey, pp. 207–8).

[19] Albrecht Adam, *Aus dem Leben eines Schlachtenmalers*, Stuttgart: Cotta, 1886, p. 153. Adam was a Bavarian artist under Viceroy Eugène's courteous patronage.

[20] Situation as of 30 June 1812 cited in Sauzey, p. 213. Note that an

additional 2,180 men were detached on various missions and 611 were listed as sick. Quote from Adam, p. 153.

[21] Captain August Prince von Thurn und Taxis quoted in Leyh, p. 198. Franz, Letter No. 15.

[22] Maillinger, pp. 71–2.

[23] Völderndorff, Book 6, p. 31. A participant as well as an historian, Völderndorff was one of Deroy's staff officers in 1812.

[24] Maillinger, p. 71. Franz, Letters Nos.14 and 15.

[25] Adam, pp. 153–4.

[26] Seyboltstorff in Auvera, p. 471.

[27] Deroy to King Max, 22 June 1812 in Uebe, p. 88.

[28] Leyh, p. 199. Seyboltstorff said that the corps received only half or quarter portions of bread after 13 June and that the 19th Division had none at all after 3 July; Wrede, however, with his additional transport, generously shared some of his division's bread with Deroy's command (in Auvera, p. 472).

[29] St Cyr, p. 41.

[30] Leyh, p. 199; and Stabsauditor Max von Stubenrauch's diary quoted in Maillinger, p. 71.

[31] Deroy to Max Joseph, 19 July 1812, in Leyh, p. 199. Uebe states that Napoleon also heard a less welcome greeting: 'Kaiser! Brod!' (Emperor! Bread!'), p. 95.

[32] Artillery battery commander Karl Baron von Widnmann in Maillinger, p. 75. Numbers for the corps vary even at this early stage: Leyh and some memoirists make the total 25,000 at the review; Holzhausen gives 20,000.

[33] Thurn und Taxis; Maillinger's recollections echo these sentiments; both in Maillinger, p. 75. Also Völderndorff, Book 6, p. 41.

[34] Maximilian Count von Preysing-Moos, 'Tagebuch des Generalmajors Maximilian Graf von Preysing-Moos', *Darstellungen aus der Bayerischen Kriegs- und Heeresgeschichte*, Heft 21, Munich: 1912, p. 27.

[35] As the 21st (3rd and 6th Regiments) and 22nd (4th and 5th Regiments) Light Cavalry Brigades, the four regiments would remain under Preysing's command, finally evaporating 'at almost the same spot near Vilna' after the crossing of the Berezina.

[36] St Cyr, pp. 45–6. Napoleon, wrote St Cyr, found the Bavarian cavalry '*fort belle*'.

[37] Seyboltstorff in Auvera, p. 474. The Bavarians also believed that the extra meat ration allocated to the men to make up for the lack of bread was a contributing factor in the growing number of sick (Leyh, p. 200). The lack of bread was a continual source of concern and complaint, see St Cyr to Berthier, 2 August and 4 August; Deroy to Max Joseph, 11 August; Wrede to Max Joseph, 13 August; and Wrede to St Cyr, 2 September, in Gabriel Fabry, *Campagne de Russie*, Paris: Chapelot, 1900–03, Vol IV, pp. 60–1,

151, 216; Vol V, pp. 238, 807.

[38] Seyboltstorff in Auvera, p. 475.

[39] St Cyr, p. 46.

[40] Numbers from official reports summarized in Sauzey, pp 216–7. Note that the numbers appear *somewhat* better when one discounts the four cavalry regiments detached on the 14th (numbering something less than 2,000 sabres); still, even leaving the chevauxlegers out of the calculation, the corps went from 23,000 to 16,000 in the course of four weeks.

[41] Deroy and Wrede to Max Joseph, 11 August 1812, in Auvera, p. 477; part in Leyh, pp. 200–01. Oudinot's comment from a letter to Marshal Berthier, 14 August 1812, in Fabry, *Russie*, Vol V, p. 295.

[42] Infantry divisions: 6th Legrand (French, Franco–German and Portuguese), 8th Verdier (French and Franco–Dutch), 9th Merle (Swiss, Croat and Franco–Dutch). Light cavalry brigades: Castex (5th) and Corbineau (6th). Doumerc's 3rd Heavy Cavalry Division.

[43] This Russian commander is most commonly known simply as Wittgenstein.

[44] Général de Brigade Valentin was commanding in place of Jean Verdier, badly wounded on the 16th.

[45] The numbers are (as usual) in dispute: Sauzey gives II Corps 12,000 infantry and 1,000 cavalry, the Bavarians 11,000; Leyh states the Bavarians numbered 12,500. Neither source is sufficiently detailed to distinguish between infantry and artillery in calculating strength figures, nor is it clear whether the numbers cited for Wittgenstein include artillery and engineers or just infantry and cavalry. The point is that the two sides were probably nearly equal in numbers during the August battles; indeed, the French and their allies may well have had a slight edge over Wittgenstein. See also Fabry, *Russie*, Vol V, Annex, p. 26ff.

[46] The high officer casualties are also explained in part by their disproportionate numbers: companies only averaged 40 to 50 common soldiers, but the strength of the officer corps was largely intact. As a result, there was a significant number of 'excess' officers on the battlefield and many of them became casualties (Völderndorff, Book 6, p. 122).

[47] Marbot, vol. II, p. 534.

[48] St Cyr, pp. 77–9. See also Christiane d'Ainval, *Gouvion St Cyr*, Paris: Copernic, 1981, p. 112.

[49] According to Marbot, he also had a second bridge hastily constructed to facilitate withdrawal if necessary (Marbot, vol. II, pp. 534–5).

[50] Pouget, p. 194.

[51] St Cyr (p. 84) and some other sources give 5 p.m. as the starting hour.

[52] Compliments from St Cyr, pp. 86, 99: 'He was nearly 80 years of age; he was the doyen and model of the generals of Europe; for some time it had seemed that he had no desire but to end his long military career on the field of honour. His death caused deep regrets in the French Army and

among the Bavarian troops.' For quote from Wittgenstein see 'Journal des Opérations du Ier Corps Russe', in Fabry, *Russie*, Vol V, Annex, p. 60.

53 Sauzey, pp. 239–41.

54 Ibid., pp. 241, 244. Note that Sauzey gives the number of detached for 28 August as 1,656, but does not list detached troops in the subsequent entries; it is reasonable to assume that a similar number (1,600 or so) remained detached on various duties throughout September. Auvera (p. 488) gives somewhat different figures (also using official sources): for 29 August, 3,088 present in the 19th Division and 3,687 in the 20th for a total of 6,775 officers and men present for duty. Leyh (p. 211) lists the 19th Division with 3,350 men at the end of August (he provides no figure for the 20th).

55 St Cyr, p. 106. Also Wrede to St Cyr, 29 August, and to Max Joseph, 2 September, Fabry, *Russie*, Vol V, pp. 806–08.

56 Marbot, vol. II, p. 560.

57 Auvera, pp. 490–91.

58 These numbers are from St Cyr, pp. 129–30 and Appendix 30 (VI Corps situation report for 15 October). St Cyr, remarks, however, that only 1,823 of the Bavarians 'were truly in a condition to serve'. He numbers the Russians at 50,000, but acknowledges his disagreement with a Russian source that placed Wittgenstein's command (including Steingell) at 40,000.

59 Holzhausen, p. 144; Marbot, vol. II, p. 566; Sauzey, p. 245.

60 Maillinger, p. 121.

61 Henri de Schaller, *Histoire des Troupes Suisses au Service de France*, Paris: Terana, 1995, pp. 171–83.

62 St Cyr, p. 178. In addition to Ströhl's Bavarians, Wrede's ad hoc command consisted of the 19th Ligne, 37th Ligne, 124th Ligne, 2nd Swiss and elements of the 11th Léger; Corbineau's Brigade (7th and 20th Chasseurs, 8th Chevau-Léger-Lanciers) was supplemented by the 7th Cuirassiers (from Wrede to Berthier, 30 October 1812, in Eduard Freiherr von Völderndorff und Waradein, *Observations sur l'Ouvrage de Mr. le Comte Ph. de Ségur*, Munich, 1826, pp. 23–47; also in Sauzey, p. 246). 'Steingell' is occasionally spelled 'Steinheil'.

63 This is a compact presentation of a convoluted sequence of events that took place over several days and was compounded by lost orders, long marches and enemy action. For a partial glimpse into this nest of confusion, see St Cyr's memoirs and the correspondence among St Cyr, Wrede, Merle and the II Corps Chief of Staff from 22 to 30 October 1812 in Gabriel Fabry, *Campagne de 1812: Documents Relatifs a l'Aile Gauche*, Paris: Chapelot, 1912, pp. 103–25.

64 Holzhausen, pp. 138–9, 147. Friction also characterised the relationship between Wrede and St Cyr. According to his biographer, Baron Alfred Ernouf, Maret was also concerned about Wrede's actions; Ernouf terms the Bavarian position 'eccentric' and argues that Wrede's behaviour not only inconvenienced Maret in Vilna, but brought disgrace to the Bavarian

general and left a history of resentment which influenced Wrede's conduct in the 1813 campaign (Alfred Ernouf, *Maret, duc de Bassano*, Paris: Didier, 1884, pp. 450–1).

[65] Strength from Auvera, pp. 494–5.

[66] Wrede to Maret, 25 October 1812, in Völderndorff, *Observations*, p. 37.

[67] Völderndorff, *Observations*, p. 32.

[68] Général de Brigade Jean Baptiste Franceschi's Brigade: 7th March (replacement) Regiment, two unnumbered cavalry replacement regiments, and an artillery detachment for a total of 2,033 infantry, 1,317 cavalry, 91 artillery and train, four 6-pounders. Général de Brigade Louis Coutard's Brigade (3rd Brigade of the 28th Division): 4th Westphalian Infantry (1,336), 1st Hessian Light Infantry (1,168), artillery and train (171), six 6-pounders and two howitzers, for a total of 2,675 officers and men. The corps also included a company of 32 mounted gendarmes from the Department of Vilna; from VI Corps Situation Report dated 16 November 1812 in Völderndorff, *Observations*, p. 95. Franceschi held his infantry in very low regard but considered the cavalry 'good troops... who desire nothing but to encounter the enemy' (Franceschi to Wrede, 12 November 1812, ibid.).

[69] Völderndorff, *Kriegsgeschichte*, Book 6, pp. 285–6.

[70] Franz, military diary for December 1812.

[71] Quoted in Leyh, p. 237.

[72] Condensed from Leyh, pp. 217–44. See also Holzhausen, vol. II, p. 140. The 'sacred squadron' was a temporary formation of cavalry assembled from the few officers and men who still had horses at this late stage in the campaign.

[73] The men were well cared for along the Dvina, presenting a stark contrast with their compatriots at Polotsk. Coming from Polotsk, the new regimental commander, Colonel Cajetan Butler, noted in his first report to King Max: 'The regiment is in the best condition, the men are healthy and fairly well supplied with equipment; what a contrast with the regiments I have just left' (Leyh, p. 254).

[74] Leyh, pp. 253–5.

[75] Ibid., pp. 255–6.

[76] Uebe treats this shift at length and provides some interesting quotations (but these must be used with care, as some are exaggerated to meet his personal predilections and others are taken out of context). See especially pp. 104–17.

[77] Völderndorff, *Kriegsgeschichte*, Book 6, pp. 234–6.

[78] According to Auvera, the 7th arrived in Glogau on the 5th.

[79] Usaci [or Uschatz to the Bavarians] was the name of both a town and a river.

[80] Although Wrede had disbanded the 3rd Brigades on 19 August, Franz continued to refer to them for some time.

81 This was the foolish act of someone in Legrand's Division. The fire spread quickly and alerted the Russians to the French withdrawal which had gone unnoticed until then. St Cyr disgustedly called this an 'inconceivable excess of stupidity' (p. 165).

82 Typhus, frequently called 'nerve fever' in Franz's day.

83 According to Franz's son Julius, Franz made this part of his journey by ambulance wagon.

84 Three replacement detachments reached Wrede in Poland in late December with a total of 2,748 officers and men on arrival; the detachments were commanded by Colonel von Rodt, Colonel von Hausmann (initially, replaced by Colonel Rummel on 7 November) and Colonel von Hoffnaass. See Heinrich Demmler, 'Die Neubildung der bayerischen Heeresabteilung nach dem Rückzuge aus Russland 1812 und die Ereignisse bis zum Rückkehr in die Heimat 1813', *Darstellungen aus der Bayerischen Kriegs- und Heeresgeschichte*, Heft 15, Munich: 1906, pp. 13–31.

85 This was Lieutenant Colonel Wilhelm von Rodt, who would command the 7th Infantry during the invasion of France in 1814.

86 Soft cloth caps were common in all armies for fatigue duty and 'casual' wear; Franz's hat was doubtless a welcome relief from the weighty *Raupenhelm.*

87 Franz routinely referred to these by the French term *hausse-col.*

88 Francis Edward James Keith, 1696–1758, a Scottish soldier who became a field marshal under Frederick II of Prussia, and was killed on 14 October 1758 at the battle of Hochkirch.

89 Letters 4 and 5 are lost.

90 Prior to October 1810, each line company in a regiment had one of the regiment's senior officers as its designated proprietor. The only exception was one line company which 'belonged' to the monarch and thus bore the title *Leibkompanie.*

91 Franz used the term *Feuerspritzen* ('fire fighting equipment' or 'fire engines'); he probably had in mind hand-operated fire pumps mounted on carts or wagons (with thanks to John Elting and Peter Hofschröer for helping to clarify this). 'Windmills' may be an exaggeration of the portable hand mills Napoleon attempted to procure for the invasion of Russia (see Elting, *Swords*, p. 577).

92 It is interesting to note that the idea of Napoleon marching to India was a topic of discussion even among junior officers in an allied contingent.

93 A reference to French foreign minister Hugues-Bernard Maret, Duke of Bassano, 1763–1839.

94 We have retained the original term 'pioneer' here. The Bavarian Army used the term *Pionier* (pioneer) for 'sapper' instead of the more common German word *Zimmermann*. Sappers were assigned on a basis of one per company (see Bezzel, p. 55; Münich, p. 246).

95 It is not clear what Franz intended to convey by this rather cryptic

sentence and the use of the abstruse term 'pancratic'. He may have been referring to the formidable reputation of Marshal Davout (Prince of Eckmühl) and his I Corps.

[96] A small portion of this page was cut away, probably when the letter was opened.

[97] As St Cyr did not want to open his attack until late afternoon (approximately 4 p.m.), Franz had most of the day to compose the previous letter to his parents.

[98] See Franz's 1829 account for additional details of this action.

[99] Auvera, pp. 481–5. Fabry translated most of Franz's narrative into French and published it in his *Russie*, Vol V, pp. 675–8, preceded by the 7th Infantry's official account.

[100] Völderndorff, *Kriegsgeschichte*, vol. III, pp. 115–16.

[101] Franz used the common German term *Relation*. Note that Franz's lengthy German sentences have been retained as much as possible in order to give the reader a flavour of the age and sense of Franz's writing style.

[102] *Schloss* in German, here meaning a large manor or estate.

[103] In French in the original; a common practice for military terms in the early nineteenth century.

[104] Franz uses here the old title of the 1st Infantry: '1ste Linien-Infanterie-Leibregiment'. Officially, however, the 1st Infantry assumed the title *König* in 1811 and lost thereby the *Leib* designation.

[105] Second Lieutenant Franz von Cetto, attached to St Cyr's staff as an ordnance officer.

[106] The Battle of Borodino, 7 September 1812.

[107] Rodt's replacement column, as well as two others, departed in October and reached Wrede in late December.

[108] Marshal Berthier.

[109] Claude Victor-Perrin, Duke of Belluno, Marshal of France, 1764–1841.

[110] This may refer to something in the 7th Infantry's history which Franz and his father would have understood; note, for example, that the regiment 'bivouacked in the woods near Anzing' in October 1805 (see Franz's diary in Chapter Two).

[111] Bavaria established a Gendarmeriekorps in October 1812 for internal police and border patrol duties.

[112] The beginning and end of this letter are missing. Letter No. 24 explains where and when it was written, however.

[113] See 1813 for more on these two replacement columns (Rodt led one, Rummel took over for Hausmann when the latter became ill).

[114] Letter No. 23 is missing.

[115] This attachment is missing.

Chapter Six

War with Europe and the Siege of Thorn

Europe's war against Napoleon did not end with his eviction from Russia. The Russians continued the conflict on Polish and German soil, joined by Prussia, Sweden and Great Britain. Although weather and mutual exhaustion brought an operational pause in the first months of 1813, the Allies were soon on the move and, by April, they were approaching the Elbe, pushing the desperate French before them. Napoleon, however, had not been idle. He stamped a new army out of the earth (including new contingents from Bavaria and his other German allies) and threw the Allies back in a pair of costly slugging matches at Lützen and Bautzen in May. With their inexperienced armies falling into increasingly poor condition, both sides agreed to an armistice in June, ostensibly to discuss peace, but in reality more directed towards resting, refitting and reinforcing their combat units.

Left behind as these grand battles raged to the west and southwest, were a number of fortress garrisons comprising thousands of French, *Rheinbund* and other Napoleonic troops. Among these was the force defending the ancient city of Thorn [Torun], an important road centre with one of the few permanent bridges over the great Vistula River. While part of the Bavarian contingent made its painful way back to the fatherland, Franz and several thousand of his countrymen were designated to garrison Thorn and hold it against the approaching Allied armies. Through his 'military diary', Franz thus grants us a rare glimpse into one of the least-known aspects of the 1813 campaign: the sieges of the Polish and Prussian fortresses.

Reorganisation, Rest and Retreat

In the wake of the Russian disaster, Napoleon's Chief of Staff, Marshal Berthier, directed the bits and pieces of the Bavarian contingent to concentrate at Plock. (Napoleon himself had gone home to France to start raising a new army.) Although almost no formed troops had come back across the Neman, Wrede had at hand some officer cadres (including Franz), small groups of individual soldiers and approximately 1,200 convalescents from the corps' depot. Most important, three columns of replacements from Bavaria made their way to the theatre of operations in the closing days of December. Using these as a basis, Wrede was able to assemble a small mixed division of two infantry brigades, a combined cavalry regiment and four artillery batteries for a total of 254 officers and 4,004 men with 20 guns (as of 1 January 1813).[1]

In addition to warm (though 'very tight and poor') quarters, order and a sense of organisation, the men found in Plock welcome supplies of clothing, money, food and medicines provided by King Max.[2] Unfortunately, sickness, principally the dysentery and typhus that had racked the contingent since August, continued to ravage its ranks, reducing strength and slowing recovery. Wrede also had to contend with shortages of infantry muskets (587 men, one seventh of the division, were still unarmed on 2 January) and artillery ammunition, deficiencies that were not overcome until early February. Two additional columns of replacements arrived on 10 and 13 January bringing the infantry a welcome increase of 2,348 officers and men. By the middle of the month then, as Wrede's command was on the verge of departing Plock, it numbered 5,840 officers and men in the infantry division, 381 in the combined cavalry regiment and 335 artillery and train personnel.[3]

The reconstituted division, however, could not remain in Plock. In no condition to resist the renewed Russian advance, the French forces in Poland and Prussia withdrew steadily to the west, taking the Bavarians along as one of the army's few combat-effective units. The division thus departed Plock on 18 January and, with frequent contact with probing Cossack patrols, made its way first to the Oder (16 February) and then to the Elbe, where it arrived north of Dresden on 9 March with only 1,813 men under arms (another 1,782 were in hospital). Unfortunately, and despite a personal appeal by Wrede, Major General Friedrich Baron von Zoller's 2nd Brigade had been detached on 16 January and sent off to garrison Thorn. Bitter and frustrated by this French decision, Wrede turned over command to Major General Joseph Count von Rechberg und Rothenlöwen on 7 February and returned home to recuperate personally and to contribute to the restoration of the Bavarian Army. Meanwhile, the main body of the division continued its trek to the west.

By the beginning of April, the French and their allies had withdrawn behind the Saale River, and it was here that welcome orders arrived directing Rechberg to march for Bavaria. Departing on 10 April, the men crossed the border into their homeland on the 17th. On the way, however, they suffered a final indignity, losing five of their remaining six guns to raiding Prussian cavalry on the night of 13/14 April.[4] Taking this humiliation and march losses into account, Rechberg's command numbered a mere 1,225 men and one gun when it reached Bamberg.[5]

Within the Walls of Thorn

Home to some 7,000 people in 1813, Thorn was an old city, founded by the Teutonic Knights in the 13th century. Lying on the north (right) bank of the Vistula, it was connected to the opposite shore by two long wooden bridges which met in the middle of the river on a small, fortified island. Napoleon, recognising its value as a base for operations in Poland and Prussia, had begun refurbishing its fortifications in 1806, but the extensive work he had required was only partially complete when Franz and his compatriots reached the city on 20 January 1813. Specially troubling to the prospective defenders were the hills north and west of Thorn which almost completely dominated the fortress. Moreover, the city's weakest side, the stretch of wall along the Vistula, was made particularly vulnerable because the frozen river allowed nearly unhindered access to the decrepit old ramparts. On the south (left) bank of the Vistula, an abatis covering some fortified houses formed a weak bridgehead of sorts. Slightly downstream on the south bank, however, the castle Dybow offered a solid, if isolated, strongpoint.

With 4,044 men, von Zoller's 2nd Brigade provided the bulk of the Thorn garrison, the remainder being a meagre 300 French infantry and some 250 French and Polish artillerymen.[6] This gross disparity in strength notwithstanding, Zoller refused the opportunity to serve as governor of the fortress. Although there were technical reasons to turn down this offer (the Bavarians lacked a suitable staff of engineers and other specialists for the proper conduct of a siege), his principal reason was the concern that the French would use him and his brigade as scapegoats if the fortress fell. Wrede applauded the refusal,

> I give my complete approval, my dear general, to your decision not to accept the government of Thorn, so that in future you will have a witness who will be in a position to do justice to the behaviour of your troops.[7]

The post of governor thus fell to Général de Brigade Jean Poitevin, Baron de Maureillan, an energetic and experienced engineer officer who had most recently commanded the engineers in Marshal Ney's III Corps during the Russian campaign. Under Poitevin's direction, the garrison immediately set about preparing for the siege that was sure to come, by strengthening the works, gathering in cattle and other victuals, conducting reconnaissances (lacking cavalry, these patrols became the responsibility of the infantry) and evacuating to Posen as many of the sick as possible.

These preparations were timely for the Russians were indeed on the move. Patrols in late January discovered nothing beyond scattered

Cossack detachments who showed no interest in engaging the garrison's infantry. By 4 February, however, the Cossacks had become bolder and the next day regular cavalry appeared for the first time, followed by infantry on the 7th. These were troops of the Russian Third Army's advance guard under Lieutenant General Efim von Tschaplitz, which had crossed the Vistula below Thorn early on the 7th and thus approached the city from the south bank.

The garrison actively opposed the Russian advance as best it could, sallying out several times between the 8th and 11th to collect information and keep the Russians at arm's length. A probe on the 11th found the enemy gone and four more days passed before new Russian troops arrived, this time advancing on both banks of the river, Lieutenant General Voinov's II Corps on the south bank and General of the Infantry Count Langeron's I Corps on the north. The Third Army's commander, General of the Infantry Mikhail Barclay de Tolly, also appeared, setting up his headquarters several miles downstream to oversee the reduction of the fortress. Although not all were dedicated to the attack on Thorn, Barclay's command numbered nearly 16,000 (of whom perhaps one third actually participated in the siege work), and it was reinforced by Prussian artillery and engineers in the course of the operation.[8]

While the Russians and Prussians observed Thorn, the active Poitevin kept the garrison busy improving the city's defences and conducting occasional sallies against the surrounding enemy. Conditions inside the fortress, however, were rapidly deteriorating. Food was one major problem. Although the garrison's larders were well stocked in terms of quantity, the quality of the rations left much to be desired. Some of the victuals had already been in storage for several years with the result that much of the meat and fruit was spoiled. The ammunition supply was another difficulty; it was adequate for the sporadic fighting that occurred in February and early March, but supplies quickly dwindled when the Allies initiated siege operations in earnest.

By far the greatest challenge for the garrison, however, was sickness. Again, as at Polotsk, the Bavarian ranks were decimated by illness, especially typhus. Franz was one of the fortunate few to recover from this ailment, which filled the shabby hospitals beyond capacity and consumed hundreds of his countrymen. An average of 21 Bavarians died from sickness every day during March, and by the end of the month, Zoller's Brigade was reduced to approximately 1,600 men under arms with another 1,700 in hospital. The sickness rate for the Bavarians thus exceeded 50 per cent for much of the siege; in contrast, the French and Poles had only some 11 per cent of their soldiers in hospital (62 of 575 total strength on 25 March).[9]

Poor conditions notwithstanding, the French, Polish and Bavarian soldiers behaved well, and Poitevin proved himself a firm, intelligent and resourceful leader. Together, they maintained a lively defence with accurate counter-battery fire throughout March and repeated forays against Russian attempts to establish positions near the fortress. Unfortunately, Thorn's resources were limited and when the Allies began formal siege operations on 7 April, the garrison's days were numbered.

The first parallel was opened the following day and Russian infantry supported by Russian and Prussian sappers made steady progress thereafter, despite the best efforts of Zoller's men. On the night of 10/11 April, for example, Captain Johann Fleischmann of the 3rd Infantry led 50 men in a brilliant counter-attack to regain a key outpost just beyond the fortifications – a deed which earned him the entry into the Max Joseph Order in 1814 and in 1825(!) the cross of the French Legion of Honour.[10]

Artillery ammunition was already running short, however, and reached a critical stage when a lucky Allied shot hit a powder magazine on the 11th and destroyed 1,000 cartridges. The French continued to reply to the Allied guns, but the attackers' advance was inexorable and Poitevin's innovative efforts to fabricate replacement artillery cartridges from infantry ammunition were time-consuming and inadequate. Furthermore, many of the fortress' better artillery pieces had been damaged or destroyed by this time, leaving the gunners with a poor selection of mostly antiquated cannon with which to respond to the heavy daily bombardment. Some 1,400 rounds came in on the 13th for instance. Resistance could not be maintained much longer.

Considering his situation – ammunition nearly exhausted, artillery pieces collapsing, garrison reduced to barely 1,600 men, food supplies insufficient, no hope of relief – Poitevin raised the white flag on the morning of 15 April. In the ensuing negotiations, the Russians refused to allow the garrison to retain its firearms, but agreed to permit an evacuation under the condition that the men would pledge not to fight against the Allies for one year. Zoller's men thus escaped the unpleasant fate of prisoners of war and departed Thorn, unarmed but unbowed, on 18 April.[11] They numbered 139 officers and 1,951 men, including a bare 200 from the 7th Infantry.[12] Making an arduous journey through hostile Prussia, neutral Austria (escaping there after Prussian partisans had repeatedly threatened the weaponless little band), and friendly Saxony, the Bavarians finally returned home on 16 June.[13]

Campaign in Germany

While Zoller's Brigade was enduring blockade and siege in distant Thorn, Napoleon called upon Bavaria to assemble yet another contingent to support the *Grande Armée*. Unable to resist Napoleon's commands but unwilling, after the Russian catastrophe, to commit his realm completely to the Imperial cause, Max Joseph temporised, responding slowly to French instructions and providing only two-thirds of the required 13,000 men. The king also deflected Napoleon's request to have Wrede named to command the contingent and placed it instead under the newly-promoted Lieutenant General von Raglovich. Nonetheless, by the beginning of April, a Bavarian division had assembled near Bamberg and Bayreuth. As in 1812, the Bavarian authorities initially gave their field army a grand title, styling it a 'corps d'observation' in the hopes of garnering thereby some degree of independence. As in 1812, however, such measures were otiose and the Bavarian troops, duly designated the 29th Division of the *Grande Armée* in Marshal Oudinot's XII Corps, departed for Saxony at the end of April approximately 7,500 strong.

Raglovich's division missed the opening struggles of the spring 1813 campaign, but joined in the slow pursuit that followed the partial French victory at Lützen. Napoleon reviewed the Bavarians for the last time as they passed through Dresden on 13 May. Parts of the division fought in the Battle of Bautzen (21 May) and the Combined Chevauxlegers Regiment participated in a number of engagements during Oudinot's abortive march toward Berlin in late May and early June. The bulk of the division, however, remained a spectator to the XII Corps' combats prior to the 5 June armistice.

Similarly, the Bavarians were held in reserve during the great battles of the autumn campaign. Although they participated in Napoleon's two failed attempts on Berlin, therefore, their roles in the Battles of Grossbeeren (25 August) and Dennewitz (6 September) were minor. The consequences of the disastrous defeat at Dennewitz, however, engulfed Raglovich's command as well as the rest of XII Corps. Between 5 and 8 September, the division lost some 2,000 men and numbered only 2,300 effectives when it was reorganised as a brigade in the middle of the month.

Reduced to four battalions, one squadron and one battery, the Bavarians now served as the Dresden garrison for several weeks before heading to Leipzig on 7 October. The men of the brigade, now under the command of Major General Maillot, the former commander of Franz's 7th Infantry (Raglovich had been called home by Max Joseph), were also spared the rigours of of the Battle of Leipzig. Guarding the army's huge artillery and baggage park 15 miles north-east of the city, the Bavarians could hear the dull rumble of guns, but took no part in the fighting. After the battle, Maillot escorted the train to Torgau, receiving en route the first rumour that Bavaria had changed sides in the war. With the co-operation of the local French commander, the chivalrous Général de Division Louis Narbonne-Lara, Maillot and his troops maintained a neutral stance outside Torgau while they waited for confirmation that their monarch had joined the Allies. A letter from Tsar Alexander soon verified the shift in Bavaria's allegiance, and the tiny Bavarian force, now a mere 1,226 strong, marched for home on 22 October.[14]

One Bavarian unit continued to serve with the French long after the monarchy had broken with Napoleon: the 13th Infantry and its attached artillery which had taken refuge in Danzig following the retreat from Russia. Here the Bavarians were incorporated into a new X Corps, a patchwork organisation under the command of Général de Division Jean Rapp and comprised of troops from all across the face of Europe. The 13th Infantry, along with other remnants of Grandjean's division from the Russian campaign, constituted Rapp's most reliable troops and served him well throughout the siege. In October, for example, when desertions among the non-French troops led Rapp to restrict outpost duty to French and Polish units, Colonel Cajetan Count Butler of the 13th protested. Pointing out that the Bavarians had had only two deserters in the course of the siege, he argued that Rapp's decision was an insult to Bavaria and requested permission to resume normal duties. Rapp relented and the 13th resumed its place in the front lines.

The regiment found itself in an extraordinarily uncomfortable situation, however, when the Russian commander sent Butler two letters (4 and 9 November) announcing Bavaria's break with Napoleon and demanding that the 13th leave the fortress. Butler, a paragon of military honour and correctness, discussed the letters openly with Rapp and asked to be relieved of further external duties; Rapp agreed and the regiment was withdrawn from the outer defences pending formal instructions from Bavaria. These arrived on 3 December in the form of a letter from Wrede directing Butler and his men to return home. On 12 December, the 13th Infantry marched to the city gates with flags flying and personally escorted by Rapp. The two sides parted with cordiality, Butler writing that, 'the mutual farewells at this gate proved the high degree of respect which the regiment had earned during its stay in this city.' The fortress capitulated three weeks later on 1 January 1814 and the remaining 16,000 men of the garrison marched off into captivity. The Bavarians, on the other hand, were granted a month's rest and headed home on 12 January, arriving in Bayreuth on 18 February with 40 officers, 331 infantrymen, 34 artillerymen and two guns after an absence of nearly three years.[15]

The Break with France

While Raglovich's division and the 13th Infantry were still fighting alongside French eagles, Wrede and others were working to convince

Max Joseph that the time was right to break out of the alliance with Napoleon and join the Allies. After considerable internal debate during the summer of 1813, secret negotiations were opened with Austria, which had itself only become a part of the coalition in August when the summer armistice came to an end. These talks, conducted by Wrede on the Bavarian side, led to the signature of the preliminary Treaty of Ried on 8 October and its ratification one week later. Among other treaty commitments, Bavaria agreed to work for the dissolution of the *Rheinbund* and to supply a contingent of at least 36,000 men to the European coalition against Napoleon under the general direction of the nominal Allied commander-in-chief, Austrian Field Marshal Prince Karl zu Schwarzenberg.

A new Bavarian Army had been slowly assembling around Munich since the spring, but the mobilisation of the force called for in the treaty proved beyond the monarchy's immediate capacity in the aftermath of 1812 and in light of Napoleon's repeated demands in early 1813. Nonetheless, Wrede marched north on 10 October with some 25,000 Bavarians and an attached Austrian corps of nearly equal strength. From this point on, the Bavarian Army would fight against its former master, and Wrede's immediate task was now to threaten Napoleon's line of communications along the River Main.

Although one battalion of the 7th was included in Wrede's command, Franz was on leave from his regiment and missed this initial foray against Napoleon. As the Austro–Bavarian force moved north toward the Main, Wrede learned that the French Army was retreating toward the Rhine after the disastrous defeat it had suffered at Leipzig between 16 and 19 October. Hoping to catch the weakened and ragged enemy before they crossed the Rhine, Wrede made for Würzburg, blockaded the fortress there, and pushed west toward Frankfurt am Main. At Hanau, on 30 October, he attempted to cut off the French but found himself opposed by Napoleon in person and suffered a clear defeat. Wrede was badly wounded and could not resume command until 14 December, by which time Allied preparations for crossing the Rhine were nearing completion. The stage was set for the invasion of France.

◆◆◆❈◆◆◆

Military Diary of
FRANZ JOSEPH HAUSMANN
for the
THORN GARRISON, 1813
For the 2nd Battalion of the
Royal Bavarian 2nd Combined Infantry Regiment
after the formation of the battalion on 4 January 1813.
Including marching days and important events
occurring at the time.

January 1813

4 January	The battalion was in cantonment at Srebno near Plock in the Duchy of Warsaw.
17 January	To Kowal.
18 January	To Wloclawek.
19 January	To Nieszawa.
20 January	Into the Thorn fortress.
23 January	A man from the picket in front of the Jacob's Gate was taken prisoner by a Cossack patrol, while he was standing guard. From this day until 7 February enemy cavalry frequently swarmed around the fortress, and during this time several sorties were made.

February 1813

7 February	Several infantry and cavalry columns approached the fortress and blockaded it.
8 February	At 2 o'clock in the morning a sortie of 200 men was undertaken, and the enemy was driven from the heights on the left bank of the Vistula.
9 February	At 4 a.m. the garrison also conducted a sortie with 700 men, during which a real battle was joined, and two officers and several men were wounded, also some people were killed. At 12 noon the enemy fired on the city from the left bank of the Vistula, during which bombardment the garrison stood to arms until 4 o'clock in the afternoon.
10 February	The enemy infantry and artillery moved away from the fortress, leaving it blockaded only by light cavalry.
12 February	A sortie of 250 men was undertaken, during which one Cossack was taken prisoner.

14 February	A sortie of 300 men was made, and the enemy entrenchments were destroyed.
16 February	The garrison conducted two sorties, namely one in which Lieutenant Colonel Fortembs led 300 men on the left bank of the Vistula in order to procure cattle in the villages of Gross- and Klein-Nierschevki. A detachment of 60 men from this commando was supposed to cross the frozen Vistula at Schwarzloch, but it was turned back again by the enemy troops, who were quite strong in this town. The commando, which had marched out at 6 a.m., arrived back at the fortress at 5 p.m. The second sortie, commanded by Lieutenant Colonel Theobald and also consisting of 300 men and two artillery pieces, went downstream on the right bank of the Vistula, but it could not reach the town of Schwarzloch that had been designated as the meeting place with Lieutenant Colonel Fortembs, because the enemy attacked it too strongly, and in the afternoon, after a small encounter with the enemy, during which three men were wounded, it therefore returned to the fortress, arriving back at 4 o'clock.
21 February	On this day because of the warm weather the ice standing on the Vistula broke up.
23 February	The so-called German Bridge leading from the island to the bridgehead was destroyed by the ice flow.
25 February	The high water tore a hole in the bridge leading from the city to the island, whereby this bridge also became impassable.

March 1813

2 March	The enemy began small arms fire and launched rockets,[16] which our outposts did not return, primarily because the distance was too great and because of the darkness of the night.[16]
4 March	During the night the enemy launched similar fire, which our outposts again did not return. In the evening the horse of one of the negotiators sent to the enemy, after throwing its rider, came up to the outposts, and, because all calls went unanswered, several shots brought it down.
8 March	The enemy shot at the fortress with three field pieces from half past midnight until daybreak, and his fire was answered by the batteries on this side. At 11 o'clock in the evening the enemy fire from five artillery pieces began again, and it lasted until after 1 o'clock.

9 March	The fortress was again fired upon during the night from 11.30 until 2 o'clock.
11 March	The cannonade again took place from 10.30 until 12.30 at night.
12 March	The firing went on from 11 in the evening until 3.30 on the morning of the 13th.
13 March	This cannonade lasted from 11.30 at night until 3 o'clock on the morning of the 14th.
16 March	The enemy fire directed at the fortress lasted from 8.30 until 2 o'clock on the morning of the 17th.
17 March	The same thing from 10 in the evening until 1.30 on the morning of the 18th.
18 March	The firing took place from 11 in the evening until 12.30 on the morning of the 19th.
20 March	The enemy cannonaded the fortress from 9 o'clock in the evening until 1 o'clock on the morning of the 21st.
21 March	The enemy fired on the fortress from 10.30 in the evening until 2.30 in the morning.
22 March	From 10 o'clock in the evening until 1 o'clock on the morning of the 23rd.
23 March	The same thing from 9.30 to 12 o'clock in the evening.
24 March	A commando of 100 men from the 2nd Regiment was sent to the village of Mokern, in order to pick up the cattle and potatoes available there.
29 March	There was a changing of the outposts at 4.30 in the morning, and the old and new outposts together made a sortie on every road. During one of the sorties in front of the Old Gate, the enemy was fired upon for several hours, and a French patrol reconnoitred the island.[17]
31 March	During this night a boat filled with bombs and shells was sent down to the second island, in an effort to destroy the enemy boats there, but it did not succeed. Also, a large number of enemy infantry were seen. At just this moment a sortie was made from the Dybow castle toward Potkusch, during which there was heavy skirmishing.

April 1813

| 3 April | In the evening the enemy moved in two columns toward the fortress, and the garrison stood to arms from 7.30 to 10 o'clock. The enemy fired on the fortress from midnight until 3 o'clock on the morning of the 4th. |

7 April	The enemy bombarded the fortress from midnight until 3 o'clock on the morning of the 8th.
8 April	The enemy infantry approached the fortress, and on this night, that is the night of the 8th, the first parallel of trenches was opened up. From this time on, the fortress was constantly fired upon.
9 April	We were continuously harassed by the enemy, whereupon we returned the fire.
10 April	The outposts changed guard at 3 o'clock in the morning. Toward noon the enemy fired several times at our batteries. In the evening, after 10 o'clock, the enemy attacked the outposts in front of the Old Gate and at the mill and forced them back. The 2nd Regiment had to stand to arms all night on the glacis. On this night the enemy approached closer with his attack in front of the Old Gate. The enemy fire at our battery, and that from the fortress at the enemy battery, continued without pause.
11 April	Toward noon the magazine next to the Kulm Gate bastion exploded because of a bomb that fell into it.
12 April	In the morning one could see a new battery in front of the mill picket again, after this post had been forced back the night before. The cannonade and the bombardment went on all day without break.
13 April	This night there was again heavy skirmishing. The entire day the Kulm Gate battery and also a part of the city were bombed and cannonaded.
14 April	On the night of the 13th the enemy attacked the outpost at the Old Gate, and it came to heavy fighting. Our outposts withdrew somewhat. The bombardment continued on the 14th.
15 April	On this day the cannonading went on until 8 o'clock in the morning, when there began a general period of calm, during which negotiations took place.
16 April	At noon the fighting started up again, but it lasted only half an hour, after which a Russian officer came to the governor, whereupon the capitulation was agreed upon, and the fortress area was immediately occupied by an Imperial Russian battalion.
17 April	A battalion of Russians entered the city to keep internal peace, and the enemy fired in victory to celebrate the surrender of the Thorn fortress.

18 April	At 5 o'clock in the morning authority was assumed by the Russians. At 9 o'clock the arms, bags and ammunition were turned over to the enemy, and at the same time the garrison marched out of the fortress, giving up its arms as it passed the arsenal, and the night was spent at Tugelwiesen.
19 April	Crossed the Vistula near Kruschi and to Gniewkowo.
20 April	To Sroczki.
21 April	Stare Radziejewo.
22 April	Sompolno.
23 April	1st Battalion Budzislav; 2nd Battalion Dimba.
24 April	Day of rest.
25 April	Brudzewo.
26 April	Muchlin.
27 April	Day of rest.
28 April	Zenkowo.
29 April	Koszielnowiesch near Kalisch [Kalisz].
30 April	Day of rest.

May 1813

1 May	To Ostrow.
2 May	To Chwaliszew.
3 May	Day of rest.
4 May	Sulow.
5 May	Seyne near Trachtenberg [Zmigrod].
6 May	Seyne, day of rest.
7 May	The 2nd Battalion to Streny; the 1st Battalion to Klein Paulwi.
8 May	Lampersdorf 2nd Battalion; Belwiese 1st Battalion. Crossed the Oder on this day.
9 May	Day of rest.
10 May	To Krumlinden [Lipny] 1st Battalion; to Kaltwasser 2nd Battalion.
11 May	To Modelsdorf 1st Battalion; to Altenau 2nd Battalion.
12 May	To Ottendorf [Ocice] near Bunzlau [Boleslawiec]. The Bobr River was crossed on this day.
13 May	Day of rest, remaining in place until
22 May	to Goldberg [Zlotoryja].
23 May	In the afternoon to Krain.

24 May	To Gerlachsdorf near Fauer.
25 May	To Freiburg [Swiebodzice] 1st Battalion; to Liebichau 2nd Battalion.
26 May	To Hermsdorf near Waldenburg [Walbrzych].
27 May	Day of rest.
28 May	Reisendorf near Waldenburg.
29 May	Broke camp at 3 o'clock in the morning and halted at Gürsdorf at 3 o'clock in the afternoon, after which the brigade marched across the Bohemian border to Braunau [Broumov], but started out again at 11 o'clock at night, and
30 May	went on to Trautenau [Trutnov], where into bivouac and had to pay cash for everything.
31 May	Bivouacked at Stangerbach.

June 1813

1 June	1st Battalion to Franzendorf near Reichenberg [Liberec]; 2nd Battalion to Oberhanigen to the 1st Regiment. Here the troops paid cash for quarters. The agreement reached for this battalion was at 4 kreuzer per person.
2 June	Again across the border to Zittau in Saxony.
3 June	Day of rest.
4 June	Spremberg near Neusalza,
5 June	Ehrenberg near Neustadt.
6 June	Reichsstädt near Dippoldiswalde. Crossed the Elbe at Pirna.
7 June	Day of rest.
8 June	Mittelsaida. Remained here until
12 June	to Wolkenstein.
13 June	To Bernwalde.
14 June	In the evening via Hundshübel and Carlsfeld until
15 June	to Neukirchen.
16 June	To Schwarzenbach [an der Saale] near Hof.
17 June	To Lanzendorf. I first learned from the newspaper about my promotion to first lieutenant.
18 June	To Bayreuth.
19 June	Day of rest.
20 June	To Büchenbach near Pegnitz.
21 June	Igensdorf near Eschenau.
22 June	To Nuremberg.

23 June	To Rittersbach near Roth.
24 June	To Ellingen.
25 June	To Eichstätt.
26 June	Into the Neuburg garrison, after beforehand crossing the Danube.

Notes to Chapter Six

[1] Report of 1 January 1813 in Demmler, 'Neubildung'.

[2] Quote from a battalion commander's report cited in ibid., p. 47.

[3] Figures from official reports of 15 January (infantry and cavalry) and 13 January 1813 (artillery) cited in Sauzey, pp. 278–81.

[4] The division had only one battery of six guns by this time; the other 14 guns that had been saved from Russia had been sent back to Bavaria in February.

[5] The foregoing narrative is condensed from Demmler 'Neubildung', and Leyh, pp. 269–76.

[6] Bavarian strengths from report of 20 January 1813. The French infantry was the debris of the 85th and 108th Ligne; the rubric 'artillery' encompasses here two French and one Polish foot artillery companies as well as small groups of sappers and various artillery artisans. The garrison's entire cavalry force consisted of nine troopers of the 1st French Chasseurs. The foregoing data from two of the appendices in R. von Hösslin and E. Hagen, 'Die Vertheidigung von Thorn', *Darstellungen aus der Bayerischen Kriegs- und Heeresgeschichte*, Heft 3, Munich: 1894.

[7] Wrede to Zoller, 28 January 1813, in Hösslin/Hagen, p. 32.

[8] Barclay's force also included a cavalry corps under Lieutenant General Sass. Numbers and organisation of the Russian forces from Carl von Plotho, *Der Krieg in Deutschland und Frankreich*, Berlin: Amelang, 1817, pp. 43-4; and Völderndorff, pp, 435–6. Plotho states that only some 3,500 Russians/Prussians took part in the siege, a figure that seems far too low; Hösslin/Hagen, on the other hand, give the besiegers approximately 6,700 men with 38 siege guns (p. 45).

[9] Hösslin/Hagen, especially reprint of 'Standes-Ausweis der Besatzung von Thorn', 25 March 1813.

[10] Ibid., p. 48; Ruith/Ball, pp. 200–01.

[11] Napoleon found the capitulation over-hasty, telling Poitevin in Dresden, 'You have served me poorly by this surrender' (Hösslin/Hagen, p. 55).

[12] The 15 officers and 1,012 soldiers who were left behind in the hospitals of Thorn made their way back to Bavaria individually. The dead numbered 929, only 7 of those from enemy action. Forty Bavarians were missing or known to have deserted.

[13] Principal source for the siege of Thorn is Hösslin/Hagen; contributing sources include: Auvera, Deifl, Leyh, Plotho (especially Beilage XII, 'Das Tagebuch der Belagerung der Festung Thorn'), Ruith/Ball, Sauzey.

[14] One of the four battalions had been detached to escort the French Imperial Guard's baggage wagons; it marched with the Guard all the way to Erfurt, whence the French sent it home with honour and courtesy. Furthermore, a few chevauxlegers accompanied Oudinot to Hanau, finally departing the marshal's entourage on 30 October after Napoleon's victory over Wrede (Sauzey, pp. 335–6).

[15] Leyh, pp. 282-94 (including quote from Butler's diary).

[16] It is not clear what Franz is describing with the term *Raketen* ('rockets'). The Russians and Prussians who besieged Thorn did not possess this sort of exotic artillery and there were no British or Austrian rocket troops anywhere near Thorn in early 1813.

[17] The Old Gate (Altes Thor) was on the western face of the fortress near the Vistula. The Kulm Gate where the powder magazine exploded was on the north-western corner of the old city wall.

Chapter Seven

The Invasion of France

The brief 1814 campaign in France often showed Napoleon at his best as a commander. With a small army – mostly young conscripts and old men huddled around a hard core of veterans – he struggled to hold off vastly superior Allied forces encroaching on French territory from all directions. Through wretched winter weather, he exploited his central position and unique unity of command to win a string of brilliant, if desperate, little victories over his often hesitant foes. But all the courage, endurance, spirit and sacrifice were not enough. In the end, he and his dwindling legions succumbed to overwhelming numbers, France's exhaustion, and his own inability to set any limits on his designs and ambitions. The result was abdication and exile, but only after one of his most skillful campaigns.

Of the vast Allied host pressing slowly into France as 1814 opened, the two most important formations were Prussian Field Marshal Gebhard Leberecht von Blücher's Army of Silesia (107,000 men) and the Main Army under Schwarzenberg (209,000 men).[1] Both were aiming for Paris, the Army of Silesia generally following the Marne River while Schwarzenberg advanced astride the Seine. After much discussion, the Allies had decided on a winter campaign and began moving across the Rhine at the turn of the year, depriving Napoleon of the time he needed to recover.

Across the Rhine

In accordance with the terms of the Treaty of Ried, the Bavarians were employed as an independent, unitary contingent under their own commander. Wrede was thus entrusted with V Corps of the Allied Main Army including the 26,400 men of his own contingent and an Austrian corps of 17,900 under General of the Cavalry Johann von Frimont. The Bavarian Army, hastily cobbled together for this campaign, was an odd mixture of two-thirds line troops and one-third newly-organised National Guard battalions known as the Mobile Legion. Like Franz, most of the officers in the line units were veterans, but the rank and file were mainly new recruits from Bavaria's third conscription of 1813. A large percent-age of the men in the Mobile Legion battalions (later renamed 'National Field Battalions'), on the other hand, had some prior military service, but the officers were frequently either brand new or not entirely fit for active campaign duty.[2] Wilhelm Hausmann is an example of this latter category: a competent NCO elevated to the officer corps to fill a leadership posi-tion with the burgeoning militia force.[3] Working to Wrede's advantage was his own personal involvement with this army. He had raised and trained it over the summer of 1813, and he had carried it through its first, albeit unsuccessful, battle at Hanau in October. Moreover, he had a fairly strong set of relatively young, yet experienced, general officers to command his divisions and brigades (the 18-year-old Prince Karl being an exception in terms of experience).[4]

Like many other line regiments, the 7th Infantry had only one full battalion available for field duty in late 1813. Under Colonel Wilhelm von Rodt, therefore, only the regiment's 1st Battalion, with 823 officers and men under arms (from a total of 1,103 effectives) on 14 December 1813, would march with Wrede in the coming campaign.[5]

The Bavarians spent most of November and December 1813 along the upper Rhine, incorporating the tiny remnant of Raglovich's Division (1,250 officers and men) and welcoming the return of Wrede, recovered from the wound received at Hanau. The corps passed over the Rhine at Basel on 22 December and headed north through Alsace in early January 1814, sending off the renowned Austrian partisan leader, Colonel Karl Baron von Scheibler with some Cossacks and one squadron each of Austrian and Bavarian cavalry to gather intelligence to the north and east of the route of march.[6] As he advanced, however, Wrede had to leave off significant detachments (Beckers' 2nd Bavarian Division and three Austrian battalions) to blockade several small but defiant French fortresses.[7] With the troops remaining (approximately 27,000 men), Wrede made his slow, somewhat halting way west on 10 January, crossing the Moselle, Meuse and Marne Rivers while providing the connecting link between the Main Army to the south and the Army of Silesia in the north.

On the last day of January, Wrede thus found himself west of the Marne, wedged between the two principal Allied armies.[8] His orders from Schwarzenberg called for him to move north-west, but he learned that morning that another Allied corps (commanded, ironically, by his old foe from Polotsk, General Wittgenstein) had discovered only insignificant detachments in this direction. Knowing that a major French force had gathered near Brienne and La Rothière, due west of his position, Wrede decided to ignore his orders and march toward the spot he rightly concluded to be the decisive point.

Wrede formed the right wing of the Allied army as it advanced to the attack over snow-clad fields at approximately 1 p.m. on the afternoon of 1 February. Opposing the 79,000 Russian, Prussian, Austrian and German troops immediately available were some 45,100 Frenchmen under Napoleon's personal command.[9] The French Emperor, recognising that he was in danger of being outflanked and overwhelmed, had directed his army to withdraw to the west when word arrived that the Allies were massing to his front. With no choice but to stand his ground until nightfall, Napoleon ordered his men back to their places and a bitter action soon developed along the entire battle line.

A brutal contest for the villages that formed the French right and centre had been in progress for some time when Wrede's men came into line on the Allied extreme right. While most of Wrede's Austrians swung right toward Morvilliers, the Bavarian 3rd Division deployed with the 2nd Brigade north of the Soulaines road and the 1st Brigade to the south with the I/7th and the two national field battalions in the first line facing the village of Chaumesnil.

Shortly before 4 p.m., Wrede ordered the 1st Battalion of the 7th and a battalion of the Austrian 1st *Szekler* Grenz Regiment[10] forward to seize Chaumesnil and take some of the pressure off the Württemberg IV Corps next in line on his left. The men of the 7th advanced in column without firing a shot and their sudden storming attack succeeded brilliantly, quickly evicting the French from the village and securing it for the Allies at the cost of three dead and 36 wounded. The 1st Grenadier Company under First Lieutenant Karl von Bienenthal performed especially well, but suffered 22 of the battalion's 39 casualties in the assault. Unfortunately, the casualties included Colonel von Rodt, who died the following day of a head wound received during the struggle. Major von Fortis assumed temporary command of the battalion.

Having wrested Chaumesnil from the French, the Bavarians and the Grenzer successfully defended it against several French counterattacks, including one by a brigade of the Young Guard led forward by Napoleon himself. The Allied troops were well supported by several Bavarian guns on a hill east of the village, and a well-executed charge by the Bavarian and Austrian cavalry captured 16 French guns, effectively ending the threat to Chaumesnil. This additional fighting cost the 7th Infantry 34 more casualties, making for a total loss of 73 officers and men during the course of the day. As night closed in, the French were in full retreat and the Bavarians (thanks to Wrede's initiative) could take satisfaction in having made a significant contribution to the Allied victory.[11]

The Allies, however, bungled the pursuit of Napoleon's battered force. Indeed, Schwarzenberg issued no orders at all for 2 February, with the result that Wrede set out on his own to find the enemy. Unfortunately

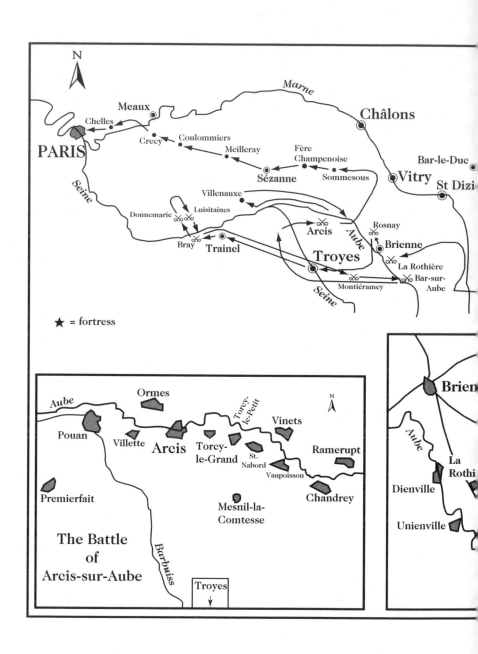

N

Marne

Meaux

Chelles

PARIS

Crecy

Coulommiers

Meilleray

Châlons

Fère
Champenoise

Sézanne

Sommesous

Bar-le-Duc

Vitry

St Dizi

Seine

Villenauxe

Donnemarie

Luisitaines

Arcis

Rosnay

Brienne

Bray

Trainel

Troyes

Aube

La Rothière

Montiéramey

Bar-sur-
Aube

Seine

★ = fortress

Aube

Ormes

N

Pouan

Villette

Arcis

Torcy-
le-Petit

Vinets

Torcy-
le-Grand

St.
Nabord

Ramerupt

Vaupoisson

Premierfait

Mesnil-la-
Comtesse

Chandrey

The Battle
of
Arcis-sur-Aube

Barbuiss

Troyes

Brien

Aube

La
Rothi

Dienville

La
Rothi

Unienville

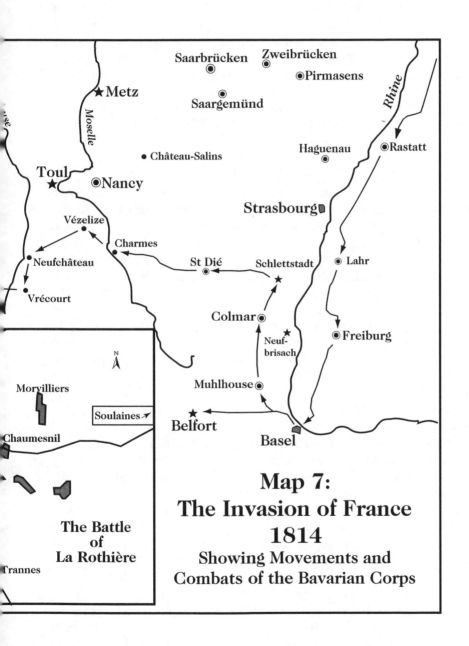

Saarbrücken   Zweibrücken

⊙Pirmasens

★Metz

Moselle

Rhine

Saargemünd

Château-Salins   Haguenau   ⊙Rastatt

Toul ⊙Nancy

Strasbourg▐

Vézelize

Charmes

Neufchâteau   St Dié   Schlettstadt   ⊙ Lahr

Vrécourt

Colmar⊙

Neuf-
brisach   ⊙Freiburg

N
⋏

Moryilliers

Muhlhouse⊙

Soulaines⬈

★
Belfort

Chaumesnil   Basel

Map 7:
The Invasion of France
1814
Showing Movements and
Combats of the Bavarian Corps

The Battle
of
La Rothière

Trannes

for the Bavarian Corps, he turned toward the town of Rosnay where French Marshal Auguste Marmont had established himself in an extremely strong defensive position. For several hours, the Bavarian 1st Division and the Austrians bravely hurled themselves at Marmont's command, but the Allies could achieve only partial successes and even those came at a heavy price. Marmont finally abandoned his position when outflanked by Austrian cavalry, but by then the Bavarians alone had lost almost 1,100 men in their fruitless attempts to storm the town. Moreover, the high losses were not justified by military necessity. The next day, Wrede was ordered to turn about and retrace his steps, leaving Rosnay and its bitter memory of pointless sacrifice behind.

The Bavarians continued west for the next ten days, passing over the Seine twice as they made their way toward Paris: first from east to west at Troyes on the 7th and then from south to north at Bray on the 12th. At Bray, the Bavarians found the bridge destroyed and a small French force deployed on the far bank. When the Schützen Company of the 7th Infantry and a cannon drove off the few French defenders, Major von Horn of the general staff embarked on a raft (the only available water craft) with seven volunteer Schützen, rowed to the north side of the river and collected enough boats to transport the rest of the Schützen across. Under the protection of the Schützen, the bridge was restored and the advance resumed on the 13th.[12]

This push north of the Seine brought the corps to within 35 miles of Paris on 16 February, but Napoleon, having hammered Blücher's Army of Silesia in three sharp victories, drove south behind V Corps and struck the Bavarians hard on the 17th. Functioning as the rear-guard, the 7th Infantry lost a few men in this action, while the 11th, more heavily engaged, suffered 270 casualties. The Allies retreated behind the Seine the following day.

South of the Seine once again, Wrede's men trudged gloomily east as the soldiers wondered why they were withdrawing from a numerically inferior foe. Inadequate provisions contributed to sagging Allied morale. Marching through regions already exhausted by the repeated comings and goings of the armies, the men found little food, little wood, less fodder and no straw for bedding in the cold, damp weather. When they arrived at Bar-sur-Aube on the 25th, for example, the troops were able to settle in and cook a proper hot meal for the first time in ten days.[13]

In addition to debilitating privations, the long, demoralising retreat also brought a sharp engagement for 7th Infantry. Serving as the army's rear-guard on the afternoon of the 24th, the battalion was under pressure as it held a bridge east of Troyes against the French pursuit. When the French finally forced their way across the bridge, Captain von Hacke of the 1st Company resorted to a desperate deception. With the darkness hiding his true weakness, he had his men sound cavalry and infantry attack signals on bugles and drums to the accompaniment of loud cries and exclamations. The ruse worked. The French believed themselves in danger of being overwhelmed and pulled back, allowing the Bavarian withdrawal to Bar-sur-Aube to continue undisturbed. This brief engagement, however, cost the battalion 89 casualties.[14]

At Bar-sur-Aube, the Bavarian soldiery again paid the price for the hesitancy, poor intelligence and weak decision-making in Allied headquarters. Ordered to continue with the retreat on the 26th, V Corps evacuated Bar at approximately 5 p.m. that evening and headed east. The last of Wrede's men had barely departed when new orders arrived directing Wrede to hold the town at all costs and to prepare for a major action on the 27th. By this time, however, the French had occupied Bar and were already busy fortifying it. Wrede's attempt to carry out his orders resulted in a fruitless night assault on the French defences which destroyed the 1st Battalion of the 8th Infantry as an effective fighting force (344 casualties left it with only around 100 men under arms) and gained the Bavarians nothing.[15]

The following day, however, ended with an undeniable Allied success. Schwarzenberg's plan called for Wrede, reinforced to 32,000 men by the addition of several Russian battalions, to fix the French from the front while Wittgenstein swung round the enemy's left flank with his 20,000 Russians. The French, numbering some 30,000, were under the command of Marshal Oudinot, so the ensuing battle brought together the three protagonists from the First Battle of Polotsk in August 1812.

Unfortunately for the Allied cause, the relationship between Wrede and Wittgenstein was characterised by tension and mistrust. Wittgenstein was thus slow to move on the morning of the 27th, and Schwarzenberg had to intervene personally to get the attack rolling. Because of this delay, Wittgenstein's outflanking move had hardly begun when the fog lifted and disclosed the Russian columns to the French outposts. Curiously, Wrede was also slow to enter the fight. Although his Russian reinforcements and some of his Austrians were committed early in the day, he did not send his Bavarians forward until 4 p.m. The Bavarians attacked with courage, but the French, though outnumbered, were determined and grimly contested every house and street corner, finally breaking off the struggle late in the evening.

Some 52,000 Allied troops thus defeated 30,000 Frenchmen, inflicting 3,500 casualties while losing only 1,900 of their own (791 Bavarians). Oudinot had again demonstrated his incapacity for any independent command. The fall of night, the tenacity of the French infantry and the absence of any coherent Allied pursuit plan saved the marshal from a much greater disaster, however. The Bavarians had again performed bravely, if not very successfully, and Wrede was rewarded with a field marshal's baton.[16] For the Allies, although the battle displayed the confusion and poor coordination that so often dogged their efforts, it also brought the painful and discouraging retreat to an end. With Napoleon focussed on the Army of Silesia, the Allied Main Army could resume its slow advance on Paris.[17]

To Paris and Peace

As March opened, V Corps, with the rest of the Main Army, marched west along the now-familiar road from Bar-sur-Aube to Troyes, reaching the latter on 4 March after some brief skirmishing with the retreating French. Wrede left one brigade to garrison Troyes and dispersed the remainder of the corps in villages to the west. Here the men (elements of the cavalry excepted) enjoyed a well-deserved and much-desired week of recuperation as Schwarzenberg probed gently toward Nogent and Bray on the Seine.

On the 14th, learning of successes by Blücher's Army of Silesia far to the north, the Main Army finally resumed its tentative move on Paris, and Wrede received orders to concentrate his corps at Arcis-sur-Aube. But the offensive ran into problems almost immediately and for the next several days, V Corps marched and counter-marched back and forth across the Seine near Arcis as the Allied leaders vacillated between advance and retreat in the light of Napoleon's latest actions. The French Emperor was indeed heading south with all speed in the hopes of getting behind the Main Army and crushing one or more of its individual corps. On the 19th, aware of Napoleon's approach but grossly overestimating his strength, Schwarzenberg directed Wrede to hold the line of the Aube against the oncoming French while the rest of the Allied host assembled at Troyes. That day, the French crossed the Aube in force west of Arcis, while Schwarzenberg, this time thinking offensively for a rare moment, drafted orders to position the army to launch a concentrated attack on the 20th.

The morning of 20 March thus found the bulk of the Allied army (III, IV and VI Corps and the Russo–Prussian reserves) moving on Arcis from the south and south-east. Wrede, on the other hand, had withdrawn from the town in obedience to his instructions and was assembling his men some six miles to the east. The French lost no time in occupying Arcis and the outlying villages the Allies had so obligingly evacuated, and Wrede, as at Bar-sur-Aube three weeks earlier, was soon forced into costly assaults against a strongpoint which his men had given up without a fight only hours before. Similarly, as at Bar and La Rothière, the corps would be caught in vicious village fighting during the upcoming battle.

The Allied plan called for Wrede's Austrians and Bavarians (with some attached Cossacks) to attack along the south bank of the Aube while Crown Prince Friedrich Wilhelm of Württemberg led the Allied III, IV and VI Corps against Arcis from the south. As usual, the combined Russo–Prussian Guards and reserves would form the army's second echelon. In all, approximately 88,000 Allied troops were in the process of descending upon some 53,000 French, of whom only 34,000 were truly available for the two-day battle.[18] On the 20th, however, Friedrich Wilhelm led his three corps astray and, with the exception of a grenadier division, a cuirassier division and some artillery, the Russo–Prussian reserves remained out of the brutal affray. As a result, Wrede's V Corps bore the brunt of the fight and suffered far and away the bulk of the casualties.

The Allied offensive ran into problems even before it started when the late arrival of the Crown Prince's troops forced Schwarzenberg to delay the start of the attack by three hours. The signal to advance was finally given at 2 p.m. and by 3 p.m., Wrede's command was heavily engaged all along its battle line: Austrians on the right, the 1st Bavarian Division in the centre with the 3rd Division 300 paces to its rear, and the combined Austro–Bavarian cavalry under Frimont on the left. While a lively mounted contest swirled over the rolling hills south-east of Arcis, the Austrian infantry attempted to gain control of Torcy-le-Grand, the key to the French position.

Although the Habsburg soldiers seized the village in their first onslaught and began to move on Arcis itself, the timely arrival of several battalions of Napoleon's Old Guard stopped them in their tracks. Before long, most of Torcy was again in French hands and a fierce struggle had begun which would continue until after 11 p.m. Fought with the utmost bravery and ferocity on both sides, the battle for Torcy consumed first an Austrian brigade (over 500 casualties) then the Bavarian II/1st Infantry and 3rd Light Battalion (163 casualties total). The combat swung back and forth, but repeated Allied assaults were never able to wrest the village from the French completely.

It was fully dark when the Austrians withdrew, exhausted and out of ammunition. Wrede decided to make yet another effort, this time throwing Franz's brigade, the 1st Brigade of the 3rd Division under Major General Georg Baron von Habermann, at Torcy. Like their predecessors, the men of the brigade fought courageously but were only able to capture and retain a few buildings on the edge of the flaming village. The battered brigade pulled back at 10.30 p.m. after losing 414 men (109 of those from the 7th Infantry), including General Habermann (badly wounded). Among the killed was Lieutenant Carl Sartorius, Franz's companion in the 7th Infantry's charge at Polotsk.[19] Two Russian grenadier battalions drawn from the reserve made a final attempt to take Torcy but, having no more success than the Austrians and Bavarians, they called off their attack sometime around midnight.[20]

The furious fighting on 20 March cost the Bavarians more than 800 men dead, wounded or missing, half of those from Habermann's 1st Brigade alone. Austrian casualties in the corps were also high and Wrede retired to his starting point that night as directed, leaving Torcy-le-Grand in the hands of the French. With no help from the Crown Prince, whose command had wandered far off to the left, and precious little assistance from the cherished Russo–Prussian reserves, V Corps had carried the main weight of the battle on the 20th, and the men now looked for an opportunity to recuperate while Schwarzenberg and his staff tried to craft orders for the following day.[21]

Although the Battle of Arcis-sur-Aube continued on 21 March with the Allies hastening Napoleon's retreat from the town, V Corps did not take part in that day's fighting. Instead, Wrede was sent back to the east to establish himself in a position to block any French effort to turn the Allied right. This march to the east, when the prize of Arcis seemed so close, apparently stirred considerable resentment among the men of the corps.[22] They did not yet know it, but the campaign was rapidly drawing to a close, and the first day's battle at Arcis would be their last significant encounter of the war.

The Allied Main Army now turned, albeit hesitantly at first, toward Paris. Along the way, Lieutenant General Osarovsky's Light Cavalry Division of the Russian Imperial Guard attached to V Corps surprised a French artillery park and captured a number of guns (23 March). Wrede, hurrying forward, spotted the tail end of Marshal MacDonald's retreating command and ordered his infantry to quicken its march, but decided not to employ the available cavalry until the foot soldiers came up in sufficient strength.[23] Although the Bavarian and Austrian infantry pressed ahead in an effort to catch the fleeing French, they arrived too late and the opportunity passed.

Similarly, the Austro–Bavarian cavalry under Frimont pushed ahead of the rest of the corps on 25 March in search of French troops withdrawing on the roads to Paris. Other Allied forces caught the French, however, and Frimont, sweeping far to the right, missed the battle at Fère Champenoise. Nor was the V Corps infantry present for this crucial engagement; it only reached the battlefield after darkness had fallen. Wrede himself, on the other hand, did play a role at Fère Champenoise. Arriving with a small escort of Bavarian chevauxlegers, he was given command of all the Russian cavalry in the area and thus made some contribution to organising the charges that finally destroyed the gallant French 'divisions' of Généraux de Division François Amey and Michel

Pacthod.[24] As the army's rear-guard (Napoleon had marched east after Arcis and thus posed a danger to the army's rear), V Corps also missed the Battle of Paris on 30 March and the triumphant entry of the Allied monarchs into the French capital the following day. Franz and his compatriots were finally afforded a view of Paris on 2 April when V Corps made its own parade through the city. Four days later, Napoleon abdicated. The war was over.

The Bavarians remained in France as part of the Allied occupation force until mid-May. During this brief sojourn, Franz's regiment learned of the death of its proprietor, Lieutenant General Prince Dominik Konstantin von Löwenstein-Wertheim, on 18 April, and the consequent change in the regiment's official title to the simple '7th Line Infantry Regiment' (no new proprietor was named). The regiment also had a new commander, Colonel von Herrmann of the 5th Light Battalion having taken over in late March while the 7th was making its way toward Paris.

The homeward march began on 16 May, but the contingent went into cantonments between Mainz and Frankfurt until the peace was formally announced in early June. While resting along the Rhine, Wrede re-organised his forces, and the I/7th came under the command of Major General Franz Xaver von Deroy (son of the renowned old war-horse who had been killed at First Polotsk) as part of the 2nd Brigade of the new 1st Division (Rechberg).

With the arrival of peace, there was no cause to keep the entire Bavarian contingent in its forward deployment on the French border, and the battalion soon headed for home. The men of the 7th thus grate-fully returned to Neuburg in late June, but the battalion remained on a war footing pending the conclusion of the Congress of Vienna.

The enormous manpower costs of the kingdom's wars since 1812, however, meant that the 7th Regiment, as most other regiments, could not organise a viable 2nd Battalion during 1814. For the remainder of the year, therefore, the regiment consisted of a staff (14), the 1st Battalion (1,010 officers and men) and the 3rd (Reserve) Battalion (306).[25] The 2nd Battalion finally came into being on 1 January 1815, but was still slightly under strength with only 822 officers and men.

The regiment's internal organisation also changed in 1814. In July King Max directed the creation of a Guard Grenadier Regiment, to be formed from the combined grenadier companies of the line regiments. New fusilier companies were formed to replace the missing grenadiers, so that under the new establishment each battalion within the 7th came to comprise one Schützen company and five fusilier companies.

The year 1814 brought one additional significant moment for the Bavarian Army – the return of the men captured during the Russian campaign. A total of 143 Bavarian officers and 680 men who had survived their harrowing captivity in Russia arrived safely at their old garrisons during the course of the year. Of that number, the 7th Infantry could welcome home three captains, three lieutenants and 57 NCOs and men. It is interesting to note that, the privations of their experience as prisoners of war notwithstanding, most of the officers and doubtless many of the men soon resumed their places within the regiment.[26]

The Bavarian contingent had therefore played a central and honourable role in the 1814 invasion of France. Together with their Austrian allies, the Bavarians under Wrede's command had made a significant contribution to each of the Main Army's victories. It was the V Corps attack that compromised Napoleon's left at La Rothière; it was the Bavarians who wrested Bar-sur-Aube from the tenacious French defence on 27 February; and it was V Corps – nearly alone – which carried the lion's share of the horrific house-to-house combat on the first day at Arcis-sur-Aube. Moreover, the senior Allied leaders clearly respected Wrede's capabilities and gave heed to his advice, repeatedly entrusting him with semi-independent missions that placed a premium on operational skill.

Given the disproportionate combat participation of V Corps as compared with the other corps of the Main Army (especially the sheltered Russo–Prussian Guard and reserve formations), one is forced to wonder if perhaps the Allied high command was intentionally using the Bavarians as cannon fodder. As Wrede himself caustically observed to one of the Tsar's adjutants after the Battle of Bar-sur-Aube,

> if it is desired that the troops fight every day and that it is always the same corps who are continually engaged with the enemy, then there should at least be bread and meat to give the soldiers and fodder to feed the horses...[27]

These misgivings notwithstanding, Wrede generally displayed the energy and enthusiasm that had marked his service under Napoleon. Even when his men could not reach the battlefield (as at Fère Champenoise), the field marshal himself endeavoured to take a hand in the action.

Despite the new-hammered nature of the contingent in 1814, despite the large numbers of new recruits, the inexperienced officers, the admixture of line and militia units, the miserable weather and the often severe logistical shortfalls, the Bavarian Army fought well during this difficult winter war, adding new lustre to the honours it had gained as a French ally. The campaign in France was thus a fitting close to the army's combat history in the Napoleonic epoch.

Military Diary of
FRANZ JOSEPH HAUSMANN
for the
FRENCH CAMPAIGN
of the
1st Battalion of the Royal Bavarian
7th (Löwenstein) Line Infantry Regiment
1813–1814

August 1813

14 August	The battalion marched along byroads via Ingolstadt and Neustadt near Neuburg; crossed the Danube near Vohburg.
15 August	Pfeffenhausen, Landshut, Vilsbiburg to Neumarkt on the Rott.
16 August	Continued through Eggenfelden to Marktl near Braunau.
17 August	Back to Untertürken near Braunau into close cantonment. Today the battalion was incorporated into the 1st Brigade of the 3rd Division.
20 August	The battalion was inspected by its brigade commander, Colonel von Rodt.
26 August	His Royal Highness Prince Carl, commander of the 3rd Division, happened to see the battalion parading and expressed his satisfaction.
30 August	The order was received to separate the unit that belonged to the Thorn Garrison from the battalion.
31 August	The detachment belonging to the Thorn garrison went to Burghausen, where from it the 4th Company of our battalion formed one battalion, and a portion [of this battalion] was given to our 1st Company along with one officer [so as to form a second new battalion]; these two newly formed battalions immediately proceeded on to the Tyrol.[28]

September 1813

1 September	The remaining group of officers and non-commissioned officers to Mühldorf.
2 September	To Haag.
3 September	To Schwaben.
4 September	To Dachau.

215

5 September To Odelzhausen.

6 September To Augsburg, where the 7th was a day of rest.

8 September To Breitenbrunn.

9 September To Krumbach.

10 September To Weissenhorn.

[The following material concerns Franz's leave from the battalion and was inserted in the diary.]

October 1813

8 October   I began my leave, going from Weissenhorn to Kempten.

14 October   From there to Munich, where I arrived on the 15th and left again on the 23rd. On the 24th I arrived back in Kempten.

27 October   Left there again and via Aichholz-Memmingen to Osterberg. In Memmingen two and in Osterberg two rations of forage.

28 October   Through Weissenhorn to Günzburg; here received two rations of forage.

29 October   Near Dillingen, two rations of forage from the quartermaster. To Donauwörth.

30 October   Via Rain to Neuburg on the Danube. Here received four rations of forage.

November 1813

1 November Via Monheim (two rations of forage) to Oettingen.

2 November To Dinkelsbühl (two rations of forage).

3 November Via Crailsheim (two rations of forage) and Ellwangen to Hall (2 rations of forage).

4 November Via Oehringen (two rations of forage) to Heilbronn. Since I left two boxes in the chaise that I took from here, Police Commissioner Schiko or Tax Director Milius will have kept them in custody.

5 November Via Möckmühl (two rations of forage) to Buchen. Here two rations of forage, and wrote to the above police commissioner.

6 November Via Walldürn to Miltenberg. Here two rations of forage.

7 November   Via Obernburg (one ration of forage) to Aschaffenburg (two rations of forage).

8 November   To Dieburg (two rations of forage), because I did not receive my marching route until the afternoon.

9 November   Via Darmstadt (two rations of forage) to Bensheim (two rations of forage).

10 November   Via Weinheim to Heidelberg. Here eight rations of forage, and met up with the battalion.

[End of insertion.]

October 1813

21 October   The remainder of the Thorn garrison marched to Dillingen.

22 October   To Donauwörth. Here across the Danube.

23 October   To Nördlingen.

24 October   To Dinkelsbühl.

25 October   To Ansbach.

26 October   To Rothenburg.

27 October   To Würzburg. Here crossed the River Main.

28 October   To Miltenberg.

29 October   To Aschaffenburg. Here crossed back over the Main.

30 October   To Hanau. Here the battalion engaged in a battle and was forced back by a Cossack volley.[29] Lost three officers dead and five officers wounded.

31 October   This unit joined up with the 1st Battalion, which was in bivouac before Hanau.

November 1813

1 November   To Frankfurt on the Main, and crossed that river.

4 November   To Pfungstadt.

5 November   To Darmstadt.

6 November   To Lauterbach.

7 November   To Weinheim.

10 November   To Heidelberg.[30]

11 November   Via Bruchsal to Langenbrücken.

12 November	To Grünwettersbach near Durlach.
13 November	To Kuppenheim near Rastatt.
14 November	To Bühl.
15 November	To Pappelwied near Appenweier.
16 November	To Griesheim 1½ hours from Kehl.
18 November	To Ichenheim and Dundenheim (and into cantonment).
21 November	The battalion staff to Dundenheim.

December 1813

1 December	Kittersburg and Goldscheuer.
2 December	Bivouacked near Sundheim in support of the outposts.
4 December	Back again to Goldscheuer in the evening. Into cantonment.
6 December	Went into cantonment in Kippenheim near Lahr and Mahlberg for the time being.
8 December	The battalion arrived in Herbolzheim.
9 December	The battalion was quartered in Forchheim.
10 December	The battalion was quartered in Neuershausen near Eichstetten. Day of rest there on the 11th.
12 December	The battalion to Kiechlingsbergen into the new cantonment.
18 December	Our battalion entered into the new cantonment as follows: the staff and four companies to Bötzingen, and the 3rd and 7th Fusilier Companies to Oberschaffhausen.
19 December	Arrived at Tunsel, and on the
20 December	day of rest there.
21 December	In Hertingen.
22 December	Crossed the Rhine at Basel, and then into quarters in Allschwill.
23 December	To Nieder-Ranspach [Ranspach-le-Bas].
24 December	To Dannemarie.
25 December	To Fontaine et Chèvremont, Phaffans, Menoncourt, Lacollonge.
27 December	To Ballersdorf near Dannemarie.
30 December	From Ballersdorf back again to Dannemarie.

January 1814

1 January	To Niederspechbach.
2 January	To Wattwiller.
3 January	To Wintzenheim.

5 January	To Dambach.
10 January	Bivouacked on the mountain behind the village of Wisembach.
11 January	At St Dié, outpost duty on the Lunéville road.
12 January	Back to St Dié, and into quarters.
13 January	To Rambervillers, the whole division into quarters.
16 January	To Socour.
17 January	To Haroué.
18 January	To Pleuvezain.
19 January	To La Neuveville [-sous-Châtenois].
21 January	To Vrécourt.
27 January	To Daillecourt.
28 January	To Bologne.
29 January	To Doulaincourt.
30 January	To Mussey.
31 January	To Trémilly.

February 1814

1 February	A battle[31] took place, in which our battalion came to be positioned at the centre. Toward 2.30 the battalion received the command to support a battalion of the Imperial Austrian [1st] Szekler Infantry Regiment, which had been ordered to storm the village of Chaumesnil. We advanced en colonne as far as the village and then immediately drove the two French battalions from their position by storm. In this were wounded Colonel von Rodt, Captain von Hacke, Lieutenants Count von Voltolini, Heilmann and Benzel, as well as one non-commissioned officer and 31 men, and further, one corporal and one private remained on the field. At night the battalion bivouacked near this village.
2 February	The battalion advanced and went into bivouac near Brienne. On this day Colonel von Rodt died at Trémilly.
4 February	In Jessains-sur-Aube.
5 February	Bivouac near Vendeuvre [-sur-Barse].
7 February	Echemines.
9 February	Avon-la-Peze.
11 February	Trainel.
12 February	Crossed the Seine near Bray and on outpost duty before the village of Mouy.

13 February	A half hour from Donnemarie the battalion joined the troops near Luistaines and remained in position in the field on outpost duty.
14 February	Bivouac near Gurcy-le-Chatel.
17 February	The Army Corps was attacked near Villeneuve and forced back. The battalion received the command to observe the right flank from its bivouac. Toward 4 o'clock in the evening the corps retreated back to our battalion, and here the battalion assumed the position of rear-guard, fighting as it withdrew; the battalion remained before Donnemarie for another three hours, crossed back over the Seine near Bray, and on the
18 February	at 2 o'clock in the morning went into its bivouac one hour the other side of Bray.
19 February	Camp near Macon close to Nogent [-sur-Seine].
20 February	Camp near Fontaines [-les-Gres]. Here the battalion took up battle position with the full Army.
22 February	At 4 o'clock in the morning withdrew in this order until two hours before Troyes.
23 February	Started out at 2 o'clock in the morning, marched through Troyes and across the Seine, and then immediately behind the latter took up position.
23 February	At 12 o'clock midnight started out and marched into camp at Lusigny [-sur-Barse].
24 February	Here the battalion was placed under the command of General of the Cavalry Baron von Frimont, who had ordered this same village on the left of the road occupied. At 5 o'clock in the afternoon the battalion withdrew en colonne as far as the bridge before Montiéramey and received the order to defend it. The entire [Allied] cavalry crossed over this bridge, and the enemy cavalry also wanted to use it to cross, but it was thrown back by [our] musket fire.

At 7 o'clock in the evening the enemy attempted to force this bridge en colonne, but he was again stopped by the well-aimed crossfire from our muskets, and it was not until after 9 o'clock that our battalion received the command to withdraw, defending itself by firing in irregular order, whereupon the enemy gave the battalion a hard chase until beyond Montiéramey, and from there allowed this battalion, which formed the rear-guard, to continue unnoticed, and thereupon the latter

25 February	proceeded into camp at Bar-sur-Aube at 7 o'clock in the morning.
26 February	Took up position behind the city in the afternoon. Toward evening the enemy took the city, pushed through the centre, to where the battalion was positioned, and was again forced back into the city by lively artillery fire.
27 February	The enemy was beaten back by the right flank of the Allies, and so he again abandoned the city. In the evening the battalion again moved into camp outside the city.

March 1814

2 March	To Vendeuvre.
4 March	To Troyes, crossed the Seine.
5 March	To Pavillon [le Pavillon Ste Julie] near Troyes.
13 March	To Premierfait.
14 March	To Allibaudières.
15 March	To Saron [-sur-Aube].
16 March	To Fait. Halted here for one hour, then marched directly to near Villenauxe, took up outposts there, and at 9 in the evening again set forth, and on the
17 March	at 4 o'clock in the afternoon to Pouan [-les-Vallées]. Here crossed the Aube near Arcis.
18 March	To Allibaudières. Crossed back over the Aube near Arcis.
19 March	At 7 o'clock in the morning to Coclois.
20 March	Advanced toward Arcis, and at some distance took up various positions. Toward 6 o'clock in the evening the battalion was directed to storm the village of Torcy-le-Grand. This was repeated three times, and each time repulsed with considerable loss, but between 8 o'clock and 9 o'clock at night entered into bivouac near Vaupoisson.
21 March	In the morning again took up battle order, and late in the evening marched across the Aube to Lesmont.
22 March	To Donnemont.
23 March	Near Bréban.
24 March	Near Courdemanges.
25 March	Near Maisons [-en-Champagne].
26 March	Near Fère Champenoise.
27 March	Near Meilleray.
28 March	Near Chailly.

29 March	Near Quincy.
30 March	Near Meaux. Here crossed the River Marne.
31 March	Near Chelles.

April 1814

1 April	Near Charenton close by Paris.
2 April	Near Rongis.
10 April	Near St Maur.
11 April	Near Gouvernern (in quarters).
12 April	In Couilly near St Germain.
14 April	To Mouron into quarters near Coulommiers.
15 April	To St Simeon near la Ferté Gaucher.
16 April	To Réveillon near Esternay.
17 April	To Sézanne.
19 April	To Ecury-le-Repos near Sommesous.
20 April	To Maisons near Vitry [-le-François].
21 April	To Contrisson.
23 April	To Bazincourt near Bar-le-Duc.
24 April	To Vaux-le-Grand near Ligny.
25 April	To Vouthon-Haut.
26 April	To Rouvres-la-Chétive.
28 April	To Grimonviller.
29 April	To Nancy.
30 April	To Hellimer.

May 1814

1 May	To Wattweiler near Zweibrücken.
2 May	To Saargemünd [Saareguemines].
4 May	To Leywiller and Altripe.
5 May	To Nebing and Torswiller.
6 May	To Chateau Salins into cantonment.
16 May	To Bissting.
17 May	To Lüchsheim.
18 May	To Buchsweiler [Bouxwiller].
19 May	To Haguenau.
21 May	To Sallenbach.
22 May	To Wörth and Pfortz close to the Rhine.
23 May	To Germersheim.
25 May	To Dudenhofen and Harthausen.

26 May	To Frankenthal.
27 May	To Eppelsheim and Hangenwiesheim.
30 May	To Bingert and into cantonment at Ebernburg.

June 1814

7 June	To Bacharach, Mannbach, Stenge, and into cantonment in Kleindibach.
10 June	To Wöhrstadt close to Mainz.
11 June	Through the city of Mainz and crossed over the Rhine at 11 o'clock in the morning; then the battalion took up quarters in Frefordt.
12 June	In Grolzimmern.
13 June	In Grossostheim.
14 June	In Milteburg.
15 June	In Wesebach.
16 June	In Würzburg.
17 June	In Ochsenfurt in the Würzburg district.
18 June	Ermatshofen close to Uffenheim in Bavaria.
19 June	In Ansbach.
21 June	In Kronheim near Gunzenhausen.
22 June	In Weissenburg.
23 June	In Dollnstein near Eichstätt.
24 June	In Neuburg on the Danube.

◆•:◎•✳•◎:•◆

LETTERS FROM
THE CAMPAIGN IN FRANCE[32]

Letter No. 5

Dannemarie
The last day
of 1813

Best of Parents,

[Yesterday] I duly received your letter of the 16th of this month, and I shall not delay in informing you at once of my [complete] good health. From a sense of filial responsibility and the certain conviction that I can never sufficiently prove to you my indebted thanks for all the things you have done for me and the good advice you have given me on every occasion, I send you my most heartfelt good wishes for the present new year. I cannot say more than to beseech the Almighty for your continuing health. I must remain silent about the feelings that fill my breast for your happiness, because I am too weak to express them. May Heaven grant us peace soon, so that I may return to the arms of my dearest parents.

By now you have probably received my Letter No. 4 of the 23rd of this month. In it I told you that we crossed the Rhine at Basel. On the 23rd we marched from Allochwier to Nieder-Ranspach, the 24th Dannemarie, and the 25th to Fontaine near Belfort, where the fortress was besieged by the First Division, while the Second Division remained by Hüningen and undertook the siege there. On the 26th, however, the well-known adventurer Colonel Scheibler, who had 600 Cossacks, 300 Szekler hussars and 300 chevauxlegers from the 7th Bavarian Regiment with him, was attacked near Colmar by 3,000 French cavalry. Because of this, on the 27th we had to retreat a quarter hour from here to Ballersdorf, in order to observe the road from Colmar, and yesterday we arrived back here.[33]

Yesterday and last night Hüningen was fired upon by 42 and Belfort by 28 heavy pieces, such as 24-, 36- and 12-pound cannon as well as howitzers. The noise has been continuously pounding around here in the midst of these fortresses all night long.

At the moment we have no news at all. With Scheibler's corps there are the following chevauxlegers left: Captain Hirschberg and a first lieutenant, as well as 60 soldiers. In short, our people have suffered most. Some sorties were made against the fortresses, in which much was lost, but, as with most sorties, their success was negligible. We did take a few prisoners, but not many.

It appears that I expressed myself poorly in my letter of the 11th

of this month, for you know my nature and my principles too well
than to think that I would allow myself to be beaten down by a chance
occurrence. It is true that many unpleasant things can make a momentary
impression on me, but I shall nevertheless stand like a man, and,
moreover, to me it does not seem a tragedy that I was even more content
in battle than before. In addition, I assure you, dear Father, that I shall in
any case act with reason and like a man.

I freely admit that if there were no overriding circumstances I could
bring myself to marry Fanny, whom you know about, and I am convinced
that you, my dear Parents, would have no objections to my choice and
would not withhold your approval, if you knew her. She comes from a
good family, has been brought up in a truly exemplary manner, and has
the most noble nature in the world. In short, I do not want to say too
much, or else you might think my prejudice spoke in her behalf. If I ever
come back, God willing, it will be time enough to [speak] of this.

My idea of having the seal sent to me was only in case one of you
was going to Neuburg. I am again sending this letter to Seipelt, so it will
not cost so much postage. By the way, I have decided to set aside 25
francs per month, beginning in January, and if it is feasible I shall allot
this amount to you. On no account shall I use it myself.

If you can get the money for the Legion of Honour, then you need
only send me the receipt, which I shall sign and send back to you.

If you should have occasion to go to the chief military cashier,
please ask him if the package that I mailed on the 18th of November has
arrived. This enclosed the separate receipts from Bienenthal and me for
the money received in Munich in recompense for the baggage lost by the
officers in question. It was addressed to the Chief Military Finance
Officer, and if he has not received it, please ask him to set our minds at
rest by returning the original receipt.

The disturbances of the Tyrolean rebels are indeed disgraceful, and
we have already read about this in the newspapers.

If after six months the capital has been correctly repaid by taxes,
then one can look forward to the interest.

Mr Caro is well and still is a clown.

My saddle is in the large package, and the gold watch is in the box.

We, too, are terribly plagued with work.

Farewell. Give my regards to Mrs Wisner, and rest assured that I
shall always be,

Your most devoted son,

Franz

The air and climate are very healthful here, in spite of the fact that for a few days now we have had snow a knife-blade high. Incidentally, if we remain in France for another three months, I shall learn French. I can already get along in it.

⋆⋅▷◦✳◦◁⋅⋆

Letter No. 8

**Camp near Brienne
in Champagne
3 February 1814**

Best of Parents,

We had a very hot day on the first of this month. Our battalion, together with a Szekler infantry battalion, had to storm the town of Chaumesnil. General Count Wrede and His Excellency Baron Frimont were very satisfied with the battalion's performance. Our good Colonel von Rodt was unfortunately wounded in the head and died of his wounds yesterday. Captain Hacke and Lieutenants Voltolini, Heilmann and Benzel were all only lightly wounded, however. Our battalion has one non-commissioned officer and one private dead, as well as one non-commissioned officer and 31 men wounded, in spite of the fact that we had only four companies, as the light infantry formed one battalion and the 7th Company had to cover the artillery.[34]

If the courier were not about to leave, I would give you a detailed description of the battle, which turned out so well for our arms. It was really fine, although also murderous. Our left flank under the Crown Prince of Württemberg seized 41 cannon, and we in the centre captured 15 cannon. Few prisoners were taken. The emperor himself was in command against us. At 300 paces he himself set three pieces against our battalion when we were in the town.

Major von Fortis of the light battalion is now in command of our battalion. Both brothers are well, and neither has had the slightest thing happen to him. All of us have only our colonel to mourn – how his good wife must be suffering.

The major begs you to tell his sister-in-law that her husband and his brother are well at the moment. Hacke and Heilmann were hit by ricochets, and Voltolini and Benzel were grazed.

I am, thank God, as healthy as a fish, although I had one misfortune. Five days ago I left my purse in my quarters that morning, because I was not feeling well. As soon as I noticed it was missing, I immediately sent someone back for it, but it was no longer there, because some Austrians had come into the quarters right afterwards. I thereby lost five or six louis d'or. Fortunately I had some silver in my belt, so I still have something at least.

All the same, I am content. God has given, and He can also take it away from me again. After all, I survived the battle, so what more can I ask? I owe God many thanks for that.

Dearest Parents, the departing courier tells me to hurry. So I wish you well. Rest assured that we shall now no longer become involved in affairs, for many Russians and Austrians have marched on ahead, and the French are constantly retreating.

I am, as always, my dearest parents' ever faithfully obedient son,

Franz

Letter No. 9

Vendeuvre
3 March 1814

Best of Parents,

Thank God, I am again able to write to you. The newspapers will have already told you about our fortunate and unfortunate incidents. In my last letter of the 3rd of February I had no time left to enclose the route we had taken, because the departing courier practically had to wait for me to finish. I therefore belatedly include it here. From Vrécourt we marched on the 27th of January to Daillecourt, where, because I did not feel well in the morning as we were leaving and even during the night, I had the misfortune of leaving behind my purse with all my gold, which consisted of about five louis d'or, and two rings that I valued highly. The next morning I immediately sent someone back to see the pastor with whom we had been quartered, but there was nothing to be found, since some Austrians had moved into quarters there right after us.

On the 28th to Bologne, the 29th to Doulaincourt, the 30th to Mussey. Here began our poor living in bivouac. On 31 January we already came across the enemy at Trémilly, where in the evening we took part in a small skirmish between the outposts, because as the First Battalion of the Third Division we usually act as vanguard, and then we remained at the outposts in Trémilly with the cavalry.

On the 1st of February we advanced to Chaumesnil, where the famous battle of Brienne[35] started, in which our battalion undertook the brilliant storming of Chaumesnil, successfully carried it through, but lost its good colonel. After the town had been completely taken, the battalion was ordered to assemble behind the last house, and the colonel, who was behind this house facing backwards, looked on, satisfied with the outcome of the attack. However, as the battalion was assembling, in what was thought to be a safe place, he was shot in the back of the head, and this caused his death.

On the 2nd the army corps advanced to Brienne, the 4th to Jessains-sur-Aube, the 5th to Vendeuvre, the 7th through Troyes and across the Seine to Echemines, the 9th to Avon-la-Peze, the 11th to Trainel, and on the 12th we advanced to Bray, where the bridge over the Seine was destroyed, crossed in boats under the thunder of cannon that the French outposts maintained on the opposite bank, and set up outposts outside the village of Mouy. On the 13th an affair began at Luistaines, wherein we again stood in the middle. According to the orders of the day the 1st Grenadier Company lost their plumes because of cowardice in this affair.[36]

During this night we remained at the outposts, the likes of which I have never seen. The entire battalion was distributed to the right and left along the road in such a way that three men stood at every 50 paces, so that we were strung out in an outpost line of three hours' march in length. On this day the enemy had taken up a very fine position, in which he could not be attacked frontally. But during the night he withdrew of his own accord, and a large number of deserters came over to us and stated that the enemy force was made up of three divisions of the army from Spain, who had been brought to this affair in wagons.

On the 14th we advanced through Donnemarie to Gurcy, up to which point the battalion continued to occupy the vanguard. On the 15th the other battalions advanced to Villeneuve. On the 17th the Russian corps under the command of Count von Wittgenstein, which had pushed on ahead of us on the right side of the road, was defeated and, at the same time that ours was attacked at Villeneuve, was thrown back on our battalion. We then took over the rear-guard, withdrew fighting to Donnemarie, held this town for two hours longer so that all the wagons and artillery had time to cross the bridge, and then withdrew that same night to Bray.

During the night of the 19th we withdrew, as the bridge had previously been destroyed, back to Macon near Nogent, and during the night of the 20th back into camp at Fontaines, where three army corps were drawn up in battle formation. Since, however, the enemy did not dare attack us but rather went around us, on the morning of the 22nd we then set out before daybreak and marched back in this formation to two hours away from Troyes.

In this same manner on the 23rd we marched through Troyes at

2 o'clock in the morning and crossed the Seine to take up a position on the other side of the river. We set out again at 12 midnight and arrived at Lusigny on the morning of the 24th. Here our battalion, and an Austrian one, were put under the command of General Baron Frimont and, with the cavalry, constituted the rear-guard as far as the bridge by Montiéramey, where the cavalry passed over the bridge in greatest haste. As the last of them crossed, the enemy cavalry also wanted to cross in our direction, but they were driven back by our fire. At night the enemy infantry came on in column and forced the bridge, but were driven back again. Since we could not sustain ourselves, however, we had to withdraw, and the enemy pursued us sniping at our heels, until after an hour we were met by others.

On the morning of the 25th we reached Bar-sur-Aube. On the 26th the enemy took the town, and we took up a position behind it. Here we met with the enemy without flinching. On the 27th quite a stiff battle took place, in which the enemy forces were defeated by the Russians on the right flank. They had to leave the city and were pursued by the Russians. We moved into our camp and stayed there until yesterday, when we marched here. Today heavy cannon fire can be heard at Troyes, and we are now standing in reserve.

I had the great good fortune to be preserved in all these dangerous moments.

Continuation on 5 March 1814 at Pavillon

Yesterday we marched out of Vendeuvre for Troyes, where we crossed the Seine and went into quarters. Today we came here, three hours' march from Troyes, where we are to remain in cantonment (as the order says), except everyone is in bivouac, because most of the houses are burned down. Only the officers may stay in the ruined houses. Here are also the division commander, General Delamotte, the brigade commander, General von Habermann, as well as General of the Cavalry Baron Frimont. Our stay here may last five or six days. On the 10th Napoleon will pronounce the ultimatum for the peace negotiations. Probably the battle in which he engages Blücher (on whom he is advancing with 40,000 men) will dictate the outcome. The weather here is still fairly raw.

Sergeant Kaiser will receive the Imperial Russian Order of St George, 5th Class, in a few days. This consists of a silver cross that has on one side the member's number and the initials of Tsar Alexander and on the other side a picture of the knight St George. Six of these decorations were given to the division. From the newspapers and army orders you will probably have seen who have received Austrian, Russian and Prussian medals.

Our battalion has again gone down quite a lot, for according to today's report there are 405 men in the field hospital. I would never have believed that such shortages could occur in this country. During the withdrawal for over one week we received no bread, no meat, no salt; in short, no food at all. And here we sustain ourselves very meagrely by foraging parties. In spite of this, those of us who are with the staff (Major Fortis, Captain Schmid, now brevet major, the battalion physician, Dr. Knittelmeier, and I) still live well, especially since we are near Troyes.

On the retreat almost all the villages on and near the road were burned down. If we have to go back the same way, it will go hard with us for two days. Bar-sur-Aube was totally plundered, because the inhabitants shot at our people with window lead. Troyes also suffered considerably at the beginning.

If only we are not forced to withdraw any farther, for otherwise we shall lose a great deal. During the affair and withdrawal of the 24th our battalion lost more than 100 men. We had two dead and 52 wounded.

When you have occasion please write me whether you have already received the 25 francs that I have had deducted since January, or why not. Captain Schenk of the Leib Regiment [1st Infantry Regiment, renamed König in 1811, but still known by its old title] was shot through the throat at Bar-sur-Aube and he cannot talk. I saw him and he asked me in writing to tell you that he sends many regards to you both. Also Captain Schmeckenbecher, First Lieutenant Zinn, in short, all the gentlemen whom you know, especially the administration chief, Economic Counsellor Knopp, asked me to send you their compliments. Lieutenant Lachner (who was shot through the cheek and nose on the 24th) also sends you his regards; he has gone back to Neufchâteau.

The bitter cold, which, along with incredible discomfort, we have to endure in this primitive cantonment, forces me to close, and I am, as always, unto death,

My dearest and best father's and mother's ever most obedient son,

Franz

When you have a chance, please tell Mrs Fortis that both Majors Fortis are hale and hearty, and give my respects to my friend Wisner and all who know me.

Letter No. 11

Couilly near Crecy
13 April 1814

Dearest Father and Mother,

Today I again have a chance to write, and this time I can do so in somewhat greater detail than on the 30th of last month, when I wrote quickly on my lap in the rain under a hut in order to communicate to you the happy event of the taking of the city of Paris.

Now we are on the way to our cantonment, which our corps will occupy in the two departments of Meurthe and Vosges, and it appears that there is no longer any possibility of war.

Upon the proclamations of the Parisian Senate, which are surely already well known, the majority of the French marshals defected with their corps, and the rest will follow, for, according to the deserters who have come to us, the whole army seems to have dissolved. Officers of all ranks, marshals, soldiers, in short everyone, ran away and came to Paris, from where everyone can go on leave.

My letter of the 5th of last month was the last time I informed you of our marching route. I shall thus continue it. We remained in Pavillon near Troyes until the 13th, when we crossed the Seine at Méry to Premierfait. The 14th we marched across the Aube at Arcis to Allibaudières, the 15th to Saron, and the 16th through Faux to near Villenauxe. Since, however, Napoleon was meanwhile moving from Chalons toward Arcis, on the evening of the 16th we then had to withdraw from Villenauxe, and on the 17th we reached Pouan, after having gone through Arcis and crossed the Aube. On this march many members of the train remained behind, all of whom were captured.

On the 18th we again advanced through Arcis to Allibaudières, where we were driven back by the enemy in the evening, and we again marched through Arcis on the morning of the 19th to Coclois. On the 20th we advanced toward Arcis and took up various positions in battle formation under the loudest cannon fire imaginable. At about six o'clock in the evening the battalion, as well as the 1st and 2nd Regiments, were commanded to storm the village of Torcy-le-Grand. Although we had the support of the Austrians of our corps, the 3rd Battalion of the Mobile Legion,[37] and numerous artillery, it was nevertheless impossible, after being driven back three times by the French guard and foot gendarmes, for us to take this village, and we therefore left it to the enemy. I told you last time what our battalion suffered on this occasion. In Paris we saw Major Gneis, who had been wounded three times, and Lieutenant Kaiser has already come back from captivity, and Major Fortis is to arrive tomorrow.

At dawn on the morning of the 21st, as also the day before, we went into battle formation and advanced in this manner. But since during the night the whole of Barclay de Tolly's[38] Corps had joined us and had raised our numbers to 110,000 men and 120 cannon, and Napoleon had only 60,000 men and 80 cannon to oppose us with, he therefore rejected this proffered battle and immediately withdrew back through Arcis toward Vitry. The Crown Prince of Württemberg pursued him, and that same evening we marched across the Aube at Lesmont, the 22nd to Donnemont, the 23rd to Bréban. On the 24th we saw the entire French army defiling along the road from Dosnon to Sompuis toward Vitry, and we accompanied them as far as Courdemanges near Vitry, keeping to their right flank. This caused Napoleon to push through at Vitry and move toward Brienne and Bar-sur-Aube, in order to mislead us, because Blücher was coming toward us from St Manhoult.

It is true that, on the 25th when we came to Villers via Loisy and could no longer find the enemy, we were in doubt over whether to pursue the emperor or not, but on our marshal's suggestion it was decided to send 20,000 men of the cavalry and artillery after him. We spent the night at Maisons and set out for Paris on the 26th. Between Coole and Soudé Ste Croix we met the enemy force, consisting of 35,000 men under the command of Marshal Marmont, who were trying to get through to the emperor, and they were then overthrown by the vanguard and relentlessly pursued. Two squares were crushed, and a total of over 10,000 men, 55 cannon and nearly 300 wagons filled with munitions, baggage, field equipment and other supplies fell into our hands.

We spent the night at Fère-Champenoise, on the 27th at Meilleray, and on the 28th at Chailly between la Ferté Gaucher and Coulommiers. On the 29th we learned that Napoleon was again pursuing us, and we remained at Quincy. On the 30th we arrived at Meaux, where it developed that Napoleon had taken the route on the other side of the Seine toward Fontainebleau. On the 31st we learned of the fall of Paris at Chelles, where we spent the night. On April 1st we camped at Charenton, half an hour from Paris. On the 2nd we passed through a part of the suburbs and across the Pont d'Austerlitz to Rongis, where we camped, and we remained there until the 10th. On this day we marched out of Paris across the Seine to St Maur in bivouac, the 11th to quarters in Gouvern near Lagny, and yesterday to here, where we have a day of rest today.

Continuation on 18 April 1814 at Sézanne

On the 14th we marched to Mourou near Coulommiers, the 15th to St Simeon near la Ferté Gaucher, the 16th to Reveillon near Esternay, and yesterday here. Today we again have a day of rest. We now know our marching route for the future. We shall go to an extended cantonment in the departments of Meurthe and Vosges. Our march there will go on the

19th to Sommesous, the 20th to Vitry, the 21st to Berthes, the 23rd to Bar-le-Duc, the 24th to Ligny, the 25th to Comercy, the 26th to Toul, which is the first town in the Department of the Meurthe. Not until we are there shall we learn of our cantonment post.

Up to now I have not received your Letter No. 5 of 26 January, and No. 6 of 12 February is also the last one I got. I hasten to answer the latter herewith.

I now no longer doubt that peace will ensue, for in the orders that we received it says that His Excellency Marshal Count Wrede will remain with the court camp of the supreme allied powers, in order to attend to the interests of His Majesty the King of Bavaria, and that we are to march into the above-mentioned cantonment during the armistice and until the subsequent final peace treaty. Further news or reports from His Excellency go so far as to say that we shall not move into this cantonment at all but shall even sooner be given the command for the final march home. This is truly most to be desired, for I am pretty fed up with war. May God in His mercy only grant that we see each other soon, and that my wishes may be fulfilled.

It is true about Steidel, and I would rather not even mention this weakness to you, because I consider it too petty.

I recall that on the address side of one of your letters there was a notation in an unfamiliar hand asking if I wanted to sell my sash, and for how much. Although I do not know who wrote this, I still wanted to ask you about it, and I forgot about it because of the hostile incidents that were still going on. But now I do want to reply to you about this, and to assure you that you well know that you can do what you wish with my things. I no longer need this sash, and you also know what it cost, so get rid of it, if you have someone who wants it.

From my Letter No. 10 from Meaux you will have seen what more we lost in the affair at Arcis. I thus add only that Major Fortis and Lieutenant Kaiser have been released from captivity.

I greatly bemoan the fate that has until now deprived me of the possibility of having the certificate issued that you wanted. I saw General Maillot only while we were under fire or en route. Major Fortis will certainly object if I ask it of him, in view of his timid nature, and furthermore you have probably already obtained it from Major Andrian, who can issue it more easily, because all the registers are with the Reserve Battalion, and it would be too late now anyway. Nevertheless, should you still not have it, please write me. I shall then approach Major Fortis about it in our new cantonment.

Captain Schmid is quite well. I spoke with him several times, and he told me much about you. He sends you his regards.

I do not lack for money, and I have all I need. Sergeant von Schmitz also joined us in time to go to Paris, for all hostile incidents were over, and he was present for only the most enjoyable part.

Now I want to tell you briefly that I liked Paris quite well. This city is fantastically large; it is more than 10 hours in circumference, and more than 800,000 people live in it. Everything that one can imagine can be bought there. It is illuminated day and night by innumerable shops or boutiques. The Palais Royal, a large rectangular square surrounded by many buildings, is a world unto itself, because there alone everything can be had. In short, I shall tell you much more about it orally, if the Almighty permits. You will have already read in the newspapers all the proclamations that were published in Paris.

Since another courier is leaving from Vitry, you will receive this letter by this opportunity, and I remain as ever and for always,

My dearest parents' most faithfully obedient,

Franz

If we should remain in the new cantonment for some time, then I shall send you my receipt for the credited half-year's pension for the decoration and ask you to withdraw it. Please extend my warmest regards to Wisner and all who know me.

Notes to Chapter Seven

[1] These Allied figures, drawn from Esposito/Elting, reflect numbers in late December; combat strength soon dropped as detachments were left off to blockade fortresses and secure lines of communication.

[2] Initially, only those Mobile Legion battalions which had participated in the Battle of Hanau were honoured with the title 'National Field Battalion'; in March 1814, all Mobile Legion units were renamed.

[3] For the difficulties encountered in filling leadership positions in the new militia see Erich Freiherr von Guttenberg, 'Die bayerische Nationalgarde II. Klasse in den Befreiungskriegen', *Darstellungen aus der Bayerischen Kriegs- und Heeresgeschichte*, Heft 22, Munich: 1913.

[4] Strength figures and notes on composition drawn from Lothar Schmidt, 'Das K. B. Korps Wrede im Feldzuge 1814', *Darstellungen aus der Bayerischen Kriegs- und Heeresgeschichte*, Heft 17, Munich: 1908. Note that these figures represent officers and men 'present under arms', the total of 'effectives'

(which included those detached or in hospital) was 32,441. The most significant detachment was the force blockading Würzburg (1,314).

[5] In early 1813, the Bavarian Army administration designated each battalion still serving in the field (that is, the remnants of VI Corps: Zoller's Brigade at Thorn and Rechberg's small division) as the 1st Battalion of its regiment; the battalions remaining in Bavaria were thus considered the 2nd Battalions of their parent regiments. Most of the battalions that marched off with Raglovich for the autumn campaign in Saxony were therefore 2nd Battalions (the II/7th for example), and the battalions reconstructed from reserves, new recruits and the returning members of Zoller's and Rechberg's commands became the new 1st Battalions. See Heinrich Demmler, 'Die Neubildung des bayerischen Heeresabteilung nach dem Rückzuge aus Russland 1812 und die Ereignisse bis zum Rückkehr in die Heimat 1813', *Darstellungen aus der Bayerischen Kriegs- und Heeresgeschichte*, Heft 15, Munich: 1906; Demmler, 'Anteil der Bayerischen Division Raglovich am Frühjahrsfeldzuge 1813', *Darstellungen aus der Bayerischen Kriegs- und Heeresgeschichte*, Heft 16, Munich: 1907; and Georg Gilardone, 'Bayerns Anteil am Herbstfeldzuge 1813', *Darstellungen aus der Bayerischen Kriegs- und Heeresgeschichte*, Heft 22, Munich: 1913.

[6] These are the Bavarian chevauxlegers Franz mentions in Letter No. 5, 31 December 1813: the 6th Squadron of the 7th Chevauxlegers Regiment (formerly the National Chevauxlegers Regiment). Scheibler's detachment was roughly handled by a strong French cavalry force on 24 December (not the 26th as Franz writes); Scheibler himself suffered three wounds, and the Bavarian squadron lost both its officers and more than half of its troopers. Scheibler's detachment was disbanded on 16 January 1814. Note that Schmidt says the detachment also included a squadron of Hessians. See Schmidt, pp. 5–7, 19; and Constant von Wurzbach, *Biographisches Lexikon des Kaiserthums Oesterreich*, Wien: Zamarski, 1856–91.

[7] Blockades were established at Hüningen, Schlettstadt [Sélestat] (both observed by Bavarians) and Neufbrisach (Austrians). The total force detached was eight Bavarian battalions, eight Bavarian squadrons and three Austrian battalions. See Schmidt, pp. 14–15.

[8] The Army of Silesia and the Main Army actually overlapped each other at this point, so that Wrede and Wittgenstein were to Blücher's right rear.

[9] Strength figures from F. Loraine Petre, *Napoleon at Bay*, London: Arms and Armour, 1977, p. 30. Another 34,000 men were posted behind the Allied main line (Russian and Prussian Guards and reserves); of these, at most perhaps 7,000 were engaged. Had the Allies wanted to develop La Rothière into a truly decisive battle, a total of some 125,000 men (possibly up to 140,000!) could have been brought to bear against Napoleon's paltry 45,000.

[10] Grenz Regiment/Grenzer: troops from Austria's 'military border' in the Balkans (*Grenze* = border).

[11] Account compiled from Auvera (pp. 547–8) and Schmidt (pp. 29–40);

supplemented by Friederich, Janson and Max Ritter von Hoen,
Die Hauptarmee 1814, vol. V of *Oesterreich in den Befreiungskriegen 1813–1815*,
Wien: Patriotische Volksbuchhandlung, 1912.

[12] The 7th Infantry was also present for an engagement on the 13th that ended in a French withdrawal. Auvera, pp. 549–50.

[13] Ibid., p. 552. Allied complaints about poor logistic support were common in this campaign.

[14] Auvera, p. 551–2.

[15] Schmidt, p. 65.

[16] The 7th Infantry was not engaged at the Battle of Bar-sur-Aube.

[17] Compiled from Schmidt supplemented by Friederich, Hoen and Janson.

[18] Janson, vol. II, pp. 275–6.

[19] Habermann survived his wound and died in 1825. See Chapter 5 for Franz's description of the 7th's charge at Polotsk.

[20] Timing from Schmidt; Hoen's account places the Russian attack much earlier in the night (approximately 8 p.m.). The Russians were from Lieutenant General Tschoglikov's 1st Grenadier Division.

[21] Schmidt (p. 111) points out that there are no reliable figures for V Corps' strength under arms on the 20th; nor was he able to uncover reasonable data on Austrian losses from the corps; the figure available (1,382) seems much too high unless it includes numerous missing and stragglers who later found their way back to their battalions.

[22] Ibid., p. 110.

[23] This account reflects Schmidt's interpretation. Janson severely criticises Wrede for not taking advantage of this moment to attack MacDonald's force (vol. II, p. 301).

[24] Wrede's actual role here is not clear. Janson (who shows little regard for the field marshal) dismisses his presence and Friederich does not even mention him. Regardless of his actual contribution, the fact that the Allied monarchs saw fit to place a large mounted force under his orders is testimony to the respect they held for him.

[25] Strengths as of 1 October 1814 (Auvera, pp. 563–4).

[26] At least five of the officers were listed with the regiment on 1 October 1814; the fate of the other is not clear from the regimental history, nor does Auvera specify how many of the NCOs and other ranks returned to their duties with the 7th. (ibid., pp. 562–5).

[27] Wrede to Max Joseph, 5 March 1814, Schmidt, p. 79.

[28] Although Franz's diary entry is unclear, it is known that the returned survivors of the Thorn garrison were used to form two provisional battalions in August 1813. Known as the 1st and 2nd Thorn Battalions, they were commanded by Lieutenant Colonels Herrmann and Merz (formerly of the 7th Infantry) respectively and were used to quell unrest in the Tyrol. Though desperately needed to rebuild his army, Max Joseph personally

decided that the men from Thorn could not rejoin their home units because they had given their pledge not to fight against the Allies. There was no hindrance on using them against the rebellious Tyroleans. See Gilardone.

[29] The reference to a Cossack volley (*Kosacken décharge*) is unclear. A 'friendly fire' situation? Franz misunderstanding events he only heard of second-hand (he was not present at the Battle of Hanau)? According to Auvera's regimental history, the battalion was roughly handled by some French cavalry during the battle, but there is no mention of Cossacks.

[30] Here Franz rejoined the battalion.

[31] The Battle of La Rothière.

[32] From this series of letters only Nos. 5, 8, 9 and 11 have been preserved.

[33] The Bavarian 7th Chevauxlegers Regiment was formed in 1813 as a militia unit with the title 'National Chevauxlegers Regiment'. It was granted the numeral and placed in sequence with the regular line chevauxlegers regiments before embarking on the campaign. The fight to which Franz refers actually occurred on 24th December, not the 26th.

[34] The Bavarians apparently formed an *ad hoc* light battalion for at least part of the 1814 campaign by pooling the Schützen companies of several battalions.

[35] Although Franz refers to this engagement as the Battle of Brienne, it is known to military history as the Battle of La Rothière. Brienne, which is nearby, gave its name to a series of engagements between Napoleon and the Army of Silesia in the closing days of January.

[36] The company involved in this incident was the 1st Grenadier Company of the 8th Infantry Regiment. The grenadiers were accused of withdrawing from a defensive position unnecessarily, and Wrede punished them by publicly denying them the right to wear the coveted red plumes (*Huppen*) on their helmets which distinguished them as grenadiers (Schmidt. p. 52; Auvera, p. 550). See illustration.

[37] Franz's use of the title 'Third Battalion of the Mobile Legion' is unclear.

[38] Prince Michael Barclay de Tolly (1761–1818) commanded the Russo–Prussian Guards and Reserves.

Chapter Eight

'The Happiest Years of My Youth'

Bavaria participated in one final war during the Napoleonic era – the campaign of the Hundred Days in 1815 occasioned by Napoleon's escape from his exile on the island of Elba. The Allied leaders from 1813–14 were still gathered in Vienna, dickering over the settlement of innumerable questions of territory and compensation, when word of Napoleon's landing in France reached them in early March 1815. Quickly putting aside their many disputes, the powers of Europe, great and small, immediately began to prepare for war against the returned French Emperor. Schwarzenberg, again designated as the overall commander, hoped to invade France in June or July, but Napoleon hit first, striking into Belgium in an attempt to defeat Blücher's Prussians and the Duke of Wellington's Anglo–Allied force before his other foes could start their operations. The ensuing Waterloo campaign brought Napoleon's defeat on 18 June and his abdication four days later. The Napoleonic Wars were over.

Bavaria contributed an army of some 60,000 men to the Allied cause in 1815. Organised into four divisions under Wrede, it was an impressive contingent, but Minister Montgelas, concerned for the kingdom's shaky financial situation, found it more than a little extravagant. In his opinion, the size of the force,

> sprang from the ambition of Prince Wrede, burdened us with the support of an over-large army, which was commensurate with neither the population nor the resources of the realm... But his desire to command, to shine thereby, and to enhance his image through a strong army; this consideration pushed every other into the background.[1]

Although this large force duly entered France on 18 June, its combat experience was limited to a few insignificant encounters with French outposts and garrisons from the 23rd to the 25th. Wrede pressed on for Paris more or less on his own initiative, but the victors of Waterloo reached the French capital far ahead of the Bavarians. In any event, Napoleon had already given up his claim to the throne, and Wrede's men were detailed off to occupation duties by the middle of July. The Allies levied a heavy war indemnity on the prostrate foe and maintained an occupation force, including approximately 10,000 Bavarians, in France until 1818 when the new regime in Paris finally managed to hand over the last sou.

Although still technically in uniform, Franz did not participate in what he called 'the military promenade to France in the year 1815'.[2] He was already on leave status, studying economics as he prepared for a new career as a civil official. In 1818, when the last of the Bavarian occupation troops returned from duty across the Rhine, Franz graduated from university and left the army. Throughout his life, however, he cherished the memory of his military service and retained an enduring pride in his achievements with 'the 7th Infantry Regiment, in whose ranks I spent the happiest years of my youth'.[3]

Franz was not alone in his nostalgia for his years in uniform under Napoleon. Despite the horror of experiences such as the retreat from Russia, despite the nationalist sentiment that swept much of Germany in the early to mid-nineteenth century, Napoleonic veterans' groups flourished in Germany in the decades following the French Emperor's second abdication. Proudly wearing their crosses of the Legion of Honour, publishing songs and poems to 'the hero Napoleon', they preserved a memory and contributed to the Napoleonic legend,

> But nothing matches the thrill
> when our bright eyes
> envisage the Emperor
> who led us to fame and victory,
> who glorified France's throne,
> and was a true father to us![4]

In his voluminous writings[5] we have no indication that Franz belonged to any such organisation, indeed it seems unlikely he would have been drawn to one, but his impression of Napoleon as 'the greatest man of our times' was shared by many German survivors of the *Grande Armée*. For Franz, as for other German veterans, this experience of service in the Napoleonic Wars, particularly those halcyon days under the Emperor himself, became the most intense, most vivid years of their lives, defining experiences of danger, camaraderie and glory that outshone the more secure but less exhilarating era they inhabited after 1815.

Notes to Chapter Eight

[1] Quoted in Junkelmann, p. 341.

[2] From Franz's account of the First Battle of Polotsk in Auvera. p. 485. *See also* Chapter 5.

[3] Ibid.

[4] Words from the song written for the Founding Festival of the Veterans' Association of Former Napoleonic Soldiers in Krefeld, August 1848; reprinted in Carl Schehl, *Vom Rhein zur Moskwa 1812*, Krefeld: Obermann, 1957. See Sauzey (pp. 350–1) for similar quotations from a book called *Liederbuch für die Veteranen der Grossen Napoleonarmee von 1803 bis 1814*, published in 1837.

[5] Other than the extracts quoted in Appendix 2, Franz's many post-1815 letters to his children are not included in this volume.

Appendix 1

BATTLES AND ENGAGEMENTS*

Including Sieges Inside and
Outside of Fortresses

* This list was compiled by Franz and provides some additional material on his campaigns and the only information from him on his service in the war of 1806–07.

1805

3 December	Battle near Stecken in Moravia, lasted 3½ hours.
5 December	Engagement near Stecken in Moravia, lasted from 2 o'clock in the afternoon [of the 5th] until the 6th.

1806/07

10 October	Besieged Kulmbach in Prussia until 11 October.
7 November	Besieged Gross-Glogau in Silesia until 3 December.
8 December	Besieged the fortress of Breslau [Wroclaw] in Silesia continuously until 7 January 1807. On 30 December some regiments of the besieging corps had an engagement with the corps of Prince Pless near Strehlen, which lasted three hours.
14 May	Crossed the Narew near Pultusk in Poland under heavy cannonade lasting half an hour.
16 May	A persistent, five-hour engagement near Pultusk.
22 June	A few insignificant vanguard skirmishes near Luski in Poland.

1809

18 April	A cannonade on the Landshut road near Mühlhausen lasted one hour.
19 April	Battle near Abensberg in Bavaria, began at 11 o'clock in the morning and lasted until almost 6 o'clock in the evening, when it was interrupted by a driving rain, but
20 April	in the morning it started up again and lasted the whole day, and as far as Pfeffenhausen.
21 April	Battle on the Schlossberg [mountain] near Landshut lasted from 11 o'clock in the morning until 5 o'clock in the evening.
22 April	Skirmishing on the Vils as far as Frontenhausen with enemy stragglers.

24 April	Stubborn and significant engagement near Neumarkt on the Rott from 11 o'clock in the morning until late at night, when the corps withdrew to Vilsbiburg.
29 April	Some skirmishing before Salzburg on the Salzach; hereupon the city was taken by storm.
11 May	The pass near Lofer in the Tyrol was taken after a two-hour encounter.
12 May	On its march to St Johann the corps was often harassed by insurgents.
13 May	A three-hour encounter at the Kleiner Zoll [toll house] near the Gratenbrück [bridge], but afterwards continuous torment from the insurgents firing from the mountains.
14 May	Took the city of Rattenburg by storm and were pursued again all day by the insurgents on the nearby mountains.
15 May	A 1½-hour encounter at the Ziller bridge, constantly accompanied by the shots of the insurgents on the side, and in the evening burned down Schwaz with howitzer fire, as also all the single houses standing on the roads.
16 May	A vigorous engagement at Schwaz, after which the town was taken by storm and no inhabitant was spared.
6 July	Battle near Wagram lasted until the 8th. Pursued the enemy on the 9th and skirmished near Laa on the Thaya.
10 July	Battle near Znaim was continued on the 11th.

1812

7 August	An engagement near Polotsk on the Dvina.
11 August	An engagement near Walenok on the Drissa.
13–15 August	Skirmishing by the outposts near Muschek.
16 August	Outpost skirmishing near Polotsk.
17 August	Battle near Polotsk
18 August	continued in the afternoon and did not become murderous until today.
22 August	Heavy engagement near Beloe.
4 September	Took the city of Disna, insignificant skirmishing with Cossacks on the Dvina and the small river of the same name [Disna].
17 October	Battle near Polotsk on the 18th and stubbornly prolonged on the 19th, and on the night of the 19th withdrew across the Dvina.
20 & 21 Oct	Continuous cannonade from both banks.

22 October	A brief Cossack attack on the night of the 22nd during the march.
24 October	In the evening an engagement near Kuplice during the retreat, lasting half an hour.
5 December	The great retreat began, and lasted until
28 December	when we arrived at Plock on the Vistula.

1813

20 January	Garrison in the fortress of Thorn, where the siege began on the 23rd and under daily shooting and raids lasted until
18 April	concluded.

1814

2 & 3 Dec	Small outpost skirmishing before the fortress of Kehl outside of Strasbourg, and on 22 December insignificant cannonade near Hüningen.
26 & 27 Dec	Skirmishing near the fortress of Belfort.
5 January	Skirmishing near the fortress of Schlettstadt.
1 February	Battle near Brienne. Storming of the village of Chaumesnil, which went on into the 2nd.
12 February	Cannonade and crossed the Seine near Bray.
13 February	Engagement near Luistaines lasted from 10 o'clock in the morning until late at night.
17 February	Rear-guard engagement from 10 o'clock in the evening until toward morning around Gurcy-le-Chatel near Bray.
24 February	Significant rear-guard engagement near Montiéramey, until on the morning of the 25th toward Bar-sur-Aube.
26 February	Battle near Bar-sur-Aube, which continued on the 27th.
4 March	Pursued the enemy near Troyes.
18 March	Rear-guard skirmishing near Allibaudières.
20 March	Battle near Arcis and three times stormed the village of Torcy-le-Grand.
24 March	A small cannonade near Courdemanges not far from Vitry-le-Français.
26 March	Engagement near Fère Champenoise and constant pursuit of the enemy.
1 April	Spent the night before the fort of Vincennes.

Appendix 2

ADVICE TO HIS SON

Franz took a lively and detailed interest in the education of all his many children, but he devoted particular attention to the military career of his eldest son, Otto Hausmann, especially in regard to finances, behaviour and prospects for promotion. He corresponded frequently and inspected practically every dimension of the young man's existence. As a cadet and later an artillery officer, Otto probably found this paternal scrutiny oppressive, but the letters also show a concerned and loving father who hoped to help his son by sharing his own experiences and deep religious faith. Of more immediate concern to modern military historians, however, are several excerpts from this extensive correspondence that shed additional light on Franz's personal history, uncover some little-known aspects of military life in the Napoleonic age and tell us something about the attitudes of small-state Germans in the years between Napoleon and Bismarck.

On Napoleon

Letter of 16 May 1844 All great men, and they should be your models, made diligent use of their youth to prepare themselves for life; only so could they become great and famous, so that they stood out above the thousands, even millions of ordinary souls. Napoleon, the greatest man of our times, was, like you, trained in a military school (Brienne). The same was true of Schiller, the greatest poet, who was trained at the Karl's School for officers' sons in Ludwigsburg and later in Stuttgart.[1]

On Promotion

Letter of 17 December 1845 Just remember that French is still the most important thing besides the general subjects of study, for this language is especially useful toward becoming an adjutant and for joining the quarter-master general's staff, and only these two branches lead to more rapid promotion.

Letter of 25 October 1850 In general, a young officer should take advantage of every opportunity to wait upon staff officers and their wives from time to time. Therefore, you should associate with such comrades as often carry out social duties.

On Military Life

Letter of 27 May 1848 As rules of conduct I give you the following for your consideration:

1) That you should not put your silver money in your chest of drawers, because one of the servants could have a key to it and steal it from you. Give it, as long as you do not need it, to your landlord to keep for you, or to one of your staff officers. Your gold, however, you should always carry on you well secured in your wallet, for a young man who still lacks experience in the world is often robbed.

2) Never let your orderly touch your trunk or chest of drawers. Never give him the key to take any clothing out. Always do this yourself. There are cases in which orderlies have stolen all kinds of possessions from their masters, and how can you take reprisals against such persons?

3) Often check through your clothing, for orderlies often wear their masters' boots, underwear, etc. and ruin them, so that very often new acquisitions are necessary, which the masters would not need if they had paid proper attention. The master must also cover the laundry cost in these cases.

4) Move into your quarters at once, as you can more easily pay the couple of days until the end of the month at the monthly rent rate than at the rate in an inn, where it costs much more, especially since for that time you would have to eat[2] at the same inn, which is also much more expensive.

5) When you get a horse, keep the forage under your strict lock and key, perhaps in an adjoining area, and allow the groom to take out only as much as he needs for each feeding, so that the stablemaid cannot throw your forage over to the cattle standing in the same stable, making the masters often wonder why their horses look so shabby, because their fodder is being taken away from them without their masters' knowledge.

6) One of your main tasks is to study the character of your comrades in whose company you find yourself. If you find them to be moral and good fun, stick with them; but if you have any doubts, then try to remove yourself little by little from their company, without thereby offending them or letting them realise that you look down on them, so that you do not end up in arguments.

7) When you are on guard duty with men from the lower ranks, you should regale the men on the watch with beer, but not so much that any of them become drunk. This might cost you each time – depending upon how many of them there are – perhaps 24, 30 or 48 kreuzer. You must not let yourself be drawn into more. Also, your comrades will perhaps visit you and drink a few glasses of beer with you, and be offered at most some bread and cheese. Only no drunken brawl should be allowed to develop, least of all with wine. A staff officer never condones such things.

Letter of 7 June 1848 When I was an adjutant and 20 years old, I bought a raw team horse and trained it for riding. Later I also always did that, and bargained for the horses the way Lieutenant Reineck probably has done, and in so doing I always so calculated that I never had a loss from horse transactions. A horse always cost me 9 to 12, never 15, louis d'or, and that was their value. Today, when they are more expensive, the handsomest cost up to 18 louis d'or. Anything above that is a luxury. For breaking them in add another 5 louis d'or at most, though I always did this myself.

Even though I accept that it is simpler for you to obtain a horse that has already been well broken in, nevertheless, the price of 30 louis d'or is much too high for someone who does not have a large fortune at his disposal. Is there in Germersheim [Otto's garrison] no non-commissioned officer who breaks horses in? In that case, you could buy a nice riding horse and have it broken in, which would not make nearly such a demand on the funds you have at hand as would the projected purchase for 33 [sic] louis d'or.

It is not very difficult to train a horse to become used to gunfire, especially in a garrison and fortress, where some exercise or other is being carried out almost daily. I have never had regular riding lessons, but by talking to experts I learned everything necessary for handling a horse, and by practising on my own I learned to ride well. After the proper training my horses stood firm, both among firing cannons and in skirmishes, and adjutants [as I was] have far less time to spend training their horses than do cavalry and artillery officers in the line and in the batteries. So think the matter over carefully (in buying a horse one should never be in too much of a hurry!).

Letter of 22 July 1848 Consider all these suggestions [on the purchase and maintenance of uniforms and other articles] from all sides of wisdom and economy. Only you must in all circumstances keep the rule in mind that the amount of your possessions should not exceed your needs, because an officer can never count on having a steady place of assignment but rather must always be ready to move at a moment's notice, and on marches, etc. too much baggage is an enormous inconvenience. How many things have been lost in this way? "One God and one jacket" was the general rule among us old soldiers, and that suited us fine, because in my day the earlier frock coats had been discontinued and the later ones not yet introduced. One uniform (with epaulettes) and one dress coat <u>were</u> our total outfit.

Letter of 7 May 1849 If you should march out into any battle, always place your complete trust in God. He will preserve those who love Him from every and all danger. Do everything demanded of you with cheerful and steadfast courage. God will always be with you if you walk unfailingly in His ways and turn away from sin. The soldier who has faith in God must not think that any ball has been poured for him, and this conviction, along with a short prayer, such as the one the old Prussian Dessauer[3] used to offer up, gives him courage. That is, undertake everything with serenity and reflection, meaning do not be too foolhardy, but also let no weapon scare you away from doing your duty, and at the right moment take considered action. The main thing for the artillery is technology, so the most important task of an officer in handling his defences, even under the mightiest thunder of the guns, is to use and apply the same calm and assurance as on the training field.

But especially be humane to your enemies. Never use your weapon to cause arbitrary destruction. Go only as far as duty and orders from above demand, especially against unarmed fellow citizens. The prisoner and defeated and unarmed person is no longer our enemy but rather our friend and brother.

Letter of 25 October 1850   The steadfast person is the pearl among officers and is always sought out, respected and loved by his superiors and comrades. This distinction fell to me when I was a lowly fourier, when I was being truly pressured to be put up for officer – which I steadfastly refused from 1806 to 1808 – and when I was still a young lieutenant, much older people, even captains, felt honoured to be my friends.

Notes to Appendix 2

[1] The Karlsschule was an academy for officer candidates established by Württemberg.

[2] Emphasis here and later in the original.

[3] Leopold I of Anhalt-Dessau (1646–1747), known as 'The Old Dessauer', was one of the leading military figures of early eighteenth century Europe, probably best known for the reforms he introduced into the Prussian Army. His prayer may be rendered as follows:

'Heavenly Father, graciously assist me this day; but if Thou should'st not be so disposed, lend not, at least, Thy assistance to those scoundrels, the enemy, but passively await the issue.'

With thanks to Philip Haythornthwaite for supplying this information.

Appendix 3

THE LIFE OF
FRANZ JOSEPH HAUSMANN

Date	Assignment/Event
25 Feb 1789	Born in Aachen.
January 1799	First mentioned in records of 4th Grenadier Regiment; assigned to 3rd Company as cadet (*Fourier-Schütze*).
1 Apr 1799	Assigned to depot of the *Leib* Regiment.
1 May 1799	Leaves service temporarily.
1 Nov 1804	Assigned to 7th Infantry Regiment as *Fourier-Praktikant*.
1805	**Campaign against Austria (diary)**
14 Sept 1805	Departs Neuburg on the Danube.
17 Jan 1806	Returns to Neuburg on the Danube.
1806–07	**Campaign against Prussia (neither diary nor letters)**
1 Nov 1806	Promoted to *Fourier* in 1st Grenadier Company.
1809	**Campaign against Austria (diary)**
17 Mar 1809	Departs Neuburg on the Danube.
1 Aug 1809	Promoted to second lieutenant in Reserve Battalion.
1 Sept 1809	Appointed as regimental adjutant in 7th Infantry.
18 June 1810	Returns to Neuburg on the Danube.
1812	**Campaign against Russia (diary and letters)**
4 Mar 1812	Departs Neuburg on the Danube.
19 Aug 1812	Temporarily assigned as brigade adjutant.
25 Sept 1812	Member of the Legion of Honour.
10 Nov 1812	Returns to duty as regimental adjutant.
Jan–April 1813	**Siege of Thorn (diary)**
1 June 1813	Promoted to first lieutenant.
26 July 1813	Returns to Neuburg on the Danube.
1813–14	**Campaign against France (diary and letters)**
8 Oct 1813	Departs on leave from regiment.
10 Nov 1813	Rejoins regiment for campaign against France.
24 June 1814	Returns to Neuburg on the Danube.
1 Dec 1814	On leave status; enters university in Augsburg.
1815	**Waterloo Campaign (no active role)**
1 Apr 1815	Adjutant in Reserve Battalion.

From 1818	**Civil Official (letters to Otto)**
21 Apr 1818	Completes university.
30 Apr 1818	Leaves army; enters civil service.
16 Sept 1824	Prison Inspector in Kaiserslautern.
17 Mar 1826	Regional Commissioner in Pirmasens.
7 Jan 1834	Regional Commissioner in Neustadt on the Haardt.
28 Oct 1843	Royal Counsellor in Neustadt on the Haardt.
1850	Royal Counsellor in Speyer.
25 Oct 1852	Knight of the Order of St Michael.
30 July 1856	Dies in Neustadt while on holiday.

Sources Hausmann family papers; Bavarian War Archives, *Personalakt* for Franz Joseph Hausmann, file OP 78406. Notes in parentheses indicate extent of surviving original material.

Appendix 4

THE LIFE OF
JOHANN WILHELM HAUSMANN

Date	Assignment/Event
16 Sept 1759	Born in Jülich.
18 July 1777	Joins 14th Fusilier Regiment as private soldier.
1780	Promoted to corporal.
1789	To 4th Grenadier Regiment.
1 Apr 1790	Promoted to sergeant.
1799	To 7th Line Infantry Regiment.
1803	Promoted to sergeant-major.

1805 — **Campaign against Austria**
Lost most vision in left eye through infection.

1806–1807 — **Campaign against Prussia**
18 Aug 1807 — Awarded Silver Badge of Honour (*Ehrenzeichen in Silber*).

1809 — **Campaign against Austria**
24 Apr 1809 — Wounded in foot at Neumarkt.
13 May 1809 — Member of the Legion of Honour.

1812 — **Campaign against Russia**
Remained in Neuburg on the Danube.

1813 — **Campaign against Europe**
1 Apr 1813 — Promoted to second lieutenant and assigned to 4th Mobile Legion Battalion of the Rezat District as battalion adjutant.

1813–14 — **Campaign against France**
Battalion adjutant, 4th Rezat District Battalion. 4th Rezat later redesignated 17th National Field Battalion.

1815 — **Waterloo Campaign**
Battalion adjutant, 17th National Field Battalion. Battalion incorporated in 5th Infantry Regiment.

From 1816 — **Continued Service**
12 Oct 1822 — Pension as first lieutenant.
1828 — Awarded Order of Ludwig after 50 years of service.
26 Oct 1833 — Granted honourary rank of captain.
19 July 1840 — Died in Neustadt on the Haardt.

Sources — Hausmann family papers; Bavarian War Archives, *Personalakt* for Johann Wilhelm Hausmann, file OP 78408 (courtesy of Dr. Fuchs); Guttenberg, p. 327.

Appendix 5

THE BAVARIAN INFANTRY REGIMENT

Rank	1804–11	after 1811
Staff		
Inhaber (Proprietor/Patron)	1	1
Oberst (Colonel)	1	1
Oberstlieutenant (Lieutenant Colonel)	1	1
Major	2	2
Adjutant	2	3
Junker (Ensign)	2	3
Regimental Quartermaster	1	1
Auditor	1	1
Regimental Surgeon	1	1
Assistant Surgeon (*1811 Battalion Surgeon*)	2	3
Apprentice Surgeon	2	3
Drum Major	1	1
Musicians	10	14
Provost	2	1
Gunsmith	1	1
Officers		
Hauptmann (*1811 Captain First Class*)	4	6
Capitän (*1811 Captain Second Class*)	5	10
Oberlieutenant (First Lieutenant)	10	16
Unterlieutenant (Second Lieutenant)	20	16
Other Ranks		
Feldwebel (Sergeant-Major)	10	16
Fourier (Quartermaster Sergeant)	10	16
Sergeant	20	32
Corporal	60	64
Fifer	2	4
Drummer	20	28
Gefreite (Lance Corporal)	120	144*
Private soldiers	2380	2048
TOTAL	2691	2437

*Includes 16 pioneers (sappers).

Organisation 1804-1811

Two field battalions per regiment plus depot with two reserve companies.
Each field battalion composed of one grenadier and four fusilier companies.

Organisation after 1811

Two field battalions per regiment plus reserve battalion.
Each field battalion with one grenadier company, one Schützen (light)
company, four fusilier companies.
Reserve battalion with four fusilier companies.

Sources Bezzel, *Geschichte*, pp. 50-56; Münich, pp. 239–46.

Appendix 6

PRINCIPAL BAVARIAN ARMY
COMBAT UNITS 1805–14

Line Infantry Regiments

1805	*1806*	*1811*
1st *Leib* Inf Regt	1st *Leib* Inf Regt	1st Inf Regt *König*
2nd Inf Regt *Kurprinz*	2nd Inf Regt *Kronprinz*	2nd Inf Regt *Kronprinz*
3rd Inf Regt *Herzog Karl*	3rd Inf Regt *Prinz Karl*	3rd Inf Regt *Prinz Karl*
4th Inf Regt *Salern*	4th Inf Regt	4th Inf Regt *Hildburghausen*
5th Inf Regt *Preysing*	5th Inf Regt *Preysing*	5th Inf Regt *Preysing*
6th Inf Regt *Herzog Wilhelm*	6th Inf Regt *Herzog Wilhelm*	6th Inf Regt *Herzog Wilhelm*
7th Inf Regt	7th Inf Regt *Löwenstein*	7th Inf Regt *Löwenstein*
8th Inf Regt *Herzog Pius*	8th Inf Regt *Herzog Pius*	8th Inf Regt *Herzog Pius*
9th Inf Regt *Ysenburg*	9th Inf Regt *Ysenburg*	9th Inf Regt *Ysenburg*
10th Inf Regt *Junker*	10th Inf Regt *Junker*	10th Inf Regt *Junker*
11th Inf Regt *Kinkel*	11th Inf Regt *Kinkel*	11th Inf Regt *Kinkel* (was 13th)
12th Inf Regt *Löwenstein*	disbanded	disbanded
13th Inf Regt	13th Inf Regt	13th Inf Regt (was 14th)
	14th Inf Regt	

Light Infantry Battalions

1805	*1806*	*1811*
1st Light *Metzen*	1st Light *Metzen* (later *Habermann*)	1st Light *Gedoni*
2nd Light *Vincenti* (later *Dietfurth*)	2nd Light *Dietfurth*	2nd Light *Treuberg*
3rd Light *Preysing*	3rd Light *Preysing*	3rd Light *Bernclau*
4th Light *Stengel*	4th Light *Zoller*	4th Light *Theobald*
5th Light *Delamotte*	5th Light *Delamotte* (later *Dallwigk*)	5th Light *Butler*
6th Light *Weinbach*	6th Light *Taxis*	6th Light *Laroche*

Cavalry Regiments

1805	*1811*	*1813*
1st Dragoon Regt *Minucci*	1st Chev Regt	1st Chev Regt
2nd Dragoon Regt *Taxis*	2nd Chev Regt *Taxis*	2nd Chev Regt *Taxis*
1st Chev Regt *Kurprinz*	3rd Chev Regt *Kronprinz*	3rd Chev Regt *Kronprinz*
2nd Chev Regt *Kurfürst*	4th Chev Regt *König*	4th Chev Regt *König*
3rd Chev Regt *Leiningen*	5th Chev Regt *Leiningen*	5th Chev Regt *Leiningen*
4th Chev Regt *Bubenhofen*	6th Chev Regt *Bubenhofen*	6th Chev Regt *Bubenhofen*
		7th Chev Regt *Prinz Karl*

Notes to Appendix 6

1 In addition to the regular formations listed above, a variety of home defence and national guard units were organised in 1805, 1809 and 1813; some of these (most notably the 'Mobile Legions' of 1813–14) also fought outside the confines of Bavaria.

2 Several new cavalry regiments (including two of hussars and one of uhlans) were being raised in 1813–14, but did not complete formation in time to participate in the invasion of France.

3 The 13th and 14th Infantry Regiments never had proprietors, so the rest of the army jocularly referred to them as 'Thunderbolt' and 'Hammerblow' respectively (1809, from Deifl, p. 42).

Sources Bezzel; Münich; Völderndorff, *Kriegsgeschichte.*

Appendix 7

BAVARIAN ORDERS OF BATTLE

The Bavarian Army on 1 October 1805

1st Brigade   Major General Vinzenz Nutius von Minucci
 1st *Leib* Infantry Regiment
 2nd Infantry Regiment *Kurprinz*
 1st Light Battalion *Metzen*
 1st Dragoon Regiment *Minucci*
 'half battery' (five guns, one howitzer)

2nd Brigade   Major General Hippolyth Count von Marsigli
 4th Infantry Regiment *Salern*
 5th Infantry Regiment *Preysing*
 5th Light Battalion *Delamotte*
 2nd Dragoon Regiment *Taxis*
 'half battery' (five guns, one howitzer)

3rd Brigade   Major General Paul von Mezzanelli
 3rd Infantry Regiment *Herzog Karl*
 7th Infantry Regiment
 2nd Light Battalion *Vincenti* (later *Dietfurth*)
 1st Chevauxlegers Regiment *Kurprinz*
 'half battery' (five guns, one howitzer)

4th Brigade   Major General Theodor von Karg
 6th Infantry Regiment *Herzog Wilhelm*
 13th Infantry Regiment
 3rd Light Battalion *Preysing*
 2nd Chevauxlegers Regiment *Kurfürst*
 'half battery' (five guns, one howitzer)

5th Brigade   Major General Franz Xaver Count von Minucci
 8th Infantry Regiment *Herzog Pius*
 12th Infantry Regiment *Löwenstein*
 4th Light Battalion *Stengel*
 3rd Chevauxlegers Regiment *Leiningen*
 'half battery' (five guns, one howitzer)

6th Brigade   Major General Heinrich Justus von Siebein
 9th Infantry Regiment *Ysenburg*
 10th Infantry Regiment *Junker*
 6th Light Battalion *Weinbach*
 4th Chevauxlegers Regiment *Bubenhofen*
 'half battery' (five guns, one howitzer)

Artillery Reserve one battery (ten guns, two howitzers)

Sources Leyh, p. 455; Völderndorff, *Kriegsgeschichte*, Book 3, pp. 226–7. Note that the 11th Infantry Regiment is not included above because it remained in Düsseldorf.

Forces near Iglau on 1 December 1805

Commander   Lieutenant General Karl Philipp Baron von Wrede

Cavalry
1st Chevauxlegers Regiment *Kurprinz*
2nd Chevauxlegers Regiment *Kurfürst*
3rd Chevauxlegers Regiment *Leiningen*
4th Chevauxlegers Regiment *Bubenhofen* (arrived 1 December)

3rd Brigade   Major General Hippolyth Count von Marsigli
3rd Infantry Regiment *Herzog Karl*
7th Infantry Regiment
2nd Light Battalion *Dietfurth*

5th Brigade   Major General Franz Count von Minucci
8th Infantry Regiment *Herzog Pius*
12th Infantry Regiment *Löwenstein*
4th Light Battalion Stengel

Artillery   one battery

Reinforcements   (arriving on 4 December)
2nd Dragoon Regiment *Taxis* (from 2nd Brigade)
two companies of 4th Infantry Regiment (from 2nd Brigade)
Wrede's other artillery battery (had initially remained at Mautern)

Source   Völderndorff, *Kriegsgeschichte,* Book 3, pp. 226–7, 293–302.

◄ ►◊►✳◄◊◄ ►

The Bavarian Army in August 1806

1st Division   Lieutenant General Bernhard Erasmus Count von Deroy
1st Brigade   Major General von Raglovich
1st *Leib* Infantry Regiment
10th Infantry Regiment *Junker*
6th Light Battalion *Taxis*
Fussjägers (two companies)
1st Dragoon Regiment *Minucci*
6-pounder battery

2nd Brigade   Major General von Siebein
 4th Infantry Regiment
 5th Infantry Regiment *Preysing*
 1st Chevauxlegers Regiment *Kronprinz*
 6-pounder battery

2nd Division   Lieutenant General von Wrede
1st Brigade   Major General von Mezzanelli
 2nd Infantry Regiment *Kronprinz*
 13th Infantry Regiment
 3rd Light Battalion *Preysing*
 2nd Chevauxlegers Regiment *König*
 6-pounder battery

2nd Brigade   Major General Franz von Minucci
 3rd Infantry Regiment *Prinz Karl*
 7th Infantry Regiment *Löwenstein*
 4th Light Battalion *Zoller*
 3rd Chevauxlegers Regiment *Leiningen*
 6-pounder battery

Reserve Division Lieutenant General Georg Count von Ysenburg-Büdingen
1st Brigade   Major General von Marsigli
 8th Infantry Regiment *Herzog Pius*
 9th Infantry Regiment *Ysenburg*
 1st Light Battalion *Metzen*[*]
 5th Light Battalion *Delamotte*
 4th Chevauxlegers Regiment *Bubenhofen*
 12-pounder battery

2nd Brigade   Lieutenant General von Kinkel
 6th Infantry Regiment *Herzog Wilhelm*[†]
 11th Infantry Regiment *Kinkel*
 2nd Light Battalion *Dietfurth*
 2nd Dragoon Regiment *Taxis*[‡]
 6-pounder battery

[*] 1st Light is missing from the order of battle in Leyh, added here based on Leisner.
[†] Later joined 2nd Brigade, 1st Division.
[‡] Later joined 2nd Division.

Sources Leyh, Anlage 2; Leisner; see also Sauzey, pp. 51–5; and Völderndorff, *Kriegsgeschichte,* Book 4, pp. 21–2.

The Bavarian 2nd Division in Poland, 1807

Commander   Lieutenant General the Crown Prince Ludwig

2nd Division   Lieutenant General von Wrede
1st Brigade   Major General Franz von Minucci
  2nd Infantry Regiment *Kronprinz*
  3rd Infantry Regiment *Prinz Karl*
  4th Light Battalion *Zoller*
  one battery
2nd Brigade   Colonel Lessel
  7th Infantry Regiment *Löwenstein*
  13th Infantry Regiment
  3rd Light Battalion *Preysing*
  two batteries
3rd Brigade   Colonel von Pierron
  4th Infantry Regiment
  14th Infantry Regiment
  Light Battalion *Braun*[†]
Cavalry Brigade   Major General Mezzanelli
  2nd Dragoon Regiment *Taxis*
  3rd Chevauxlegers Regiment *Leiningen*

[†] This unit was formed under Major Braun (later Major Peter Palm) from two
  companies of the 6th Light and a Fussjäger company. The other half of the 6th Light,
  also with a Fussjäger company, remained under Lieutenant Colonel Count von
  Thurn und Taxis with Deroy's 1st Division.

Sources Leyh, p. 103; and Völderndorff, *Kriegsgeschichte,* Book 4, pp. 89, 166-7.

◆ ▸◑◈▸◐◂ ◆

Bavarian forces in early April 1809

VII Corps   Marshal François Lefebvre, Duke of Danzig

1st Division   Lieutenant General Crown Prince Ludwig
1st Brigade   Major General von Rechberg
  1st *Leib* Infantry Regiment
  2nd Infantry Regiment *Kronprinz*
  1st Light Battalion *Habermann*
2nd Brigade   Major General von Stengel
  4th Infantry Regiment
  8th Infantry Regiment *Herzog Pius*

Cavalry Brigade   Major General von Zandt
   1st Dragoon Regiment (two squadrons)
   1st Chevauxlegers Regiment *Kronprinz*

Artillery   one light and two line batteries

2nd Division   Lieutenant General von Wrede

1st Brigade   Major General Franz von Minucci
   3rd Infantry Regiment *Prinz Karl*
   13th Infantry Regiment
   6th Light Battalion *Laroche*

2nd Brigade   Major General von Beckers
   6th Infantry Regiment *Herzog Wilhelm*
   7th Infantry Regiment *Löwenstein*

Cavalry Brigade   Major General von Preysing
   2nd Chevauxlegers Regiment *König*
   3rd Chevauxlegers Regiment *Leiningen*

Artillery   one light and two line batteries

3rd Division   Lieutenant General von Deroy

1st Brigade   Major General von Vincenti
   9th Infantry Regiment *Ysenburg*
   10th Infantry Regiment *Junker*
   5th Light Battalion *Butler*

2nd Brigade   Major General von Siebein
   5th Infantry Regiment *Preysing*
   14th Infantry Regiment
   7th Light Battalion *Günther*

Cavalry Brigade   Major General von Seydewitz
   2nd Dragoon Regiment *Thurn und Taxis*
   4th Chevauxlegers Regiment *Bubenhofen*

Artillery   one light and two line batteries

Corps artillery   One light and three reserve batteries

In the Tyrol   Lieutenant General von Kinkel

Infantry
   11th Infantry Regiment
   2nd Light Battalion *Wreden*
   3rd Light Battalion *Bernclau*
   4th Light Battalion *Donnersberg*

Cavalry
   1st Dragoon Regiment (two squadrons)

Artillery   one battery

Source   Gill, *Eagles*, table 2-2.

The Bavarian Corps in June 1812

VI Corps   Général de division Gouvion St Cyr

19th Division   General of the Infantry von Deroy

1st Brigade   Major General von Siebein
  1st Infantry Regiment *König*
  9th Infantry Regiment *Ysenburg*
  1st Light Battalion *Gedoni*

2nd Brigade   Major General von Raglovich
  4th Infantry Regiment *Hildburghausen*
  10th Infantry Regiment *Junker*
  3rd Light Battalion *Bernclau*

3rd Brigade   Major General von Rechberg
  8th Infantry Regiment *Herzog Pius*
  13th Infantry Regiment ‡
  6th Light Battalion *Laroche*

1st Cavalry Brigade   Major General von Zandt
  1st Chevauxlegers Regiment ¶
  3rd Chevauxlegers Regiment *Kronprinz*
  6th Chevauxlegers Regiment *Bubenhofen*

Artillery   four batteries: two light, one line, one reserve

20th Division   General of the Cavalry von Wrede

1st Brigade   Major General von Vincenti
  2nd Infantry Regiment *Kronprinz*
  6th Infantry Regiment *Herzog Wilhelm*
  2nd Light Battalion *Treuberg*

2nd Brigade   Major General von Beckers
  3rd Infantry Regiment *Prinz Karl*
  7th Infantry Regiment *Löwenstein*
  4th Light Battalion *Theobald*

3rd Brigade   Colonel von Habermann
  5th Infantry Regiment *Preysing*
  11th Infantry Regiment *Kinkel*
  5th Light Battalion *Butler*

2nd Cavalry Brigade   Major General von Seydewitz
  2nd Chevauxlegers Regiment *Taxis* ¶
  4th Chevauxlegers Regiment *König*
  5th Chevauxlegers Regiment *Leiningen*

Artillery   four batteries: two light, two line, one reserve
Corps artillery   One light and three reserve batteries

‡ In Danzig with one line battery. ¶ Detached to III Cavalry Corps (17th Light Cavalry Brigade). Remaining cavalry regiments were detached under Seydewitz in July.

Source   Völderndorff, *Kriegsgeschichte*, vol. III, Beilage 1.

The Thorn Garrison, 25 March 1813

Governor   Général de Brigade Jean Poitevin, Baron de Maureillan

French Troops
   Elements of 85th and 108th Line Regiments
   Artillery and sapper detachments (including one Polish battery)

Bavarian Troops
2nd Brigade   Major General Friedrich von Zoller
   2nd Light Battalion
   4th Light Battalion
   5th Light Battalion
   1st Combined Infantry Regiment (from 2nd and 6th Regiments)
   2nd Combined Infantry Regiment (from 3rd and 7th Regiments)
   3rd Combined Infantry Regiment (from 5th and 11th Regiments)

Sources Hösslin/Hagen; and Demmler, 'Frühjahrsfeldzuge'.

The Bavarian Observation Corps[§], 30 March 1813

Commander   Lieutenant General von Raglovich
1st Brigade   Major General von Beckers
   II/3rd Infantry Regiment
   Res/13th Infantry Regiment
   II/4th Infantry Regiment[◊]
   II/8th Infantry Regiment
   Combined 3rd/4th Light Battalion
2nd Brigade   Colonel (later Major General) Maillot de la Treille
   II/5th Infantry Regiment
   II/7th Infantry Regiment
   II/9th Infantry Regiment
   II/10th Infantry Regiment
   Combined 5th/6th Light Battalion
Cavalry   Combined Chevauxlegers Regiment
Artillery   Two foot batteries (12 6-pounders, 4 howitzers)

II = Second Battalion of the regiment shown. Res = Reserve Battalion of the regiment shown.

[§] Later 29th Division of the *Grande Armée*. [◊] This battalion remained behind in Bavaria to watch the border with Thuringia and discourage domestic unrest.

Source Demmler, 'Frühjahrsfeldzuge'.

The Bavarian Corps in 1814
(part of V Corps of the Allied Main Army)

Bavarian Corps   General of the Cavalry Count von Wrede [*]

1st Division   Lieutenant General von Rechberg

1st Brigade   Major General Prince Karl
  1st Infantry Regiment *König* (I, II)
  3rd Infantry Regiment *Prinz Karl* (I)
  10th National Field Battalion
  3rd Combined Light Battalion

2nd Brigade   Major General Maillot de la Treille
  2nd Infantry Regiment *Kronprinz* (II)
  10th Infantry Regiment *Junker* (I)
  11th National Field Battalion
  15th National Field Battalion
  2nd Combined Light Battalion

1st Light Cavalry Brigade   Major General von Vieregg
  1st Chevauxlegers Regiment
  2nd Chevauxlegers Regiment *Taxis*
  7th Chevauxlegers Regiment *Prinz Karl*

Artillery   Two batteries

2nd Division   Lieutenant General von Beckers

1st Brigade   Major General von Zoller
  4th Infantry Regiment *Hildburghausen* (I, II)
  4th National Field Battalion
  9th National Field Battalion
  4th Combined Light Battalion

2nd Brigade   Major General von Pappenheim
  6th Infantry Regiment *Herzog Wilhelm* (I, II)
  13th National Field Battalion
  14th National Field Battalion
  1st Light Battalion *Fick*

2nd Light Cavalry Brigade   Major General von Elbracht
  3rd Chevauxlegers Regiment *Kronprinz*
  6th Chevauxlegers Regiment *Bubenhofen*
  two artillery batteries

3rd Division   Lieutenant General von Delamotte

1st Brigade   Major General von Habermann
  7th Infantry Regiment *Löwenstein* (I)
  11th Infantry Regiment *Kinkel* (I, II)
  1st Lower Danube District Battalion
  1st Iller District Battalion

2nd Brigade   Major General Franz Xaver von Deroy
                       (later Colonel von Treuberg)
  5th Infantry Regiment (I)
  8th Infantry Regiment *Herzog Pius* (I)
  9th Infantry Regiment *Ysenburg* (I)
  5th National Field Battalion
  6th National Field Battalion

3rd Light Cavalry Brigade   Colonel von Diez
  4th Chevauxlegers Regiment *König*
  5th Chevauxlegers Regiment *Leiningen*

Artillery   Two batteries

Corps artillery   four batteries

Roman numerals in parentheses indicate which battalions from each regiment participated in the campaign. For example (I) = 1st Battalion only.

* Wrede also served as commander of V Corps which included approximately 17,900 Austrian troops under General of the Cavalry Baron Frimont. Wrede was promoted to field marshal during the campaign.

Source   Völderndorff, *Kriegsgeschichte,* Book 8, Beilage 1; Janson, vol. I, Anlage IV.

The Bavarian Corps of the Allied Main Army, 1815

Commander   Field Marshal Prince von Wrede

1st Infantry Division   Lieutenant General von Raglovich

1st Brigade   Major General Count Pocci
  3rd Infantry Regiment *Prinz Karl* (I, II)
  5th National Field Battalion
  10th National Field Battalion
  4th Light Battalion

2nd Brigade   Major General von Deroy
  7th Infantry Regiment (I)
  14th Infantry Regiment (I, II)
  11th National Field Battalion
  Upper Danube District Jäger Battalion

2nd Infantry Division   Lieutenant General Count von Beckers

1st Brigade   Major General Baron von Habermann
  9th Infantry Regiment (I, II)
  14th National Field Battalion

15th National Field Battalion
5th Light Battalion

2nd Brigade   Major General von Treuberg
    5th Infantry Regiment (I, II)
    12th Infantry Regiment (I, II)
    2nd National Field Battalion

3rd Infantry Division   Lieutenant General Baron von Delamotte
1st Brigade   Major General Count von Spreti
    6th Infantry Regiment (I, II)
    1st Light Battalion
    6th National Field Battalion
    16th National Field Battalion

2nd Brigade   Major General von Bernclau
    11th Infantry Regiment (I, II)
    2nd Light Battalion
    4th National Field Battalion
    9th National Field Battalion

4th Infantry Division   Lieutenant General Baron von Zoller
1st Brigade   Major General von Radenhausen
    4th Infantry Regiment (I, II)
    8th Infantry Regiment (I, II)
    1st Combined Battalion of the Lower Danube District

2nd Brigade   Major General von Butler
    10th Infantry Regiment (I, II)
    13th Infantry Regiment (I, II)
    Main District Jäger Battalion

Reserve Infantry Brigade   Major General Maillot de la Treille
    Grenadier Guards (I)
    1st Infantry Regiment *König* (I, II)
    2nd Infantry Regiment *Kronprinz* (I, II)
    Rezat District Jäger Battalion

1st Light Cavalry Division   Lieutenant General Prince Karl
1st Brigade: Major General Count von Pappenheim
    1st Chevauxlegers Regiment
    3rd Chevauxlegers Regiment

2nd Brigade   Major General Baron von Diez
    4th Chevauxlegers Regiment
    5th Chevauxlegers Regiment

2nd Cavalry Division   Lieutenant General Count von Preysing
1st Brigade   Major General Baron von Vieregg
    1st Hussar Regiment
    2nd Chevauxlegers Regiment

2nd Brigade: Major General Baron von Elbracht
 2nd Hussar Regiment
 6th Chevauxlegers Regiment

Reserve Cavalry Brigade:
 Garde du Corps
 1st Cuirassiers Regiment
 1st Lancer Regiment

Roman numerals in parentheses indicate which battalions from each regiment participated in the campaign. For example (I) = 1st Battalion only.

Source Völderndorff, *Kriegsgeschichte,* Book 9, Beilage 4.

COMPARATIVE MILITARY RANKS

Bavarian, Austrian and Russian Ranks Used Here	Original Bavarian and Austrian Ranks	Contemporary French Ranks	Modern British or U.S. Equivalents
Field Marshal	Feldmarschall	(no equivalent rank)	Field Marshal or General
General of the Infantry, General of the Cavalry	General der Infanterie, General der Kavallerie or Feldzeugmeister	(no equivalent rank)	Lieutenant General
Lieutenant General	Generallieutenant or Feldmarschall-Leutnant	Général de Division	Major General
Major General	Generalmajor	Général de Brigade	Brigadier or Brigadier General
Colonel	Oberst	Colonel	Colonel
Lieutenant Colonel	Oberstlieutenant	Major	Lieutenant-Colonel
Major	Major	Chef de Bataillon or Chef d'Escadron	Major
Captain	Hauptmann or Kapitän	Capitaine	Captain
First Lieutenant	Oberlieutenant	Lieutenant	Lieutenant, First Lieutenant
Second Lieutenant	Unterlieutenant	Sous-Lieutenant	Second Lieutenant

1 All comparisons are approximate, protocol and functions could vary widely.

2 Later sources commonly use 'Leutnant' in place of 'Lieutenant' in all of the above (e.g. Oberst-Leutnant). Additionally, 'Obrist' was often used in place of 'Oberst' (e.g. Obrist-Lieutenant).

3 The rank of Feldmarschall-Leutnant was unique to the Austrian Army.

4 In the French Army, the title 'Major Général' indicated a function rather than a rank and was unique to Berthier.

5 The French title of 'Marshal' was an appointment rather than a rank.

Bibliography

Adam, Albrecht. *Aus dem Leben eines Schlachtenmalers*, Stuttgart: Cotta, 1886.

Aichner, Ernst. 'Das bayerische Heer in den Napoleonischen Kriegen', in Vol. III/1 of Hubert Glaser, ed., *Krone und Verfassung*, Munich, Hirmer, 1980.

Ainval, Christiane d'. *Gouvion St. Cyr*, Paris: Copernic, 1981.

Auvera, Premierlieutenant. *Geschichte des Kgl. Bayer. 7. Infanterie-Regiments*, Vol. I, Bayreuth: Ellwanger, 1898.

Berg, Franz. *Geschichte des Königl. Bayer. 4. Jäger-Bataillons*, Vol. I, Landshut: Rietsch, 1887.

Bezzel, Oskar. *Geschichte des Königlich Bayerischen Heeres unter König Max I. Joseph von 1806 (1804) bis 1825*, Vol. VI/1 of *Geschichte des Bayerischen Heeres*, Munich, Schick, 1933.

Coignet, Jean-Roche. *The Note-Books of Captain Coignet*, London: Greenhill, 1989.

Corti, Egon. *Ludwig I of Bavaria*, trans. Evelyn B. Graham Stamper,London: Thornton Butterworth, 1938.

Dauer, Joseph. *Das Königlich Bayerische 10. Infanterie-Regiments*, Vol. IV, Ingolstadt: Ganghofer, 1901.

Deifl, Josef. *Infanterist Deifl: Ein Tagebuch aus napoleonischer Zeit*, Eugen Frauenholz, ed., Munich, Beck, 1939.

Demmler, Heinrich. 'Die Neubildung des bayerischen Heeresabteilung nach dem Rückzuge aus Russland 1812 und die Ereignisse bis zum Rückkehr in die Heimat 1813', *Darstellungen aus der Bayerischen Kriegs- und Heeresgeschichte*, Heft 15, Munich, 1906.

Demmler, Heinrich. 'Anteil der Bayerischen Division Raglovich am Frühjahrsfeldzuge 1813', *Darstellungen aus der Bayerischen Kriegs- und Heeresgeschichte*, Heft 16, Munich, 1907.

Döderlein, Oberstlieutenant. *Geschichte des Königlich Bayerischen 8. Infanterie-Regiments*, Vol. II, Landshut: Rietsch, 1898.

Döring, Hans von. *Geschichte des 7. Thüringischen Infanterie-Regiments Nr. 96.*, Berlin: Mittler, 1890.

Dormann, Hasso. *Feldmarschall Fürst Wrede*, Munich, Süddeutscher Verlag, 1982.

Elting, John R. *Swords Around A Throne*, New York: The Free Press, 1988.

Ernouf, Alfred. *Maret, duc de Bassano*, Paris: Didier, 1884.

Esposito,Vincent J., and Elting, John R. *A Military History and Atlas of the Napoleonic Wars*, New York: Praeger, 1968.

Fabrice, F. von. *Das Königlich Bayerische 6. Infanterie-Regiment*, Vol. II, Munich, Oldenbourg, 1896.

Fabry, Gabriel. *Campagne de Russie*, Paris Chapelot, 1900–03

Fabry, Gabriel. *Campagne de 1812: Documents Relatifs a l'Aile Gauche*, Paris: Chapelot, 1912.

Friederich, Rudolf. *Der Feldzug 1814*, Vol. III of *Die Befreiungskriege 1813-1815*, Berlin: Mittler & Sohn, 1913.

Furtenbach, Friedrich von. 'Die Generale des Bayerischen Heeres im Feldzuge gegen Russland 1812/13', *Darstellungen aus der Bayerischen Kriegs- und Heeresgeschichte*, Heft 21, Munich, 1912.

Gilardone, Georg. 'Bayerns Anteil am Herbstfeldzuge 1813', *Darstellungen aus der Bayerischen Kriegs- und Heeresgeschichte*, Heft 22, Munich, 1913.

Gill, John H. *With Eagles to Glory*, London: Greenhill, 1992.

Gill, John H. 'What Do They Intend? Austrian War Aims in 1809', in *Selected Papers of The Consortium on Revolutionary Europe 1996*, series editor Donald D. Horward, Florida State University, 1996.

Guttenberg, Erich Freiherr von. 'Die bayerische Nationalgarde II. Klasse in den Befreiungskriegen', *Darstellungen aus der Bayerischen Kriegs- und Heeresgeschichte*, Heft 22, Munich, 1913.

Hoen, Max Ritter von. *Die Hauptarmee 1814*, Vol. V of *Oesterreich in den Befreiungskriegen 1813–1815*, Wien: Patriotische Volksbuchhandlung, 1912.

Holzhausen, Paul. *Die Deutschen in Russland 1812*, Berlin: Morawe & Scheffelt, 1912.

Holzhausen, Paul, ed., Maillinger, Joseph. 'Tagebuch des Hauptmanns Joseph Maillinger im Feldzuge nach Russland 1812', *Darstellungen aus der Bayerischen Kriegs- und Heeresgeschichte*, Heft 21, Munich, 1912.

Hösslin, R. von, and Hagen, E. 'Die Vertheidigung von Thorn', *Darstellungen aus der Bayerischen Kriegs- und Heeresgeschichte*, Heft 3, Munich, 1894.

Janson (no forename given). *Geschichte des Feldzuges 1814 in Frankreich*, Berlin: Mittler und Sohn, 1903.

Junkelmann, Marcus. *Napoleon und Bayern*, Regensburg: Pustet, 1985.

Kircheisen, Friedrich M., ed. *Feldzugserinnerungen aus dem Kriegsjahre 1809*, Hamburg: Gutenberg, 1909.

Koch, Jean Baptise, ed. *Mémoires d'André Masséna*, Paris: Bonnot, 1966.

Leisner, Georg. 'Die Bayerische Brigade Vincenti in Schwedisch-Pommern und auf Rügen im Jahre 1807', *Darstellungen aus der Bayerischen Kriegs- und Heeresgeschichte*, Heft 16, Munich, 1907.

Leuschner, Peter. *Nur wenige kamen zurück*, Pfaffenhofen: W. Ludwig Verlag, 1980.

Leyh, Max. *Die Feldzüge des Bayerischen Heeres unter Max I. (IV.) Joseph von 1805 bis 1815*, Vol. VI/2 of *Geschichte des Bayerischen Heeres*, Munich, Schick, 1935.

Madroux, Ludwig von. 'August von Floret', *Archiv für Offiziere aller Waffen* Band II, Munich, 1846.

Mändler, Friedrich. *Erinnerungen aus meinen Feldzügen,* Franz Joseph Schneidawind, ed., Nürnberg: Lotzbeck, 1854.

Marbot, Jean Baptiste. *The Memoirs of Baron de Marbot,* London: Longmans, Green and Co., 1905.

Münich, Friedrich. *Geschichte der Entwicklung der bayerischen Armee seit zwei Jahrhunderten,* Munich, Lindau, 1864.

Napoléon I. *La Correspondance de Napoléon Ier publiée par ordre de l'Empereur Napoléon III,* Paris: Plon, 1858-1870.

Paulus, G. 'Bayerische Kriegsvorbereitung, Mobilmachung und Einleitung zum Feldzuge 1809', *Darstellungen aus der Bayerischen Kriegs- und Heeresgeschichte,* Heft 2, Munich, 1893.

Petre, F. Loraine. *Napoleon at Bay,* London: Arms and Armour, 1977.

Plotho, Carl von. *Der Krieg in Deutschland und Frankreich in den Jahren 1813 und 1814,* Vol. I, Berlin: Amelang, 1817.

Pouget, François-René. *Souvenirs de Guerre,* Paris: Plon, 1895.

Preysing-Moos, Maximilian Graf von. 'Tagebuch des Generalmajors Maximilian Graf von Preysing-Moos, Führer der Bayerischen Kavallerie-Division, im Feldzuge nach Russland 1812', *Darstellungen aus der Bayerischen Kriegs- und Heeresgeschichte,* Heft 21, Munich, 1912.

Prielmeyer, Max von. *Geschichte des k. b. I. Infanterie-Regiments König,* München: Huttler, 1881.

Reichold, Nikolaus. *Soldaten-Sohn und das Kriegsleben von 1805 bis 1815,* Munich, 1851.

Ruith, Max. *Das k. bayerische 10. Infanterie-Regiment 'Prinz Ludwig',* Ingolstadt: Ganghofer, 1882.

Ruith, Max. *Das K. Bayer. 12. Infanterie-Regiment 'Prinz Arnulf',* Ulm: Ebner, 1902.

Ruith, Max and Emil Ball. *Kurze Geschichte des K. B. 3. Infanterie-Regiments,* Ingolstadt, 1890.

St Cyr, Laurent Gouvion. *Mémoires pour Servir a l'Histoire Militaire sous le Directoire, le Consulat et l'Empire,* Vol. III, Paris: Anselin, 1831.

Sauzey, Camille. *Nos Alliés les Bavarois,* Vol. V of *Les Allemands sous les Aigles Françaises,* Paris: Terana, 1988.

Schaller, Christian. *Fragmente aus dem Feldzuge gegen Oestreich im Jahr 1809,* Augsburg: Bürgeln, 1810.

Schaller, Henri de. *Histoire des Troupes Suisses au Service de France sous le Règne de Napoléon Ier,* Paris: Terana, 1995.

Schehl, Carl. *Vom Rhein zur Moskwa 1812,* Krefeld: Obermann, 1957.

Schmidt, Lothar. 'Das K. B. Korps Wrede im Feldzuge 1814', *Darstellungen aus der Bayerischen Kriegs- und Heeresgeschichte,* Heft 17, Munich, 1908.

Schröder, Bernd Philipp. *Die Generalität der deutschen Mittelstaaten,* Osnabrück, 1984.

Schroeder, Paul W. *The Transformation of European Politics*, Oxford: Clarendon Press, 1994.

Uebe, Kurt. *Die Stimmungsumschwung in der bayerischen Armee gegenüber den Franzosen 1806-1812*, Munich, Beck, 1939.

Völderndorff und Waradein, Eduard Freiherr von. *Kriegsgeschichte von Bayern unter König Maximilian Joseph I.*, Munich, no publisher given, 1826.

Völderndorff und Waradein, Eduard Freiherr von. *Observations sur l'Ouvrage de Mr. le Comte Ph. de Ségur*, Munich, 1826.

Wertheimer, Eduard. 'Berichte des Grafen Friedrich Lothar Stadion ueber die Beziehungen zwischen Oesterreich und Baiern (1807-1809)', *Archiv für Oesterreichische Geschichte*, Vol. 63, Vienna, 1882.

Wolf, Gustav. *Der Eilmarsch Wrede's von Linz bis Wagram*, Innsbruck: Wagner, 1909.

Wurzbach, Constant von. *Biographisches Lexikon des Kaiserthums Oesterreich* Wien: Zamarski, 1856-1891.

Xylander, Rudolf Ritter von. *Geschichte des 1. Feldartillerie-Regiments*, Vol. II, Berlin: Mittler & Sohn, 1909.

Zoellner, Hauptmann. *Geschichte des K. B. 11. Infanterie-Regiments 'von der Tann'*, Munich, Lindau, 1905.

Index

Page references in *italics* refer to Franz's writings; those in plain figures refer to the editorial commentary.